A DANCE
WITH DEATH

A DANCE
WITH DEATH

Soviet Airwomen in World War II

Text and contemporary portraits by

ANNE NOGGLE

Introduction by Christine A. White

Texas A&M University Press

COLLEGE STATION

The paper used in this book
meets the minumum requirements
of the American National Standard
for Permanence of Paper
for Printed Library Materials
z39.48-1984. Binding materials
have been chosen for durability.

∞

Library of Congress Cataloging-in-Publication Data

Noggle, Anne, 1922–
    A dance with death : Soviet airwomen in World War II / text and contemporary
portraits by Anne Noggle; introduction by Christine A. White.
        p. cm.
    ISBN 0-89096-601-X (cloth) —ISBN 1-58544-177-5 (pbk.)
    1. World War, 1939–1945—Aerial operations, Soviet. 2. Women air pilots—
Soviet Union—History. 3. World War, 1939–1945—Participation, Female.
4. Women—Soviet Union—History—20th century. 5. Air pilots, Military—
Soviet Union—History. 6. Flight crews—Soviet Union—History. 7. World
War, 1939–1945—Personal narratives, Soviet. I. Title.
D792.S65N64 1994
940.54'4947—dc20
                                                                        94-1301
                                                                        CIP

ISBN-13: 978-1-58544-177-8 (pbk.)

To fly a combat mission is not a trip under the moon
Every attack, every bombing is a dance with death.

Serafima Amosova-Taranenko
Pilot, deputy commander of the regiment in flying
46th Guards Bomber Regiment

Contents

Preface

In the fall of 1990 I traveled to the Soviet Union to photograph and record the stories of women Soviet Army Air Force veterans, the first women ever to fly combat. My sponsor was the Aeronautical Society of the Soviet Union, whose representative, Aleksandr Panchenko, put me in touch with the personnel of the regiments, scheduled the interviews, and provided a translator. Panchenko himself acted as our interpreter at times, and his expertise in aviation was extremely helpful. Margarita Ponomaryova, an English-language teacher at the military academy in Moscow, did the bulk of the translating and traveled with me to Kiev and Leningrad, where we also interviewed.

In the spring of 1991 I was again in the Soviet Union to continue the interviews. Margarita came to the United States that summer for two months while we worked further on the translations. In 1992 I returned to what had now become Russia, to listen to a few more stories and enjoy the company of my new friends.

When first on my way to the Soviet Union, with the whole process of logistics behind me, I finally had time to reflect on my intentions: what was this commitment? During World War II just over a thousand of us in the United States won our wings, graduating from what must be thought of as an experimental flight training program, and became officially known as Women Airforce Service Pilots—women military pilots—our country's first. Most of us were very young, and our thoughts were not on the historical significance of what we were doing but on the flying assignments that lay before us and of doing well at fulfilling them.

In 1989 I had written a book, *For God, Country, and the Thrill of It: Women Airforce Service Pilots in World War II*, and looked forward to returning to my love affair with photography as a more personal and art-oriented medium. Fate, in the form of an article telling of the Soviet women who flew combat in the war, decided otherwise.

All of us serving as Women Airforce Service Pilots (WASPS) wondered how we would fare if we were called upon to fly combat. We talked about it in our barracks during our six months of flight training, training conducted in the same aircraft and with the same basic routine as the male cadets. Our questions and speculations were purely hypothetical. Now I would see and hear from the Soviet women who had such experience, who knew the reality of it from those long years of combat.

I thought then, on my way to their country, that these stories would cut across all boundaries and that our gender-relatedness was a key—our sameness as girls and women, past and present, would be more significant than our differing cultural backgrounds. That proved to be true. As they told their stories, their voices and gestures spoke even before the translated words. For a people held mute for almost all the years of their lives by terror and despotism, the communication of the spirit has never been silenced.

I spent an hour or two, and at times much longer, with each veteran, and as I interviewed I had the extraordinary experience of being warmly accepted as a fellow pilot who had done my best to help win the war, known to the Soviets as the Great Patriotic War. Both the Soviet women pilots and crews and the American women pilots suffered the loss of friends while fulfilling wartime duties in their respective armed forces. This bond made it possible for me to share their reminiscences, their feelings.

I interviewed sixty-nine women who held various positions, titles, ranks, and duties in the Soviet Army Air Force. These women are looking back some fifty years to their own personal remembrances of that conflict. The recent changes wrought in the Soviet Union itself have made it possible for its citizens not only to speak to foreigners but to speak frankly with us.

The Soviet Union and its people have long been a mystery to us in the West. Although the participation of these airwomen in World War II is the central issue, the narrative also presents insights into the workings of the Soviet mind and the philosophical underpinnings of their society. But most of what has emerged is not political: it is an immense pride in their contribution to the defense of their country, and it avows their single-minded will to defeat the Germans without regard for their own lives or well-being.

The stories are about young women in combat. They are also stories of friendship, humor, and courage. These are women that make us take pride in being a woman. It takes effort not to be awed by them.

This is not a history but an account—personal, and at times emotional—of what it was like to spend nearly four years flying combat, from the early days of devastation and retreat to the victory paid for with so many millions of lives. None of the airwomen came out of the war unscathed. Everyone had lost someone, somewhere, some way. What saw them through was their unflagging determination, stoicism, and, dearest of all, their romanticism. Central to their lives is drama. Acceptance of their fate is rooted in their culture. They say it all so simply in a few words, words repeated over and over by them all—life is life.

Acknowledgments

I wish to thank Ray Graham, Susan Lyon, Sally Scott, Carol Wood Saas, Browning Coke, Robert Heyman, Kris Jensen, Robin Rule, and Cidney Payton for their belief and support in this endeavor and without whom this book would never have happened. Special thanks to Howard Sandum, my literary representative, for his intelligent criticism and patience; Lanny Smith and Bill Colbert, for their aeronautical expertise; Reina Pennington, former airforce intelligence instructor in Soviet fighter tactics, for introducing me to Soviet military history; Camille North and Texas A&M University Press, for their most enthusiastic support and guidance; Morgan Kuzio, for his photographic assistance; my sister, Mary Pease, and my niece, Dale Pease, for their humor, encouragement, and love.

I am indebted to Wes Kennedy, my assistant in 1990, for his good and tender care of me when I fell ill with pneumonia in Moscow; and James Holbrook, my longtime friend and assistant in 1991 and 1992, who traveled with me and had the good fortune of celebrating his fortieth birthday in a nightclub at the Izmailovo Hotel in Moscow.

I am especially grateful to my dear friend Margarita Ponomaryova, who translated for me in the Soviet Union and later visited me in the United States, where she had the time to do a thorough translation.

No one but Christine White could have written this introduction. Russian history professor at Pennsylvania State University and fellow pilot, she is currently working on her own manuscript, "Women in Early Russian Aviation, 1910–1939."

I wish to thank the many Soviet people who have helped me: photographer Yevgeni Khaldei, for granting me permission to include his war photographs of the 46th Guards Bomber Regiment; Aleksandr Kotenkov and Aleksandr Panchenko of the Aeronautical Society of the Soviet Union, who sponsored me; Nadezhda Popova and the Veterans Council; Yekaterina Polunina, archivist for the 586th Fighter Regiment; Irina Rakobolskaya, chief of commanding staff, 46th Guards Bomber Regiment; and Galina Chapligina-Nikitina of the 125th Guards Bomber Regiment. Most of all, I thank the sixty-nine women veterans who told me their stories.

A DANCE
WITH DEATH

An Introduction

by Christine A. White

The antiaircraft guns fired at us fiercely from all directions, and suddenly I felt our aircraft hit. My foot slipped down into an empty space below me; the bottom of the cockpit had been shot away. I felt something hot streaming down my left arm and leg— I was wounded. Blinded by the searchlights, I could discern nothing in the cockpit. I could feel moisture spraying inside the cockpit; the fuel tank had been hit. I was completely disoriented: the sky and earth were indistinguishable to my vision. But far in the distance I could see the sparkle of our regimental runway floodlight, and it helped restore my orientation. An air wave lifted us, and I managed to glide back over the river to the neutral zone, where I landed the aircraft in darkness.

> —Senior Lieutenant Nina Raspopova,
> 46th Night Guards Regiment

Such is one brief episode in the many experiences recorded in this volume of the women who served in the Soviet Army Air Force during the Great Patriotic War—World War II. Little is known in the West about the achievements of these Soviet airwomen, who are credited with being the first of their sex to serve in combat.[1] How did they come to be trained as combat pilots, mechanics, navigators, and ground crews? Where and when did the women pilots receive their flight training? How were they perceived? Was this use of women in combat a reflection of the desperate state of military affairs in the USSR in the summer and early autumn of 1941? Or was it merely an exercise in public relations or, worse, a propaganda ploy by Stalin? And finally, why is so little known about these women and the contributions they made? The memoirs contained in this volume address these questions by providing insight into the experiences and the characters of the women who flew, the training they received, and the

3

friendships that bound them together through one of the greatest cataclysms the world has known.

Although the Second World War stands as the first instance where women were officially employed in combat in any large-scale fashion, it was by no means "the first." Russian women have had a long tradition of serving beside men—and sometimes even leading them. The legendary Amazons—whose existence and activities were recorded by the ancient Greeks—were a community of women who dominated the south of Russia between the Don River and the Caucasus Mountains.[2] Much later, during the Napoleonic Wars, Nadezhda Durova disguised herself as a man and commanded a Russian cavalry to victory against the French revolutionary forces. Though she was ultimately found out, Emperor Alexander I allowed her to continue to serve and even awarded her the Cross of St. George.[3]

Although the later revolutionary governments routinely permitted the participation of women combatants, the Tsarist government had no consistent policy on this score. Though not officially allowed to serve, women were listed as new recruits in increasing numbers throughout the First World War. As early as 1915 there were an estimated four hundred women bearing arms in Russia.[4] But it was in the field of military aviation that Russian women truly stood out as firsts. Though largely ignored in most historical literature, these women were most certainly present on the front. Even though a number of accomplished Russian women pilots were refused permission to fly in the service of their country, at least two women were given special dispensation by the Tsar to serve as military pilots in the Imperial Russian Air Service. Where permission was not forthcoming, ingenuity took over. One young woman reportedly "borrowed" a male friend's military medical certificate and, disguised as a young man, joined the Imperial Russian Air Service, where she qualified as a combat pilot. The first woman ever to be wounded in aerial combat, she received injuries in the spring of 1915. Subsequently, her true sex was discovered, and she was "grounded." Her services were recognized, however, as she reportedly received the Cross of St. George for her bravery.[5]

It was not until the February revolution of 1917 that Russian women were actively recruited for the armed services. The best known of the revolutionary all-female regiments was Maria Botchkareva's controversial Women's Battalion of Death. It was only one of a number of such infantry units that were formed under the Russian provisional government in Petrograd, Moscow, Odessa, Ekaterinodar, and Perm.[6]

Although War Minister Alexander Kerensky clearly sought to utilize women's patriotism, his call to arms was really nothing more than an expression of support for what had already been happening for some time—that is, women actively engaged in combat. Under Kerensky, women who were previously barred from military flying under the Imperial government were now allowed to serve.

The Bolshevik Revolution in October, 1917, and the subsequent Civil War had, in theory at least, opened up new opportunities for women in areas that had previously been dominated by men. In particular, women were now free to take active service in the military. In 1920, at the height of the Russian Civil War, there were sixty-six thousand women serving in the Red Army, the majority as volunteers.[7] Although the number of female troops engaged in military aviation by the Bolsheviks is open to speculation, there can be no doubt that the Red Air Force was desperately in need of trained pilots. At least one of the prerevolutionary aviatrixes was known to have served in the training squadron of the Red Air Force and to have flown several missions for the revolutionary forces during the Civil War.[8]

According to Marxist ideological doctrine, women were considered to be equal citizens in both rights and responsibilities. Though not obligated to military service, the new Soviet woman was certainly free to participate in the revolution and subsequent Civil War. By the middle of the 1920s, however, women were again being encouraged into more traditional roles.[9] To be sure, the universal military service laws of 1925 and 1939 continued to allow women to enlist as volunteers, but they were actively discouraged from doing so.[10] Military service and, indeed, war—with the exception of the more traditional female support roles—were again considered outside the scope of women's affairs.

Although a very small number of women did manage to serve in the Soviet military as pilots in the early 1920s, aviation as a career—both military and civil—remained largely a male domain throughout the interwar period.[11] At the same time, however, the Soviet government was placing an increased importance on the development of aviation. Air transport was viewed as essential in such a vast and rugged country, and efforts were made to heighten public awareness and enthusiasm for aviation as well as to train proficient pilots and mechanics to serve the projected industry.[12] Though women were not specifically targeted in this effort, they were certainly not immune to its effects; by the mid-1930s women were making their presence felt in sports aviation.

Most women pilots received their training through the aero clubs set up by the paramilitary organization Osoaviakhim (Society of Friends of Defense and Aviation-Chemical Construction). Founded in 1927, the Osoaviakhim provided training to young adults in marksmanship, powered flight, gliding, parachuting, and aircraft mechanics, among other things. Though officially encouraged to participate in this training, young women often met with considerable opposition. Women who applied often found the male instructors of the aero clubs to be "less than enthusiastic" about their participation. Many young women remained undaunted, however, as their growing aero club membership and activity reflect.

The 1930s stand as the Soviet Union's "Golden Age of Aviation." There was a surge in aviation programs, both civilian and military. The second Five-Year Plan called for a tremendous increase in both number and distance of civil aviation routes. Geologic surveys and Arctic missions were now conducted by air, and Soviet accomplishments in sport and military aviation received heightened attention. By 1935 an estimated 150 aero clubs had been established under the auspices of the Osoaviakhim, and women were taking increased advantage of the opportunities available to them.[13]

In September, 1938, three Soviet women made history when they flew nonstop from Moscow to the Soviet Far East. Valentina Grizodubova, Paulina Osipenko, and Marina Raskova established a world record for women, logging twenty-six hours, twenty-nine minutes and more than six thousand kilometers in their plane, the *Rodina*. The first women to be honored with the title Hero of the Soviet Union, these women were irrepressible role models for young Soviet women. Marina Raskova in particular struck a chord with the population.

Initially trained as a navigator in 1933, Raskova went on to become an air navigation instructor for the air force. In 1937 she became the first female staff instructor at the Zhukhovski Air Academy.[14] Having gained world recognition as the navigator of the *Rodina* in 1938, Raskova was apparently permitted to enter the M. V. Frunze Academy, a prestigious Soviet military staff college. Raskova subsequently learned to fly light aircraft but was still a relatively inexperienced pilot when she took instruction in the complex and unforgiving twin-engine Pe-2. Attractive, strong-willed, and above all successful, Raskova was a hero for many of the young women who went on to serve as military pilots and navigators.

By the end of the decade women had made an indelible mark on Soviet aviation. Not only had Soviet airwomen claimed more women's aviation world records than those of any other nation, they also now accounted for nearly one-third of all the pilots trained in the USSR.[15] Moreover, Stalin himself had taken a particular interest in the women aviators. No doubt keenly aware of the tremendous international propaganda value of the accomplishments of Soviet female fliers, Stalin also seemed to have a genuine personal interest in the women and their record-breaking flights. His acquaintance with Raskova and her achievements no doubt helped to influence his ultimate decision to allow her to form all-female combat regiments in October, 1941.

In the days immediately following the Nazi invasion of the Soviet Union in June, 1941, Raskova was reportedly deluged with letters from young women pilots asking how they could put their skills to use in the service of their country—more particularly, how they could get to the front, preferably in an airforce unit.[16] Many of these women were flying instructors or had considerable experience in civil aviation. As their memoirs reveal, many felt compelled by a "fever of patriotism" to do something and so rushed to volunteer for active duty. Though they were initially turned away, it did not take Raskova long to persuade Stalin that the women were a valuable asset that could play a useful role in the war effort. The 122nd Composite Air Group was the result.

The young women who were recruited for the 122nd came from a variety of backgrounds. They reported to the Volga town of Engels, where they were divided into four groups according to previous experience: potential pilots, navigators, mechanics, and armorers. Although a number of women, especially those who were to serve as armorers and mechanics, had to be trained from scratch, a significant proportion of the women were university students when the war broke out and had already received considerable training through the Osoaviakhim. A minimum of 500 flying hours was required of women who desired to serve as fighter or bomber pilots. Though this standard was quite high, there were many more pilots than navigators, and a number of young, qualified women pilots were disappointed to discover that they had been assigned as navigators. All of the volunteers were subjected to an extremely rigorous training program, and in the case of the pilots, one that crammed nearly three years of flying experience into several months.[17] Time was of the essence.

The women's instruction, equipment, and ultimate assignment were identical to those of their male counterparts. There is nothing in the designation of the regiments that were later formed out of the 122nd—the 586th Fighter Regiment, the 587th Bomber Regiment, and

Map of Eastern Europe. Prepared by Cartographics, TAMU.

the 588th Air Regiment—to indicate that these were female units.[18] That they were not perceived as being essentially different from any of the male regiments is evident from the fact that they were given exactly the same coverage as the male air regiments in the official history of the Soviet Army Air Force in the Second World War.[19]

The three regiments were activated in early 1942. The 586th Fighter Regiment became operational in April, 1942, over Saratov on the Volga River, where it soon played an important role in the Battle of Stalingrad. In addition to protecting vital transportation and communication lines, the regiment provided air cover for advancing Soviet troops, harassed enemy positions, and guarded military installations. Equipped with Yak fighters, the regiment's operations extended as far west as Vienna and the Danube River.[20]

Because their mission was primarily defensive, the 586th was not routinely used in combat—a fact that explains the regiment's relatively low number of enemy "kills." In no way should their combat record be taken as an indication of any shortcoming. Eight of the women were detached to serve with the 73rd Fighter Regiment. The male fighter pilots obviously respected these women's capabilities, because they flew as trusted wingmen of veteran pilots. Further, two of these women—Lilya Litvyak and Katya Budanova—went on to earn the title "ace" while flying as "lone wolf" fighters.[21] Though the

586th never won the coveted "Guards" title, all of the women of the regiment were decorated. It deserves mention that, by the closing months of the war, women accounted for more than 12 percent of the Soviet fighter aviation strength.[22]

The 587th Bomber Regiment, later known as the 125th Guards Bomber Regiment, was likewise dispatched to commence operations in Saratov on the Volga River. They flew the fast, sophisticated, twin-engine Pe-2 dive bomber. Though many of the women's arms and legs were too short and their physical strength not always sufficient to fly the aircraft comfortably under all conditions, most of the women came to like the plane. Reflecting the joy that most pilots experience when flying a challenging, responsive aircraft, one member of the 125th described the Pe-2 as "astonishingly beautiful in flight."[23]

Although the regiment was used as a ground-support weapon when Russian forces broke through in the northern Caucasus in 1943, its primary mission was offensive bombing. It was used to attack enemy positions and strongholds, to destroy enemy installations, and harass troop concentrations. In January, 1943, the 125th regiment reached the front-line airfield at Novo-Georgeyevka. Their airfield was situated near an all-male bomber regiment whose members were less than confident in the women's skills and bravery. It did not take long, however, for the women pilots to win their respect. The authorities apparently agreed with them, for in the spring of 1944 the regiment was granted the coveted title of "Guards" and renamed the 125th M. M. Raskova Borisov Guards Bomber Regiment. The regiment was collectively awarded the Orders of Suvorov and Kutuzov in recognition of their skill and bravery in battle, and five members were named Heroes of the Soviet Union. Its campaigns took the 125th through Belorussia and into the Baltic area, ending as far west as eastern Prussia. On the way, the crews of the 125th flew up to three bombing sorties a day—1,134 sorties for the duration of the war—and dropped some 980,000 kilograms of bombs.[24]

Perhaps the best known of all of the Soviet women's air regiments, the 588th Air Regiment, later known as the 46th Guards Bomber Regiment, officially began operations in the spring of 1942. Commanded by Yevdokiya Bershanskaya, the 46th regiment was the only one of the three regiments formed from the 122nd Composite Air Group to remain entirely female throughout the war. The regiment received a great deal of publicity both during and after the war. It was frequently the subject of Western and Soviet journal articles, and after the war its members actively promoted the regiment's history through memoirs, collected accounts, and even documentary and feature films.

The 46th experienced a rather inauspicious start: the regiment had already suffered the loss of two crews during training, an event that delayed its departure for the front. Further, when the women arrived at their new forward base of operations in May, 1942, they were discovered to be insufficiently trained and poorly prepared for aviation combat conditions at the front. The divisional commander, D. D. Popov, despaired at having the women sent to him. His superior, however, advised patience and additional training for the regiment.[25] The women of the 46th were not to disappoint.

The 46th was equipped with a modified version of the popular U-2 trainer. Though later redesignated as the Po-2, the aircraft remained essentially unchanged from its original design in 1927. It was easy to fly, its fuel consumption was low, and it was capable of landing virtually anywhere. It carried a crew of two and between six and eight bombs—approximately one thousand kilograms—and was sometimes armed with a machine gun in the rear cockpit.[26] Made predominantly of wood and fabric, the aircraft was a fire hazard in combat. Many of the accounts related by the crews of the night bomber squadrons are focused on their fear of the aircraft catching fire.

The regiment began its operations in the Don region, where it was used to assault bridges, enemy strongholds, fuel and ammunition dumps, and enemy troop concentrations. It saw action in the Crimea, north through Belorussia and Poland, and as far west as Berlin. Between May, 1942, and May, 1945, the 46th Guards Bomber Regiment flew an estimated twenty-four thousand combat sorties, through every kind of weather and conditions. The women—pilots and ground crews alike—lived on the verge of physical collapse, managing a bit of sleep or a meal whenever they could.[27]

In February, 1943, the regiment was renamed the 46th Taman Guards Bomber Regiment, thus becoming the first female "Guard" unit. It was awarded the Orders of the Red Banner and Suvorov III Class for skill and bravery. The most highly decorated of the three women's regiments, the 46th regiment also produced twenty-three Heroes of the Soviet Union.

It should be noted that a significant proportion of the ground crews attached to these regiments were women as well. Responsible for maintaining and preparing the aircraft for their sometimes numerous daily missions, the armorers and mechanics handled ammunition boxes and machine-gun belts, made quick-time repairs, and attached heavy bombs, often working without cover in subzero weather. In the course of one night the armorers with the 46th would haul up to four tons of bombs each. In short, the ground crews were as dedicated as their aircrews. They often became so close to their pilot and aircraft that, if something happened to the plane, they felt they had failed somehow. ("We worried until our planes returned.")[28]

Although there were some who viewed the women's regiments with contempt and even made life difficult for the airwomen they encountered, many male pilots and regimental commanders did come to appreciate the skills of their female colleagues. Indeed, the record of the women's air regiments compares favorably with that of the men. The three regiments flew a combined total of more than thirty thousand combat sorties, and of the ninety-two women who were bestowed the title Hero of the Soviet Union in recognition of their outstanding service to their country in the Second World War, nearly one-third were airwomen. There were at least three fighter aces among the women pilots, and two of the regiments received the coveted "Guards" designation—an honor not given lightly, even during the war.[29]

Aside from being the accounts of the first women to engage in combat in any numbers, there is something else that makes the recollections contained in this book special: they illustrate a commonality of purpose among the women who served in the Second World War. The stories cut across national boundaries in a variety of ways. There is, for example, a striking similarity in attitude between the Soviet women pilots and that of the women who served as military pilots in the United States. There were, to be sure, some very major differences between the two groups, the most obvious being that the Soviet women were engaged in actual combat while the Women Airforce Service Pilots—the WASPS—were restricted to noncombat missions. Moreover, unlike their American counterparts, the Soviet women's air regiments were fully militarized, and the women who served did so for the duration of the war. An immediate and striking similarity can be found in the desire of both groups of women to serve—to offer their skills as pilots in the defense of their country. A sentiment shared by many of the women whose memoirs are recounted here is that they had to do something. The women who volunteered did so freely—some even lied about their experience and training in order to gain entrance to the program. Although many of the young Soviet women pilots volunteered as a result of an initial overwhelming surge of patriotism, they quickly came to realize that the war was nothing less than a national life-or-death struggle.

There is also a striking degree of similarity between the two groups in the camaraderie that the women shared. There is a closeness—a community of being—that approaches the relationship of family. It is not surprising to note that both groups developed their strongest ties during periods of great stress: the WASPS during their training, and the Soviet women while in the field.

Finally, without dwelling unduly on the issue of politics, the Soviet women were subjected to incredible political pressures. The recollections of some of the women contain grim reminders that life in Soviet Russia in the 1930s was complicated and potentially very dangerous. The same system that nurtured their love of flying and encouraged them to explore aviation was also capable of destroying them. That these women are now able to speak so freely about the difficulties faced by themselves and some of their colleagues is in itself a remarkable achievement. The fact that there is so little bitterness expressed stands as testament to their stoic determination and patriotism. Their country needed them in time of war, and they responded—fully, unreservedly, and sometimes with their lives. The overwhelming pride they share in having served their country—of having made a difference—is evident in all of the women's stories.

Though strictly speaking not a history of the Soviet women who flew in combat, this book represents *their* history—the hopes, fears, and experiences of the young women who embarked on a most deadly adventure, which combined the joyous freedom of flying with the horrors and destruction of war. Their stories are powerful, moving, and enlightening.

The women whose reminiscences are recounted in this book represent the first instance of the widespread employment of women in combat by a major power. The successes of these young women, their fears, their friendships, and their courage are captured here in their own words, seasoned with the passing of half a century. Their wartime contributions, like those of the WASPS, are only now being given the attention they so richly deserve, and the passing of these women makes the task of gathering these memoirs critical. Their stories—as their past deeds—speak for themselves.

Only a pilot can understand how it feels to be in the air without the instructor. Only a pilot knows the whole scope of feelings and sensations you experience when face-to-face with the sky and aircraft!
—Senior Lieutenant Nina Raspopova, 46th Night Bomber Regiment

Notes

1. One of the best studies to date is J. K. Cottam, *Soviet Airwomen in Combat in World War II* (Manhattan, Kans.: Sunflower University Press, 1983). There are a number of promising works in progress on the topic and increasing numbers of translations of memoirs and accounts published in Russian. There is, however, ample room for further research with the opening of Soviet archives on the Second World War.

2. Dorothy Atkinson, "Society and the Sexes in the Russian Past," in Dorothy Atkinson, Alexander Dallin, and Gail Lapidus, eds., *Women in Russia* (Stanford, Calif.: Stanford University Press, 1977), pp. 3–4.

3. Nadezhda Durova, *The Cavalry Maiden: Journals of a Russian Officer in the Napoleonic Wars*, trans. Mary Fleming Zirin (Bloomington: Indiana University Press, 1988), pp. ix, xxviii.

4. Anne Eliot Griesse and Richard Stites, "Russia: Revolution and War," in *Female Soldiers—Combatants or Noncombatants? Historical and Contemporary Perspectives*, ed. Nancy L. Goldman (Westport, Conn.: Greenwood Press, 1982), p. 80; "Young Girls Fighting on the Russian Front," *Current History* (May, 1916); and the *New York Literary Digest* as cited in Julie Wheelwright, *Amazons and Military Maids: Women Who Dressed as Men in the Pursuit of Life, Liberty, and Happiness* (Boston: Pandora Press, 1989), p. 33.

5. *Flight*, April 16, 1915.

6. Only those women's regiments in Perm and Petrograd were used in combat. See Maria Botchkareva, *Yashka: My Life as Peasant Officer and Exile* (New York: Frederick A. Stokes Co., 1919), pp. 154–71; and Reina Pennington, "Wings, Women, and War: The Formation and Development of Soviet Women's Military Aviation Regiments, 1941–42." Seminar paper, Department of History, University of South Carolina, p. 3 (n. 40).

7. Barbara Evens Clements, "The Birth of the New Soviet Woman," in *Bolshevik Culture*, ed. Abbott Gleason, Peter Kenez, and Richard Stites (Bloomington: Indiana University Press, 1985), p. 220.

8. *Aviatsiya i Rossiya* (Moscow: Mashinostroenic, 1968), p. 316.

9. Richard Stites, *The Women's Liberation Movement in Russia: Feminism, Nihilism, and Bolshevism, 1860–1930* (Princeton, N.J.: Princeton University Press, 1978).

10. Ellen Jones, *Red Army and Society* (Boston, Mass.: Allen & Unwin, 1985), p. 99, as cited in Pennington, "Wings, Women, and War," p. 6.

11. Pennington, "Wings, Women, and War," p. 9; and Cottam, *Soviet Airwomen*, p. 1.

12. "Agitprop " flights were made a common phenomenon, with membership and fund-raising drives by the Society of Friends of the Airfleet recruiting some 2 million members and raising more than 5 million rubles by June, 1925. See William E. Odom, *The Soviet Volunteers: Modernization and Bureaucracy in Public Mass Organization* (Princeton, N.J.: Princeton University Press, 1973), p. 60.

13. Cottam, *Soviet Airwomen*, p. 1. According to Osoaviakhim's publication

Samolet, 19 percent of the pilots in the USSR in 1935 were women. For the same year, only 370 or 3 percent of the 14,177 pilots in the United States were women. *Samolet* (Mar., 1935), p. 22.

14. *Bolshaya Sovestskaya Entsiklopediya,* (3rd ed.), vol. 21, p. 466.

15. Marina Chechneva, *Nebo Ostaetsia Nashim* (Moscow: Voenizdat, 1976), pp. 9–10; V. Mitroshenko, "They Were First," *Soviet Military Review* (Mar., 1969), pp. 20–22; and Pennington, "Wings, Women, and War," p. 10.

16. Alexei Flerovsky, "Women Flyers of Fighter Planes," in *Soviet Life* (May, 1975), p. 28.

17. Cottam, *Soviet Airwomen,* p. 317.

18. Pennington, "Wings, Women, and War," p. ii.

19. The women's regiments, like all others are mentioned only in the context of the action in which they participated. See *Sovetskiye Voenno-vozdushnye sily v Velikoi Otechestvennoi Voine 1941–1945* (Moscow: Voenizdat, 1968).

20. M. A. Kazarinova and A. A. Polyantseva, eds., *V nebe frontovom. Sbornik vospominaniy sovietskikh letchits uchastnits Velikoy Otechestvennoy voyny* (Moscow: Molodaya Gvardiya, 1962), pp. 186–96; and Cottam, *Soviet Airwomen,* pp. 4–5.

21. Flerovsky, "Women Flyers," p. 28; Cottam, *Soviet Airwomen,* p. 6; and V. S. Murmantseva, *Sovetskiye zhenshchiny v velikoy Otechestvennoy voyne* (Moscow: Mysl', 1974), p. 180.

22. Cottam, *Soviet Airwomen,* p. 7.

23. Cottam, *Soviet Airwomen,* pp. 11–12.

24. Murmantseva, *Sovetskiye zhenshchiny,* p. 85; Kazarinova and Polyantseva, *V nebe frontovom,* p. 26; Cottam, *Soviet Airwomen,* pp. 9–14.

25. Cottam, *Soviet Airwomen,* pp. 18–19.

26. Cottam, *Soviet Airwomen,* pp. 16–18.

27. Cottam, *Soviet Airwomen,* pp. 16–17, 19–20.

28. Cottam, *Soviet Airwomen,* p. 22; and Senior Sergeant Galina Drobovich, regimental mechanic of the 586th.

29. Pennington, "Wings, Women, and War," pp. 29–32.

One
Major Marina Raskova
1912–43

The American Committee for Aid to the Soviet Union in the
war against Nazi Germany announced that on June 22, 1943, a
supply ship would be launched at one of the wharfs in Califor-
nia. It would be named "Marina Raskova" in memory of the
heroic Russian Air Force pilot.

Pravda, Moscow, June 10, 1943

Marina Raskova was loved and venerated in the Soviet Union much
as Amelia Earhart was in the United States. She was a navigator by
profession. In that capacity, along with two women pilots, V. S.
Grizodubova and P. O. Osipenko, she flew from Moscow to the Far
East in 1938, opening up the route across Siberia and establishing a
new nonstop distance record for women. During the course of this
mission, overcast skies completely obscured all visual landmarks,
leaving radio signals as the only means of orientation. When the radio
station ceased transmitting, there was nothing to do but continue on,
eventually to run out of fuel. Raskova's crew position in the nose of
the aircraft was hazardous for a crash landing, and she was ordered to
parachute from the plane over the *taiga*, a dense, swampy, forested
area of Siberia. She landed in the swamp and struggled through the
taiga for ten days before she finally came to the site of the aircraft.

The story of this flight was widely publicized, and her courage and
stamina caught the imagination of the people. When the women
returned to Moscow, Stalin bestowed upon them the nation's highest
award, the Gold Star of Hero of the Soviet Union. They were among
the first women to have ever received that honor. Raskova was not
only intelligent and brave, she was a most beautiful young woman.

Marina Raskova's fame and influence were crucial to the formation and training of women's combat regiments in World War II.
When the war began, she joined the People's Defense Committee and
was aware that letters were pouring in from women pilots all over the

15

Marina Raskova, 125th Guards Bomber Regiment

country begging to be taken into the army air regiments. She proposed to the government that female air regiments be formed with volunteer women pilots and that these pilots, along with other volunteers selected by the Komsomol, be trained as mechanics, staff personnel, gunners, and navigators.

Raskova's proposal was approved, and she was appointed commander of the training unit with the rank of major. Everyone in the USSR knew of her, and the women considered it to be the greatest honor to serve under her command. About one thousand women were selected. They gathered in Moscow and were then transported to the training airdrome in Engels, a city on the Volga River. This took place in October, 1941.

Having been trained as a navigator, Marina Raskova was not a highly experienced pilot. After training, she was given her choice of regimental command, and she chose to lead the 587th Dive Bomber Regiment, later designated the 125th Guards Bomber Regiment. She trained herself in the Pe-2 dive bomber aircraft, considered to be a difficult and unforgiving plane to fly. Only the most experienced women pilots had been assigned to fly it.

When the regiment was activated, Major Raskova, as commander, led a flight of three aircraft to the front, flying in formation. One of the women pilots in that formation, Galina Tenuyeva-Lomanova, tells the story of this last flight. Marina Raskova and her crew crashed and were killed; thus, she never reached the front to lead her regiment in combat.

Her death greatly affected the women of the regiments. She was given a hero's funeral, and her remains were interred in the Kremlin Wall, a place of high honor.

Without Marina Raskova it is doubtful that there would have been any women air regiments in the Soviet Union during World War II.

Two
The 46th Guards Bomber Regiment

Introduction

The 588th Air Regiment was activated in the summer of 1942 and was honored in 1943 by being designated a "Guards" regiment, henceforth known officially as the 46th Taman Guards Bomber Regiment. The mission of the night bomber regiment was to destroy tactical targets located close to the front lines, such as fuel depots, ammunition dumps, ground troops, support vehicles, bridges, and enemy head-quarters. Members of the regiment were also used on occasion to fly supplies and ammunition to Soviet front-line troops. Initially this regiment comprised two squadrons; later it added a third squadron plus a training squadron.

Major Yevdokiya Bershanskaya, a civilian pilot before the war, was the regimental commander. She was the only woman to remain in com-mand of a women's regiment throughout the war. The regiment was equipped with the Polikarpov U-2 biplane, later designated the Po-2. The plane was fitted with an M-11, five-cylinder radial engine of 100 HP. This open-cockpit aircraft made of fabric and wood cruised at 60 MPH and was originally designed in 1927 as a training plane. Both front and rear cockpits were equipped with controls. The instrument panel held only the most basic instruments, and there was no radio communication.

The Po-2 was used extensively in the war, and one of its designa-tions was "night bomber." In this capacity it was fitted with bomb racks and a light machine gun in the rear cockpit. Flying over heavily defended targets on or near the front lines, it depended on stealth and the dark of night for protection. It was equipped with a noise and flare muffler to approach the target undetected. The aircraft of the regi-ment flew to the assigned target at precise intervals, making it possi-ble for the Germans to anticipate when the next plane would be over the target. This made it unusually dangerous for the flight crews, but it was a procedure deliberately practiced by the Soviets to disallow the Germans any peace during the night.

46th regiment. *Foreground, second from right:*
Yevdokiya Bershanskaya. Photograph by Khaldei

Important ground targets were guarded not only with antiaircraft guns but with numerous searchlights. If the searchlights could pinpoint and hold the aircraft in their beam, it was quite easy to shoot down this slow-moving plane. The pilot, blinded and disoriented by the powerful lights, would maneuver to sideslip out of the light. The sideslip moved the normal trajectory of the aircraft toward one side, and often it escaped in this manner. But the best defense was to approach from a high elevation, throttle back the engine to idle, fly in over the target soundlessly, and drop the bombs almost before the enemy was aware of their presence.

One other particularly dangerous approach was to have two aircraft flying together toward the target. One arrived noisily with the engine powered up to attract the attention of the ground defenses, while the other approached silently and undetected to drop bombs on the target.

The Po-2 aircraft was easily set on fire by either the antiaircraft or machine-gun tracers, and the plane was almost always doomed. The crew could not escape, because parachutes were not provided until the summer of 1944. The crew positions were tandem with the pilot

Po-2 prepares for a night mission, 46th regiment. Photograph by Khaldei

in the front cockpit and the navigator in the rear. The typical pattern flown on a mission was that of a long, narrow racetrack, with the outgoing aircraft at one altitude and incoming aircraft at another, each spaced about three minutes apart. The returning aircraft landed, refueled, and rearmed, and it immediately took off again to the target. Thus there was a continuous stream of these small planes, one bombing every few minutes. Their missions started at dark and ended at dawn. In the winter, of course, they flew many more missions than on short summer nights.

Flying at such a slow speed required an auxiliary airfield closer to the front lines in order to fly the maximum number of missions. Armament and fuel were transported to the auxiliary field after dark, and the aircraft flew out of this field until their missions ended at dawn and they returned to their home airdrome.

The 46th was the only all-women regiment in the Red Army during the war, with a total cadre of over two hundred. Thirty air crew members perished during the war in 1,100 nights of combat. The regiment flew a total of 24,000 combat missions. The most decorated of the women's regiments, twenty-three of its members were awarded the Gold Star of Hero of the Soviet Union, their nation's highest award. Five of them were honored posthumously.

Senior Lieutenant Nina Raspopova,
pilot, flight commander
Hero of the Soviet Union

I was born on December 1, 1913, in a settlement in the Far East. After the introduction of Soviet rule, the local population suffered famine and complete destruction like everywhere else in the country during that period. Whole families died of disease and poor nutrition. My father was an unskilled worker in the gold mines; my mother was a housewife. When I was ten years old my mother died, leaving our family of ten children, and my youngest sister was only nine months old. At the age of thirteen I was accepted as a cook in one of the gold mines. I was not good at cooking and often prepared inedible meals, either oversalted or overfried. To escape dismissal from my position, I buried the spoiled food somewhere in the woods and cooked meals anew. I often recall now how much food I wasted.

When I was fifteen the Komsomol sent me to the town of Blagoveshchensk to go to the mining technical school. But girls were not accepted into that school; the profession of a mining engineer was not considered women's labor. I had a great desire to learn so I decided not to leave the town, and for two months I sat on the stairs of the technical school in hope that I would be admitted. By that time eight other girls had arrived to enter the same school, so the admissions board permitted us to take the entrance examinations. On the first exam I felt completely miserable and humble; I couldn't make any mathematical calculations, having finished only four grades of primary school. Some other older and cleverer applicants felt sorry for me, alone with my grief, and they solved all the sums for me. In this way I was enrolled. At the end of the academic course I was sent to the gold mines for practical study. We girls proved to be as well-trained and industrious as the boys. I was among the most active Komsomol members of the mining technical school; and I, among other excellent students, was recommended for admission to the Irkutsk Mining–Engineering College without entrance examinations.

But in 1932 the Soviet government appealed to its youth to join aviation, and in March the Regional Komsomol Committee sent me to the Military Commissariat, where they offered to train me as a pilot in one of the civil pilots' schools. I had never seen an airplane, but I liked the idea immensely from the very start. Two girls and

some boys from my region arrived in Khabarovsk to enter the pilots'
school. The staff of cadets had already been training there for five
months. The cadets were males of twenty-one to twenty-four years,
and I was only seventeen, very small and fragile. In my entrance
record I had added three years to my age. The commander of the
school said he wouldn't admit us because we were girls, but the
government said they must admit us, so I was enrolled.

We had very little theoretical training but soon began flying. By
that time I had already fallen in love with the airplane; we flew a U-2
aircraft, and I made my first solo flight in March, 1933. Only a pilot
can understand how it feels to be in the air without the instructor;
only a pilot knows the whole scope of feelings and sensations you
experience when face to face with the sky and aircraft! On my first
solo flight I sang, cried, and sobbed with happiness. I couldn't believe
I was manning the plane. In 1933 I finished the pilots' school and was
assigned to a glider school as a pilot-instructor. It was there that I
mastered parachuting; in 1934 I made my first parachute jump.

The year of 1937 is well-known as the beginning of massive repri-
sals against the population of the whole country. I, along with fifteen
Komsomol members of my glider school, was denounced as an enemy
of the republic. We were suspected of being spies. I was fired from my
position and from the Komsomol League, and I stayed at home in
total isolation from the outer world. Nobody dared even to talk to me
or look in my direction. Everybody was scared to death to be thought
of as a friend of an enemy of the republic. It was a witch-hunt at that
time, and many innocent people perished. The only ones who supported me in that tragic situation were some pilots from the glider
school. They helped me with money and food. One of the fifteen was
sentenced to death and was killed. This situation lasted for fifteen
days. Then they returned my Komsomol membership card, and I
came back to the glider school, where I was reenlisted. In 1939 I began
the courses of the commanding staff in the Central Air Club in Moscow. On finishing these courses I was appointed a pilot-instructor at
that same air club, where I trained future pilots.

When the war started I voluntarily joined Raskova's regiments on
October 7, 1941. I flew in the 46th Guards Bomber Regiment. I made
857 combat missions during the war, and I was awarded the title of
Hero of the Soviet Union. I left the army in 1946, with a total of about
four thousand flying hours.

Early in the war, when we were retreating, extremely severe battles were waged. We were bombing the enemy, and they were advanc-

ing very rapidly. In that circumstance we were fearful when landing our aircraft after a mission, because we never knew if the landing strip was German- or Soviet-held. This situation was compounded by the insufficiency, primitiveness, and defenselessness of the U-2 aircraft; no ground communication, no parachutes, and a limited number of primitive instruments in the plane. Although this aircraft was initially designated the U-2, when the designer of the aircraft, Polikarpov, died in an air crash, it was renamed the Po-2. That was in 1943.

I was shot down twice during the war. One of our most dangerous missions took place in the area of Mozdok, on the Terek River. The enemy was solidly fortified, and they used antiaircraft guns, aviation searchlights, and unceasing fire. On December 9, 1942, our regiment was given an assignment to not let the enemy ferry across the Terek River. My navigator, Larisa Radchikova, and I completed the first mission, but on the second one we were caught by enemy searchlights after we had dropped our bombs.

The antiaircraft guns fired at us fiercely from all directions, and suddenly I felt our aircraft hit. My left foot slipped down into an empty space below me; the bottom of the cockpit had been shot away. I felt something hot streaming down my left arm and leg—I was wounded. Blinded by the searchlights, I could discern nothing in the cockpit. I could feel moisture spraying inside the cockpit; the fuel tank had been hit. I was completely disoriented; the sky and earth were indistinguishable to my vision. But far in the distance I could see the sparkle of our regimental runway floodlight, and it helped restore my orientation. An air wave lifted us, and I managed to glide back over the river to the neutral zone, where I landed the aircraft in darkness.

The Germans could see us in that zone and went on firing at us. We got out of the cockpit with difficulty, because both of us were wounded; I was bleeding all over. Large splinters were sticking out of my body. My navigator was wounded in the neck, and even after she was operated on, her head was set onto one side. So with both of us bleeding we walked so very slowly toward the hills where our troops were supposedly located. I gave Larisa my few pilot belongings and had only my pistol with me. Even a map holder made my movements unbearable and impossible. Larisa was wearing army high boots, and they were squeaking and making so much noise that I made her take them off so we would not be detected by the enemy. All the way from the landing place to the Soviet lines she walked through mud and impassable roads with nothing on her feet but her socks. We walked on and on, never having even a short rest. I knew if we sat down for a moment, we would never stand again. Bit by bit we two cripples made our way: I was trying to take care of her, and she was trying to take care of me! We came to a bridge over a small mountainous river. We feared to step on the bridge, thinking there could be an ambush on the other bank. We stood for a few minutes trying to decide what to do when a sentry came out of the darkness and questioned us in Russian with a thick Kazakh accent. "Stop, who is coming?" Larisa replied in shock, "Are you Russian or German?" and they were Russian! We were taken to their dugout. I had a piece of shrapnel sticking out of my arm, and one of the soldiers wanted to help. He tried to pull out the shrapnel with a pair of pliers, but he couldn't get it out.

It was a number of hours before we arrived at a field hospital where severely wounded soldiers were waiting their turn to be operated on. I had lost much blood and was very weak. We sat on a bench awaiting our turn for surgery. We were opposite a deep pit and watched dead bodies covered with white cotton sheets being thrown into that huge communal grave. This scene shocked me to the bottom of my heart. As long as I live I'll never forget mortally wounded soldiers whispering to us to jump the line and go ahead of them for surgery, because their minutes were numbered. After surgery we were to be transported to the rear, but we managed to return to our regiment where I was bedridden for two months. When I returned to duty and was assigned a mission, it was terribly difficult for me to return to combat.

Another episode happened in 1942. The Germans were still advancing very quickly, and our regiment was retreating with the army. One of our pilots made a reconnaissance flight with my aircraft, and upon landing she hit the propeller and knocked off part of one blade. The enemy tanks were closing in on our airfield, and the regimental commander ordered us to redeploy to another location. There was no time to replace the propeller, and I had a choice of destroying the aircraft and leaving on a truck or flying it out if possible. I had the mechanic quickly cut off part of the opposite blade of the propeller to reduce the vibration.

I got the aircraft into the air, and it was shaking so fiercely that only by holding the control stick with a strong grip could I manage to fly it. On my seat I was like a peanut jumping in boiling oil in a frying pan! I was escorted by the other planes of the regiment, but what was the use of that protection? If I fell down, nobody could save me. It was really moral support. I've been living all my long life with the eerie feeling of that plane trying to shake itself to pieces, and I still don't understand how I survived that flight.

The second time I was shot down was in 1943 over Kerch in the

Tatyana Makarova, Hero of the Soviet Union (*left*), and
Vera Belik, Hero of the Soviet Union, 46th regiment

battle to liberate the Crimean Peninsula. In order to knock out the
well-fortified fascist troops from the area, the Soviet marine landing
force had to capture the peninsula. To prevent the enemy from detect-
ing the marine force landing, our regiment was given the assignment
of creating a noise screen over the strait. But unfortunately the landing force was detected and crushed by the enemy. In the cockpit, I saw
the sailors, marine officers, military ships, and boats dying in the cold
waters of the strait. It all looked incredible from above, as if millions
of worms swarmed in the raw meat of minced human bodies. I prayed
to God to stop that slaughter.

Suddenly the fuel tank of my aircraft was hit, and the engine
choked, coughed, and quit. I just managed to get back over the Kerch
Strait and was about to land on a village road when I noticed all the
approaches to the sea had been bombed and the roads ruined with
trenches. There was no way out; I had to land there. Only God knows
how I escaped death and made it down on that destroyed road. At the
end of the landing run a metal construction, an antitank device,
pierced the cockpit floor. The left wheel stopped over the edge of a
deep trench. My friends told me I was born in a lucky undershirt! I
also ascribe it to destiny.

At the end of my story I want to tell everybody who is going to read this: don't believe those who say they had no fear in the war. I did fear the war, and death—I feared each combat mission. After bombing and having escaped the enemy's fire, I couldn't pull myself together for ten or fifteen minutes. I was shivering, my teeth were chattering, my feet and hands were shaking, and I always felt an overwhelming striving for life. I didn't want to die. I dreamed of a small village house, a piece of rye bread, and a glass of clear river water. And never again a war! That is why today's hardships seem to me a trifle in comparison to what we had to go through in the war. I am grateful to each passing day for the life it gives me.

After the war I married, had two sons, and did not fly anymore. One of my sons is a helicopter navigator; the other is an engineer of the air defense aviation.

Major Irina Rakobolskaya,
navigator, chief of the commanding staff, deputy commander of the regiment

Irina Rakobolskaya,
46th regiment

I come from a family of teachers. My father was a physicist, and my mother taught Russian. I was born in a very small settlement called Dankov, 300 kilometers from Moscow, in the Lipetsk region. My father died when I was only eleven, and my mother raised my sister and me. Before his death we moved to Moscow, and I finished secondary school here. In 1938 I entered Moscow University Physics Department and was a third-year student when the war started. Earlier I wasn't interested in aviation, but I attended a parachute school and jumped several times just out of curiosity. I was mostly interested in poetry and theater.

When the war broke out we realized that our country needed

soldiers, not physicists, and our one aim was to defend our country. Marina Raskova was forming the women's air regiments, and I was drafted as a volunteer into the regiment. I was then twenty years old.

We were piled into trucks in Moscow and taken to the train where we departed for Engels. At that time the country had a lot of female pilots, but unfortunately there were very few women navigators, gunners, or mechanics. Those of us who were to train in these fields were taken from civilian colleges. I was immediately assigned to the group training as navigators.

Our regiment, the 46th, was formed in December, 1941. At that time a commanding staff of the regiment was appointed, and that staff comprised mainly navigators. I was appointed chief of the commanding staff. I cried because I wanted to fly. Raskova told me that she didn't want to hear civilian talk, only military, and that I must abide by army regulations. If I was appointed chief of the commanding staff, then I was to obey orders and do my duty!

We did not fly in formations with a leader but instead flew one after another in a line toward the target. We then looped back to the field to rearm, took off again, and flew another mission with the same pattern. There were no radios in the aircraft and thus no communication while the planes were in the air. That was the pattern of our particular night missions. The commander's duty was to coordinate the whole effort, and so she flew very few missions. She could not be in command if she flew a mission.

Until 1944 our regiment flew without parachutes. Our pilots thought the plane itself to be like a parachute and felt they did not need them. Over our own territory we could get down quite easily, and over the German lines we felt that it was much better to burn up than to be captured by the Germans. But then one of our outstanding crews was shot down over Soviet territory by a German fighter and burned to death, and only then was it ordered that all Po-2 crews must wear parachutes.

In 1945 the lives of Rufina Gasheva and Olga Sanfirova were saved by parachutes. Rufina was the navigator and Olga her pilot, and commander of the squadron, when they were shot down over Polish territory. The plane was set on fire, and they both jumped. They landed on neutral territory between the Germans and the Soviets, and Olga stepped on a mine and was killed. A Soviet soldier saw that happen, and he went out and took Rufina in his arms and carried her from the mine field.

For our regiment, airdromes were not constructed at all: we used

just fields. When we advanced into Poland it became extremely difficult, because the fields were so muddy our aircraft, the Po-2, could
not take off—the wheels stuck in the mud. The fuel trucks could not
move in the mud, either. We took apart log fences and laid them
down to make runways. The crews would seize the wings of the plane
and hold on while the pilot revved up the engine; then, when she
signaled, they would let go, and the plane took off. When they landed,
it was in the mud where the crews again seized the wings and pushed
the plane back to the log runway. It was then refueled by carrying the
fuel in jerry cans to the plane. The bombs had to be carried by hand to
the planes also. Trucks couldn't come to the aircraft, so everything
had to be carried to it. Each night the ground crews hand-carried
three tons of bombs to the planes. The lower wing panel was quite
close to the ground, which made it especially hard for the girls to
carry them under the wing and fix them to the plane. They crawled
on their knees with the bombs in their arms.

Our regiment made 300 combat missions from that field in those
conditions. The total combat missions flown by our regiment during
the war was 23,000. I personally made 23 combat missions as a navigator, and Bershanskaya made 35. We lost about thirty members of our
regimental air crews. For us, those were great losses; for the army, it
was not considered heavy losses.

Our whole regiment took to embroidering. We had no threads, no
real cloth, but we had underwear, usually of a blue material, and we
had cloth—not socks—that you put your foot into and then pulled on
the boots. You see, the boots were very large for us, and these cloths
made them fit comfortably. We embroidered flowers on those cloths
with thread made out of the blue underwear.

When we moved forward into Poland and Germany, we found
many pictures of beautiful flowers to use in our embroidery. My
mother would send colored threads to me at the front. Once I came on
inspection to one of the dugouts because there had been much rain,
the dugouts were flooded, and we wanted to repair the trench to make
it more livable. I saw that the floor was covered with water and that
water was streaming down the walls. There was a table near the light,
and I saw one of the girls standing on the table embroidering, obliv-
ious of the conditions in the room.

The squabbles that went on between the flight squadrons were
almost always about who was to take off first. The first to take off
usually flew the most missions, and they were competitive. The
spirit in the female regiments differed greatly from that in the male

regiments. But we were quite ordinary people, and we sometimes violated the strict code of army discipline. It was required that we always fly with flares, which came with a parachute attached to slow their descent so we could see where to land. Once two of our navigators, who did not use the flares while on a mission, separated the parachutes from the unused flares. They used the material to sew underwear and pants, because we were supplied with only male underwear. These crew members were brought to trial in the regiment for destroying military ammunition and were each sentenced to ten years' imprisonment. They were allowed, however, to stay with the regiment to show their ability to settle down and be adequate military officers through their work. One of them was killed in action, and the other survived the war with her chest covered with decorations and orders. At that time the girls agreed with their sentence and thought it to be quite just!

There were a few cases when the aircraft would be over the target, and a bomb would stick and not drop. The navigator would get out of the cockpit, stand on the wing, and reach down with her hands to try to push it loose. The women were as brave as the male crews.

We had parties and danced and sang, and we had amateur contests and wrote poetry. The first slogan of the regiment was: You are a woman, and you should be proud of that. When weather caused the cancellation of a mission, everyone stayed at the airfield and danced. It would never come into any man's head to do that, while waiting for permission to fly.

When I was appointed deputy commander of the regiment, it was a part of my duties to give orders to the girls that I had trained with and to know that they had to stand up when I entered the room. We were friends, and this was a shock to me and was the hardest thing I had to endure during my first year of army service. Later on the regiment was reinforced by girls I didn't know personally, and it was easier.

Once I lost the seal of the regiment. I thought life would end—life was over for me. The only thing left to do was shoot myself in the head. Just as I knew I had to tell that I had lost it, I found it! But I remember feeling as though I were standing on the edge.

As the deputy commander, I stayed at an advanced temporary airfield all night while the combat missions were being fulfilled. I had a special map that showed what time each crew was to fly over the target and return, and we were so near the front lines that each aircraft over its target was visible from the airfield. There were occasions when I saw our planes shot down and on fire, and I could look at that map and calculate who it was burning in the air. It was the most grievous torture I endured in the army during the war—to calculate who was dying.

My good friend Yevgeniya Rudneva, who was awarded the Gold Star (Hero of the Soviet Union) posthumously, was an astronomer and a poet and was fond of fairy tales. When we were not on missions, she would gather us all together at the airfield and recite fairy tales by Zhukovsky. When she was burning in the air over Kerch, I was standing at the airdrome watching it. I was losing my friend, she was burning away above my head, and I could do nothing to save her. Grief paralyzed me—I was blind and deaf. I could hardly pull myself together to keep on handling the combat of the regiment on the ground.

There were 200 women in the regiment. We were the only regiment in the whole of the Red Army without any men serving in it. Once a male was assigned to us for one month to install air-to-ground communications. He was very shy and quiet and even ate by himself. At one time he was supplied with female underwear, because his surname was one whose ending could be either male or female. On that day he said that not one single day would he remain after he finished with the installation!

Our aircraft flew 1,100 nights of combat. We started the war with two squadrons and finished the war with four. We trained our personnel at the front and had one auxiliary squadron used only for training. Usually we were assigned the combat mission for that night during the day, and I was responsible for receiving those missions from the army. Normally both the target and the number of combat missions directed at that target were indicated. The peculiarity of our missions was that we always bombed the front line of the enemy. The planes flew to the target at one altitude and back at another. One night an aircraft returning from a mission was approaching for a landing, and it let down on top of another aircraft, also landing. Three of the crew members were killed, and one survived with a broken leg.

Sometimes we used flares to see our target, and sometimes a Soviet searchlight directed our aircraft to the target. These two methods were used when our troops were moving and their location constantly changing. Otherwise we bombed in the dark. It is complicated, this lesson in tactics. It was impossible for our planes to bomb from a low altitude, because the explosion would damage our own aircraft.

We bombed from at least 600 meters up to 1,200 meters and never used delayed fuses, because the enemy could pick them up and take them away. We usually started from an altitude of 1,300 meters, then throttled back and glided silently down to about 600 meters so the enemy couldn't hear us approaching the target. We suffered losses not so much because of the antiaircraft guns as because of the German night fighters. Six crews were shot down by German night fighters. In one episode over Poland, Polina Makogon was killed when her aircraft collided with a German night fighter.

NOTE: Irina Rakobolskaya is chair of the Physics Department at Moscow University. Her son teaches physics at Stanford University.

Major Mariya Smirnova,
commander of the squadron
Hero of the Soviet Union

I was born in 1920 in a peasant family. Until I was thirteen years old I went to a village school. Then my family moved to Tver, on the Volga River. At the age of sixteen I completed the three-year course at a teachers' college and taught at a primary school. In the neighborhood there was an airdrome, and every day I saw the planes flying. Thus was born my decision to train as a pilot.

In 1937 I began my flying and continued on to become an instructor. Among one hundred cadets I was the only girl. In 1939 I began training cadets. After the Great Patriotic War started, on November 1, 1941, I joined the regiments formed by Marina Raskova.

I was appointed deputy squadron commander of the 46th Guards Bomber Regiment. We flew to the front on May 2, 1942, and we didn't know our exact destination because the front was very unstable—liquid, so to speak. The situation might change several times a day. We were assigned to an airforce division, and the pilots were not enthusiastic when they heard that a female flying regiment was to link up with them. They accepted us with great mistrust, and each of us was flight-tested by a male pilot. My record in the logbook was "excellent!"

On the first combat mission we lost our commander of the squadron, and I was appointed to take her place. There were ten pilots and ten navigators in my squadron; eight pilots became Heroes of the Soviet Union. Two crews were shot down, and they perished. All of the pilots made more than 800 combat flights—I made 935. We carried out very risky assignments. We flew through the front lines, breaking through three defense lines fortified with German artillery to bomb targets such as fascist airdromes, railway stations and tracks, field headquarters, and bridges. We flew in a line three minutes apart, and the enemy was well aware of our timing. They had to be on the alert all night long—they didn't have a wink of sleep. This strategy was deliberate to tire the enemy around the clock.

46th regiment. *Front row, left:* Mariya Smirnova;
third from left: Yevgeniya Zhigulenko

We faced risks every night. You shouldn't misinterpret my words
and think we faced death openly and bravely—it is not true. We never
became accustomed to fear. Before each mission and as we approached the target, I became a concentration of nerves and tension.
My whole body was swept by fear of being killed. We had to break
through the fire of antiaircraft guns and also escape the searchlights.
We had to dive and sideslip the plane in order not to be shot down. All
this affected my sleep enormously. When we returned from our missions at dawn, I couldn't fall asleep; I tossed in bed and had anxiety
attacks. We slept two to four hours each day throughout the four
years of the war. Once my regiment sent me to a recreation center for
medical treatment to restore my health. But I ran away after three
days because I couldn't stay when the others were risking their lives,
so I returned to my regiment. Fear was always an inseparable part of
our flights, but we knew we had to go through it for we were liberating our motherland. I feared for my squadron; each night when I
climbed into the air, I thought not so much about the assignment as
of the possibility of crashes and death.

On a mission near Novorossijsk, I had just dropped my bombs on the railway tracks and was turning away when I saw a German fighter, a Focke Wolf, flying toward me. I managed to dive and make a sideslip. Only pure chance saved me, and I escaped the enemy's fire. But the aircraft behind me, piloted by Dusya Nosal, was caught by the enemy fire. She was killed in her cockpit. Her navigator, Irina Kashirina, in the back cockpit knew how to fly and took over the controls, but the dead pilot had slumped forward over the control stick, and she was not able to use the controls. So she had to reach forward and hold the dead body by the collar with her left hand and control the aircraft with her right hand. The rough air over the Crimean hills almost caused her to crash, but she brought the plane with the body of the dead pilot back to the regimental airfield. She was in a state of shock.

On the Taman Peninsula the Germans had a strongly fortified line known as the Blue Line, stretching from Novorossijsk to Timruk. This line was firmly backed by strong antiaircraft defenses, and the whole territory was networked by searchlights, antiaircraft batteries, and machine guns. Here and there were spread the enemy airdromes with fighter aircraft on alert. The Blue Line was stuffed with German staff, and our regimental task was to bomb this concentration of enemy troops and weapons. My crew was the first to map the route for the regiment and simultaneously reconnoiter the disposition of the enemy troops.

Usually, on my way to a target when the searchlights were off, I tried to approach and hit the target before they knew my aircraft was there. I would idle the engine and glide over the target noiselessly. But when a searchlight lit up and caught me in its web other searchlights also lit up, and I would find myself in their cross of lights. To escape the searchlights, I idled the engine and sideslipped down into the darkness. Even though it was a slip into pitch darkness, I could always determine the angle in relation to the ground. I never used flares to clarify where I was; I was never disoriented because the searchlight mirrors and the ground itself were my orientation. No matter how blinded I was by the lights, I had to think and act quickly to level out the aircraft. The next moment the enemy was fiercely trying to locate my plane again, combing through space.

On this flight the antiaircraft guns were silent. I sensed something very uncommon about that and then thought of the only reason for the silence—German fighter aircraft! We had not been attacked in this way before; we had not developed tactics to counter the attack of fighter planes. I had considerable experience in combat and maneuvered to escape the searchlights, for to escape the searchlights was to escape the fighter. But behind me flew young, inexperienced crews— reinforcements who did not escape. Four of the aircraft following me were shot down. The tracer bullets set their planes on fire; our planes were so vulnerable they were burning like sheets of paper. We were not equipped with parachutes at that time, so eight girls burned in the air. One was Irina Kashirina, who had landed the aircraft with the dead pilot. It is a horrible scene when a plane is burning. First it explodes; then it burns like a torch falling apart, and you can see particles of fuselage, wings, tail, and human bodies scattered in the air. The other crews who were in the air at that moment witnessed that tragedy. I saw it with my own eyes as I returned from the mission.

In the morning, when we realized that the girls had perished and we would never see their smiling faces, never hear their voices, horror seized us. We didn't sleep that day and the next night fulfilled our combat missions without a wink of sleep. The everyday ration of vodka in the army was 200 grams, and we were daily allowed 200 grams of dry wine. But the regimental commander forbade us to drink, and we gave our word of honor not to break her order. Even after that tragedy we kept our word.

Our airdrome was occasionally attacked from the air. In the Crimea our field was bombed by a group of fascist fighters at dawn, when we were in the field mess eating breakfast. We were at a new location, and the logistics battalion hadn't yet camouflaged the airfield and planes. We rushed from the mess to our planes, which were dispersed on the field, and we flew off in all directions in order to save the aircraft. I must confess that when I am telling you all these stories, I am shivering as if going through hell over and over again. If I talk about my war experiences, I cannot sleep afterwards, so much is my agitation.

In the Taman area I was assigned to bomb a column of enemy trucks and weapons moving along the road. The night was moonlit, and this was not in our favor. The altitude was low, and the silhouette of the aircraft was clearly discernible to the Germans, but for awhile they masked and didn't fire at me. We dropped three flares to light the area. Hardly had my navigator, Tatyana Sumarokova, dropped half of the bombs when four antiaircraft guns burst out firing at us in rapid succession. These were Oerlekon tracer missiles. All of the tracers hit the aileron wires, and I lost control of the ailerons. The tracers also hit the bomb wires under the left wing, and we couldn't drop those bombs. The most urgent necessity was to get out of the fire zone. But I couldn't maneuver because of the aileron damage; the only possible escape was to dive. My altitude dropped from 600 to 200 meters. That made it especially risky, because at that altitude we could be hit by submachine gun fire, or even by a gun! My navigator was wounded in the forehead and was blinded by blood. Without her to guide me, I headed back to our airdrome. I didn't know to what extent our aircraft was damaged. We were lucky to have no wind that night; if the wind had banked our plane, I would have never been able to level it. The bombs still attached to the left wing were pulling the aircraft to the left. I held the plane with my right rudder. But how to land the plane? The landing strip was ninety degrees from my heading, and somehow I had to turn. Using the rudder, I kept applying pressure to the right. Soon I saw the airdrome, and I shot three red rockets to indicate an emergency landing. Since we were landing with the bombs still under the left wing, I made a decision to land a distance from the other planes so as not to blow them up if we exploded. When the altitude dropped to six or eight meters, I completely lost control and stalled. The fact that we didn't fall flat saved us from exploding. The aircraft went to pieces: the fuel tank fell on my right foot and squeezed it; I hit my head against the control panel and lost consciousness. Our ground personnel ran to our plane and extracted the navigator from her cockpit, but they couldn't pull me out because I was trapped by the fuel tank, which was too heavy to lift. So they had to axe the fuselage to break into the cockpit. I was happy to remain alive.

I can't help trembling when I recall an accident that happened in my squadron, for in recalling, it again comes alive. It took place on a mission over the Taman Peninsula. A very young crew of pilot and navigator came into my squadron as reinforcements. I always escorted new, unskilled crews to the target on their first flight, so after takeoff, I joined up with them. Our target was Mitridat in the Crimean. We dropped our bombs and made a turn to fly back when I saw a very low overcast rapidly advancing from the Black Sea. I idled the engine and dove to escape the overcast, but the clouds were growing incredibly fast, like a snowball, in front of our eyes. For awhile we could dive into the holes between heavy clouds, but they soon disappeared in that gray, scary mass. The wind increased, and I could see we were drifting. I made a sixty-degree drift correction, for the wind was strengthening, and there was extreme turbulence. I came out of the overcast at 300 meters. Below me was the sea—no shore in sight. The

Taman Peninsula separates the Black Sea from the Sea of Azov. I understood that I had not corrected my heading enough, and I had been blown to the Sea of Azov! The overcast pressed me lower to the water, and the aircraft was shaking heavily from the extreme turbulence. I corrected my course to fly back; I was thrown back and forth, up and down. I could hear the sounds of the water splashing below me, the sea spray streamed off the waves—my insides were throbbing and jumping. Around me was nothing but pitch-black emptiness, and the head wind was almost equal to the speed of my aircraft. For three hours I was suspended in the air and seemed not to move. Then, in the distance, I saw land; I prayed to the skies to help me to the land. Finally, I was able to land on the Taman Peninsula. I feared for the young crew, for there was no news of them—I knew they had crashed. A month later their bodies were found on the shore of the Sea of Azov. They ran out of fuel and fell into the sea.

On another mission over the Kerch Strait the engine quit. I couldn't even think of making a forced landing on the waters of the strait because it was winter, and our heavy fur overalls made it impossible to float to the surface. I throttled back to save on fuel and took advantage of the tail wind to make it to land. It was night, and I had to land in an area that had been mined by the Germans; the land was uneven, torn by explosions. I landed at minimum speed to reduce the landing roll. When we came to a stop, I was so happy and relieved that I jumped out of the cockpit and immediately fell into a deep trench! Fortune had smiled on me again.

When we were flying in the northern Caucasus, we would take off in clear weather and often return in dense fog that reached from the ground up to fifty meters. We found the location of the airdrome by orientation, for we knew all the terrain landmarks. On those foggy nights, the ground personnel would shoot a red flare to indicate the landing strip and a green one if they thought the aircraft was not in position to land. Landing in thick fog, I would enter that milky sheet, and when the cockpit began to darken, it was a sign that the land was close. Then I would pull the nose up and sink to the ground for a landing.

In Belorussia the Soviet troops began their major offensive on all fronts, pushing the enemy to the west. The front-line troops advanced very fast, and small numbers of enemy troops were encircled and scattered in the Belorussian woods. They were hiding there and were trying to fight back the attacks of the Soviet army. Our new location was a clearing in the woods, and when we landed, some of the girls went into the forest and saw very closely—nose to nose—German tanks masked among the trees! Our aircraft were short of fuel because the logistical battalion had been detained. But we had to leave because at any moment we could be attacked by the tanks, so we flew away. The situation itself was ridiculous. Here we were, encircled by the German tanks, while their tanks were encircled by the advancing Soviet army!

What did we all think then, the girls from the flying regiments? Was the war a woman's business? Of course not. But then we didn't think about that. We defended our fair motherland, our people whom the fascists had trampled. We won the greatest victory of the twentieth century! I never dreamed to see the victory. We sensed it, but by then I had a feeling I would not live to see it. Now having gone through that hell it has become priceless to me as never before.

There is an opinion about women in combat that a woman stops being a woman after bombing, destroying, and killing; that she becomes crude and tough. This is not true; we all remained kind, compassionate, and loving. We became even more womanly, more caring of our children, our parents, and the land that has nourished us.

After the war our regiment was released, and we all wanted to fly in civil aviation. I applied to the medical board, but I could not pass the medical examination. I had undermined my physical and mental health at the front; I was completely exhausted by the four years of war and combat. There was a period when we went without a day off for one hundred days.

I have always been a devoted Communist, and I have worked for the benefit of my people.

Lieutenant Polina Gelman,
navigator
Hero of the Soviet Union

When the war broke out I was a sergeant, and when I retired I was a major. I didn't fly after the war, but I still served. My pilot, Dusya Nosal, was killed, and the night she was killed I didn't fly with her. She was training another young navigator, and the navigator brought the plane back. Dusya was the first woman pilot to become a Hero of the Soviet Union in the Great Patriotic War. My next pilot was Maguba Syetlanova, a Tartar.

We flew one after another over the target every three minutes. The Germans liked to sleep at night, and they were very angry with the planes. They spread the rumor throughout the army that these were

Polina Gelman, 46th Guards
Bomber Regiment

neither women nor men but night witches. When our army advanced again, the civilians said to us that we were very attractive and that the Germans had told them that we were very ugly night witches!

The English book *Night Witches* is fictionalized; only the names are real. The book by Raisa Aronova of the same title was written during the war, tracing our path. She collected the events associated with a particular place and wrote chapters about the different personalities: a true chronicle. She herself flew in the regiment as a pilot and carried out 960 combat missions.

I was born in 1919 and grew up in the first postrevolutionary period. Right after the revolution it was like in your Civil War: everything was burning. I read the book *Gone with the Wind*, describing the events between the South and North, and it was all burning. We didn't know exactly what was going on then, we didn't know the real truth, the real roots of the events, but still it was a kind of an adventure for us. We were young, we had a very good time—we enjoyed it.

My father was killed in our Civil War when I was only five months old. My mother raised me by herself. She didn't have much education, but she was a very cultured woman who was well-read. She participated in the revolution in October, 1917, as a nurse. I remember her telling me how she brought bread, tobacco, and papers to the revolutionary prisoners, pretending to be a rich lady, and she also got clothes and false papers to the prisoners to help them escape. This all happened in the Ukraine region when power was switching from the Reds to the Whites, back and forth.

In 1919, when my mother was giving birth to me, a shell from the air destroyed half of the hospital, and my mother was in the half of the building that was safe. I consider it to have been a good sign because I am still alive! I went to a secondary school, finishing ten grades with excellent marks. When I was in ninth grade, my girl-friend and I decided to enter a glider school that had started in our town. In the glider school we first jumped with parachutes. On my first flight in the glider, the instructor told me to do a maneuver that he had shown me, and I had difficulty reaching the controls. I was very low in the cockpit, and he couldn't even see me, and that fright-ened him because I had disappeared! When we landed he called me such bad, dirty names that I have never heard again, and he said that I couldn't fly anymore because I was too little. I was in love with aviation and wanted to devote my life to it, but I was so unhappy that I could not become a pilot that I chose to go to Moscow University and study history.

On the day the war started, I was about to take my exams for my third-year courses. It was a Sunday, and when we heard the war had started, all the professors and students gathered at the university. We were patriotic and wanted to do something, to enlist or whatever. When we women applied to join the army along with the men, we were not accepted because the army would not draft women. We protested that we were brought up to believe that women were equal to men, and we thought that we should be allowed to go into the army, too. That summer all we could do was dig trenches around Moscow and put out fires, started by the fascist bombs, on the roofs of buildings.

In October, 1941, we learned that three women's air regiments were to be formed and trained, with Marina Raskova, Hero of the Soviet Union, as the commander. By this time there were many experienced women pilots in the USSR, but few women trained as navigators and mechanics. The women they wished to train in those fields were those who had completed at least a few years in universities, glider schools, or parachuting or aviation technical schools.

I applied and was accepted for training in the regiments and was selected to become a navigator. I was then assigned to the 588th Air Regiment, later to become the 46th Guards Bomber Regiment. We hated the German fascists so much that we didn't care which aircraft we were to fly; we would have even flown a broom to be able to fire at them! But we didn't fly brooms: we were given a biplane, the Po-2, to do our night bombing, without even any optical sights to indicate when to drop the bombs. Instead, we devised a method of visual sight-ing by making a chalk mark on the wing of the aircraft to indicate when to drop the bombs. This sight was unique in that each of us, being of different heights, would make a mark in a slightly different place—a personalized mark, it could be called—to help us in bombing accurately. This method proved to work extremely well in practice.

The slow speed of this aircraft, only 100 kilometers per hour, made us a target from both small-arms fire and antiaircraft guns. The plane was covered with fabric, and the fuel tanks were not shielded, which made us very vulnerable to being set on fire if we were hit. We wore no parachutes until late in the war.

In Mozdok, in the Caucasus, where we flew missions attacking the headquarters of the German staff, they had the most powerful searchlight we had yet encountered. If a searchlight caught our planes in its beam, we couldn't see anything—we were blinded. The pilot flew with her head very low in the cockpit because she could see nothing outside, and when we managed to get out of the beam we were still blinded for a few moments. It was difficult to even maintain the aircraft in level flight, because we flew only by visual references. The numerous searchlights caught and held us in their beams as spiderwebs hold a fly. They followed us even after we crossed the front line, and the guns followed us also. When we returned to the main airdrome and examined our aircraft, we found so many holes in it that it was like a sieve.

Later on we devised new tactics for our missions. We flew two planes at a time to the target. The first attracted all the searchlights and antiaircraft guns, and the other would glide in over the target, with its engine idling so the Germans couldn't hear it, and bomb the target. With all the attention on the first plane, the second could make a successful attack.

We carried flares with us on our night missions that were equipped with parachutes, so we had maximum use of their brilliant light as they drifted down to earth. We sometimes used them to find an emergency field, to light our airfield, or to locate a target. When we were to use a flare, I had to screw a pin out of the cylinder with my fingers, and when the pin was removed, I had just ten seconds before the flare was activated. So I immediately threw the flare over the side. In the winter we were provided with fur gloves, but I couldn't complete the procedure with the flare unless I removed the gloves. It was very cold, and my skin would stick to the metal of the cylinder. That was also true when I used the machine gun that was on a swivel rail on the back of my cockpit. Our aircraft was very primitive, and other planes more sophisticated than ours were provided with a mechanical means to drop the flares. There was a hook on the cylinder for use by those aircraft.

Once when we were on a mission, I was to drop a flare to make sure we were over the target, and I had taken off my gloves to activate the flare. In order not to lose my gloves, I always had them tied together with a leather cord. When I had activated the flare I tried to throw it over the side, but I couldn't because the hook had caught in the cord. I had ten seconds before we would have been on fire from the flare. The pilot was calling out that she was blinded by the searchlights and needed my help to orient herself, and I had to think what to do. So I stopped trying to free the flare and threw the flare with my gloves attached over the side. When the Germans had our plane in the searchlights and my pilot was disoriented, the only way she could orient herself was to have a flare light up the landscape. She would then be able to see in spite of the searchlights.

Once we were given a holiday on November 7 to celebrate the anniversary of the October Revolution. This was one of our few holidays, and we were constantly flying missions without any break. On this day we celebrated the holiday with wine. We were so out of the habit of drinking anything alcoholic that we got drunk immediately. In the middle of the celebration, about 10 P.M., the Germans began maneuvering, and the commander of the regiment ordered us to fly a combat mission. We put on our men's flying suits, which were too large for us, and the fur boots, which were very heavy and much larger than our feet. We were stationed in the Kuban region, and there was mud everywhere on our airdrome.

While we were running toward our planes, we sank into the mud. I felt quite drunk, and I would say to my pilot I wouldn't go; I would take another step and sink again into the mud, and my pilot came to me and dragged me out of the mud by the collar of my flying suit. In this way we finally got to the aircraft. She placed me in the cockpit, and we took off for the mission. It was overcast, and we were told to return if the overcast was lower than 560 meters. It really was lower but we continued. We felt very jovial and were not at all serious about the mission. When we saw the shadow of our aircraft on the clouds, we thought it was another plane flying along with us. We saw that when we turned right it did also, and when we turned left again it turned with us, and it made us laugh to see it. We laughed so much we didn't notice that we were flying over the target. We only realized it when the German searchlights caught us. Our interphone quit, and in order to warn the pilot that we were over the target, I had to lean forward and shout into her ear.

When we completed the mission and returned to our airdrome, the commander was very curious about what we were doing all this time. The overcast was below our limits, and all the other planes had turned back. The reason we were not to fly at lower altitudes than those specified was that dropping the bombs from any lower altitude would endanger our plane, because the explosion would blow upward and hit us. Upon inspection, our plane had been hit. There were two large holes that proved to our commander that we had really completed our mission and at a lower altitude than allowed.

We were in Germany in May, 1945, and everybody knew that the end of the war was near, and no one wanted to die. We were assigned to a mission within the range of 100 kilometers. Normally our missions were not to be more than 50 kilometers, but our commanders were impatient to finish the war as soon as possible. On this mission our engine overheated, and two of our engine cylinders lost their heads. According to regulations, we were supposed to find an unpopulated place to just drop our bombs and return to our airdrome. The visibility was zero, we could see nothing on the ground because of the fog, and we couldn't see where to drop the bombs. It could be on our own troops, on civilians, or on anyone. So we decided to land with the bombs still attached. We did not want to die, to risk our lives, but we had to do it even though we couldn't see the landmarks at the airdrome, only the red spots of the lights. The airdrome was near an old church, and it was the church spire that gave us our orientation. When we landed, we were not near the runway but on the edge of the forest. We stopped just one meter from the start of the forest. Out of joy that we were safe and alive, we jumped out of the cockpit and started an Indian dance.

There were other narrow escapes. Once when we were fulfilling a mission, a shell hit below my cockpit, and it stopped inside the parachute I was sitting on! God saved me. Another time a shell came through my high boot, but it did not even hit my foot or leg.

We were assigned a combat mission on May 8, one day before the victory. Everything was ready, the bombs loaded and the crews on their way to the aircraft, when suddenly we saw the mechanics run up to our aircraft and do something. What they were doing was deactivating the bombs. The Germans had surrendered; the war was over. I burst out crying. Everybody cried that day.

After the war I returned to Moscow University and received my degree in history and simultaneously graduated from the Academy of Military Interpreters. I worked as an interpreter and didn't like it. I studied economics and received a Ph.D. in economics. Then I was sent to Cuba to study the Cuban economy. I was there one year right after their revolution. The Cubans were very polite and nice to me. They would ask if I was a labor hero or a war hero, and when I said a war hero, they were fascinated.

Senior Lieutenant Serafima Amosova-Taranenko,
pilot, deputy commander of the regiment in flying

Serafima Amosova-Taranenko,
46th regiment

I was born in Siberia. An airplane once made a forced landing at our village, in a very distant rural area far from any city, and that was the first airplane I had ever seen. We were so excited, we ran around it, touching it; we were village children and didn't know anything about civilization. I couldn't even dream of becoming a pilot. After I finished seven grades in school I was sent to the city to study technical courses, and I was made a leader of small children. I was leading them down a street, teaching them about street signs, when I saw a model of an airplane on a sign hanging on a building. I went closer and saw that it was a flying club. Young volunteers could train in aviation before the war.

I entered the flying school at age eighteen, and I flew well and got excellent marks in glider school. Because I was an excellent pilot, I was allowed to open the air show there at our airdrome. We had no catapult, but the soldiers, who had been invited to stretch the elasticized rubber, stretched it very tight, and the glider took off much sooner than I expected. The plane pulled up into a vertical position and stalled over onto its back; then entered into a spin so the controls didn't respond, and it dove into the ground. People ran to get out of the way. I was injured and was taken to the hospital. At the hospital the medical staff ridiculed me and said I shouldn't have stuck my nose into male business anyway. Lying in bed, I secretly cried all night. I was very sorry for myself and my glider. This was in June, 1933.

In August, the government appealed to the young people to join a civil aviation school. I was then working as a Young Communist League leader in the regional Komsomol Committee, and I was appointed chief of the board selecting students for civil aviation school. I secretly put my name on the list to be admitted to the program. When the committee saw my name they refused to let me go, because they wanted me to perform Komsomol activities there. So I went to a higher level of the party, and they let me do it. I was the only woman in the class, and there were ten men. I was the only woman in the whole school! The boys there respected me, they worshiped me, and even loved me. They didn't even dare to touch me. I studied there for three years with excellent marks, and they said I could choose where I worked. I chose the western Siberian area so I could fly over my father's house; I wanted him to see me flying the plane. I went home when I graduated, and to my grief I learned my father had died in May. It was August, and no one had told me of his death!

In August, 1936, I began flying on the longest route in civil aviation, from Irkutsk, Siberia, to Moscow. I flew the aircraft that carried mail, a Pe-5. Then I flew as an airline pilot in a single-engine aircraft that carried nine passengers and a crew of two. In 1941, before the war, when I had been flying for five years as a civil pilot, I was drafted into a pilot training school to teach young men to fly. We trained boys whose knowledge was very limited and who had not even seen a steam engine before! It was during graduation exercises that we heard that war had broken out. Before the war, people would say the smell of powder was in the air, for war had already started in Europe. When the war began, I decided to join the army voluntarily. I was a pilot, second class. The army told me that no women were to fly in combat. In November, 1941, I received a cable saying that I should be released from my duties and report to the regiments being formed by Marina Raskova.

At the training base in Engels, I was taught to bomb targets in the Po-2 aircraft. I was appointed squadron commander in the 588th Air Regiment of night bombers. We trained for six months, eighteen hours a day. We were sent to the front in the Donetsk region in the Ukraine. Our objectives were to bomb front-line German depots, headquarters, ammunition supplies, troops, and other targets. We flew at night at a maximum altitude of 1,200 meters or, in cloudy

weather, at 600 meters minimum. The planes were fabric and plywood, and that, coupled with their slow speed, made them danger-
ously easy targets—a bullet could explode them.

When we arrived at the front, the first combat mission was made
by the regimental commander and the squadron commanders and
their navigators in crews of two. When we took off there were coal
deposits on fire, and coal burns constantly for years. On the way to
the target, no one fired at us. I recognized the landscape, and we had
no trouble. We flew back to the reference point, a torch that was
illuminated for us, and decided to make a second pass over the target.
When we flew over the target the second time, still no one fired at us.
We decided to release our bombs over the forest where the German
troops were concentrated, and when the bombs exploded, searchlights rocketed into the air, and antiaircraft guns began firing at us.
Going back, we had difficulty finding the airdrome because the area
was covered with smoke, and there were only three small sources of
light at the airfield. When we landed, our fellow pilots began hugging
and kissing us. We waited for the third crew to return, but it had been
shot down over the target—it was the commander of the second
squadron. We didn't give way to our grief, but we painted on the
fuselage of our planes: Revenge to the Enemy for the Death of our
Friends.

We were retreating to the east with furious battles. In the northern
Caucasus we bombed ferries crossing the Don River, and afterward
we had to land on another airdrome in the mountains because the
Germans were rapidly approaching. It was difficult to land in the
mountains at night because our airfield was near sea level, and we had
to descend in circles. I flew 555 combat missions.

When I became the deputy commander of the regiment in flying,
my main mission was to find airfields that we could use. The front
was fluid, and we were constantly moving from one airfield to another. Normally, we used two fields for our regiment: one, the home
airdrome; and the other, an auxiliary field about fifteen kilometers
closer to the front lines. We only landed there to rearm and refuel
during the night and then returned to our home airdrome before
daylight. The Germans couldn't find these bases close to the front
lines, because we left them before daylight when their reconnaissance planes came over our lines.

My other mission was to train new pilots. No reinforcements
came from the rear, and we had to retrain there at the front: navigators as pilots, and mechanics as navigators. I ran a flying school, so

to speak. We lost thirty pilots and navigators in our regiment during the war.

One night, as our aircraft passed over the target, the searchlights came on, the antiaircraft guns were firing, and then a green rocket was fired from the ground. The antiaircraft guns stopped, and a German fighter plane came and shot down four of our aircraft as each one came over the target. Our planes were burning like candles. We all witnessed this scene. When we landed and reported that we were being attacked by German fighters, they would not let us fly again that night. We lived in a school building with folding wooden beds. You can imagine our feelings when we returned to our quarters and saw eight beds folded, and we knew they were the beds of our friends who perished a few hours ago. It was impossible not to cry. It was a great loss and pain but none of us surrendered, and we were full of anger and decided to pay the enemy back for the loss of our friends.

On one airfield where we were stationed there were two regiments, one female and one male. We had the same missions, the same aircraft, and the same targets, so we worked together. The female regiment performed better and made more combat flights each night than the male regiment. The male pilots before a flight started smoking and talking, but the women even had supper in the cockpit of their aircraft. Once one of the German prisoners said, "When the women started bombing our trenches we (Germans) had a number of radio nets, and the radio stations on this line warned all their troops, 'Attention, attention, the ladies are in the air, stay at your shelter.'"

Nobody knows the exact date when they started calling us night witches. We were fighting in the Caucasus near the city of Mozdok; on one side of this city were Soviet troops and on the other, German. We were bombing the German positions nearly every night, and none of us was ever shot down, so the Germans began saying these are night witches, because it seemed impossible to kill us or shoot us down.

Once when I was looking for an auxiliary airstrip for a night landing, I couldn't know from the air that there were a lot of mines on this field. I landed, and an officer, calling to me and waving his hands, approached my aircraft and said, "Can't you see this field is mined!" Then I saw there were mines, but fortunately I landed between the rows of them. When I chose a field, it had to be convenient for landing and taking off at night. It also needed some space for about two hundred ground personnel and the maintenance battalion with its fuel, bombs, and ammunition. I had to take care that there was camouflage at night and to foresee all those things. And you are landing on this field with fear, but it is your duty.

The women in the regiment were very friendly and caring with each other, and it helped us to stand our situation. When I would see that one crew was caught by artillery fire and spotlights and I was flying behind them, I would start bombing these projectors and positions and help them to escape death. So friendship, mutual support, and love of our motherland helped us to endure and to await the victory. It is a surprise that during the war none of us had ever asked for a rest at the hospital for some illness. They paid attention to the women's situation in our regiment, and the girls had the right not to fly. But the women didn't report to the regimental doctor or tell anybody about their problems—they kept on flying. After the war we had a lot of headaches, could not relax, and had very hard problems with our sleeping, because for nearly three years we turned over the day and night. During daytime we could sleep for only about four hours, and that is not enough. Then, with training and briefing, there were a lot of sleepless nights. For the first year after the war everyone had problems with sleeping, and I know there were no sleeping pills. I couldn't sleep for at least three months.

I could go on talking about it because we had been fighting for one thousand nights—one thousand nights in combat. Every day the girls became more courageous. To fly a combat mission is not a trip under the moon. Every attack, every bombing is a dance with death. In spite of this, every girl knew the danger, and none ever refused to fly her mission or used a pretext to avoid participating in the bombing. Our feelings were that we were doing a simple job, just a job to save our country, to liberate it from the enemy. I don't know what was in the hearts of these girls when they were climbing into and sitting in the cockpit before their flight. I don't know, but you could not read on their faces any fear or feeling of danger, and they performed their duty with an open heart and very honestly and bravely.

After the war, I continued to fly for two years; then, because of the condition of my health, I retired. In 1947 I married a military man and had to change my domicile from Rostov to the Ashkhabad town area. There was an earthquake in Ashkhabad in 1948 when Stalin was in power, and he ordered us not to tell anybody. Even in our own country nobody knew the situation! They announced there was an earthquake and there were no victims, as usual. In the U.S., Canada, and Mexico there would be lots of victims, lots of damage; and in this country there was no information, no damage, no victims at all. So no help was sent.

After the war our country was destroyed, and we didn't have any help from anyone. Ashkhabad was completely destroyed. Only the mosques, the building of the party organization, and some other buildings built before the war survived the earthquake. I saw Kerch city in the Crimea when the city was destroyed during the war, but the picture in Ashkhabad was completely the same. It was destroyed. My daughter was born in August, and she died in this earthquake. It took place late at night. There are a lot of mosquitoes in that area, and when they bite you they leave scars and wounds on your body. So I decided to put her near the wall, and during the earthquake the building crashed completely.

Forty-five years have passed since the war, and the women that took part in it are still friends. We are very happy when we come together, and we get together often to celebrate some occasion. We help each other financially and in morale, and we write a lot of letters to each other. We send postcards to each other on VE Day with poems, pictures, or drawings.

NOTE: Serafima Amosova-Taranenko died in 1992.

Captain Klavdiya Ilushina,
engineer of the regiment

I was born in 1916 in Moscow in the family of a worker. I finished secondary school in Moscow and entered a technical college, studying engineering and electronics. After my third year I was sent to Gorky to help build an automobile manufacturing plant. This was my practical training, to work in actual construction. This period just before the war was one of developing heavy industry in our country, and there was much construction of industrial plants.

After graduation I was sent to the region of Noginsk to work in an electrical station. I realized that I lacked knowledge, so I wanted to learn more in my field and decided to go on with my studies. I submitted my documents to the aviation department of a military engineering academy. I chose that particular department, because since my childhood I had been dreaming of connecting my life with aviation. The competition was severe. There were forty-seven men and women who submitted their documents to study there, and only three were to be admitted to the academy. And I was one of them!

These were the most magnificent, most wonderful years of my youth. I lived the very process of acquiring knowledge; it brought me mental satisfaction. The staff of the department were very friendly to me because there were only two women in the department. Women then, as women today, had absolute equal opportunity with men. The faculty found me to be one of the brightest cadets, and I graduated with flying colors.

When I entered the academy my health was very poor, caused by the poverty of our country, because I had starved a lot in my youth. The academy treated this problem with sympathy and understanding and sent me to a sanatorium several times. They also gave me breaks at the third, fourth, and fifth courses just to give me a time to relax. I graduated from the academy in May, 1941, and I was twenty-five years old.

When the war broke out I was drafted to an aircraft plant. I was on the board that tested the aircraft and examined the planes and the equipment. But I didn't want to be in the rear; I wanted to be in active army service, and I requested that I be drafted to the front. I was given an option to either stay at the aviation plant or to go with the regiments then being formed by Marina Raskova. I chose the regiments.

I was immediately drafted as the engineer of the regiment. Then I found myself in the 46th Guards Bomber Regiment. I was in that regiment from its origin until the last day of the war. In August, 1946, when the regiment was released, I returned to Moscow with the rank of captain.

My duty during the war was as engineer of the equipment installed in the aircraft, and I was responsible for its maintenance and proper operation. The equipment in the Po-2 was quite simple, but I had a heavy work load because the regiment had many planes, and each night I had to see to each one.

When I first came to the regiment, I was not pleased. I wasn't used to working with girls, for I had always worked with men. The girls seemed noisy, and some of them were naughty. The ground personnel, I mean the mechanics, were from a very common strata of society: from factories, from working families. The pilots and navigators and technical staff all came from universities and colleges, and they were not homogeneous. It irritated me in the first period of my service, but later on, after I was in closer contact with the girls, we all became like sisters. Up to the present day we call all members of our regiment sisters.

Every day held anxiety and concern, for we lost one-third of the regiment in a very short period, and among them were my closest friends. Each night was a kind of torture. We prepared the aircraft for combat missions, and at times they flew ten or more missions in a night. That was twenty or thirty aircraft to be refueled and rearmed ten times a night. Each night I moved to the auxiliary field in one of the regimental vehicles, where I oversaw the preparation of the aircraft during the night. We never had enough sleep; not for the whole war did we have sufficient sleep. The mechanics prepared the aircraft for combat all during the night, and they repaired and tested them in the daytime. We averaged two hours of sleep at the end of the night's bombing missions. It would have been impossible to carry out that schedule if we had not had some breaks. When the weather was very bad the planes didn't fly, and on a few occasions we had a holiday.

I had married while I was at the military academy. My husband was drafted into the army in the very first days of the war, and then he was killed in action. I had no time for love during the war.

At one point we were stationed in the Caucasus in an area that was very close to a swamp. There were lots of mosquitoes, and I was bitten so severely that I was ill, and my body was covered with red spots. The regimental doctor decided to take me to Rostov on the Don for examination and consultation with another doctor. While we were on our way to that military hospital, we were bombed and fired upon. When we came to the hospital, there was another very severe bombing. The Germans were bombing the hospital, and people were being wounded and killed. They were carrying the wounded out of what had been the hospital, but it was completely destroyed; I was so shattered by what I was witnessing that I broke down completely. It was a carnage! The doctors were totally engaged in caring for the dying and wounded, and our doctor decided that we should return at once to our regiment.

On our journey back, I looked down at my body and saw the disease had vanished—all the red spots had disappeared completely! It must have been the trauma of the bombing, but I left the regiment absolutely sick and returned absolutely healthy. Out of that terrible tragedy came a small comedy.

Another time we were stationed in Belorussia, and the area was in a state of flux. First our troops were encircled, then they were not. The Germans and our troops were all mixed in close proximity, and an area would be first under our control, then under German troops. We were sleeping in tents at the airfield, and just before dawn, we saw a group of people moving toward us. We didn't know what to do. Were they the enemy or Soviet troops? We got ready to fire at them, and at that moment they displayed a white flag. It turned out that they were Soviet troops who had gotten lost in the woods. The white flag saved their lives and our lives: we would have fired at them. There were so many units encircled and milling around with the Germans that even the commanders had no clear idea of the situation.

In the Crimea we were advancing, and we moved into a Ukrainian settlement, a village; we were billeted in their houses. I was in a house where I was treated to a very good meal, and it was Easter time. The housewife cooked special cakes and eggs and other good things to eat. We were so excited and happy that we at last were going to have substantial meals and a good sleep. By then all I could think about and dream about was a full night's sleep. So at last I fell into bed and went to sleep. I dreamed that the aircraft in the regiment were being bombed by the fascists. Then the housewife shook me by the shoulder and said, "You must get up, your airfield is being bombed, your aircraft are burning!" Well, the dream coincided with the truth. I had a fortune-telling vision in my dream!

We all rushed to the airfield to save our planes. I threw on my clothes and shoes in the darkness and ran out of the house, and it wasn't until I was running toward the airfield that I realized I had on my high heels. I lost the heel of one shoe, and at that moment a German plane came down the road, following me with tracer bullets. He was flying at such low altitude that I could see his face. I threw myself flat on the ground, and he flew over me.

When I came to the airfield many of our planes were damaged, some burning and some destroyed. The Germans had gone. I jumped into the cockpit of one of the aircraft to check the damage, and the German planes returned and continued bombing. I dove out of the cockpit onto the ground and lay under the wing. There were no trenches in which to hide, the bombing was heavy, and all of us lay on the ground with no protection, waiting for it to stop. When they flew away two or three of the girls were wounded, and our planes sustained heavy damage.

Before that episode, the regiment was inspected by the commander of the front. He was not satisfied with us because he did not like the underwear and linen hung out on clotheslines, nor was he satisfied with the combat readiness of the regiment. The second time he came to inspect he was completely satisfied with our readiness, and he decided to reward the girls with suits, coats, skirts, and a pair of high-heeled shoes. So they were ordered and given to all the girls in the regiment. And that is why I had high-heeled shoes at the front!

While we were stationed in the Crimea, we were flying from our air base to the auxiliary airfield when we were attacked by a German fighter. The Po-2 had four of us, the pilot, navigator, myself, and a mechanic, squeezed into the two cockpits. I could hear the zinging of the bullets passing by my head, but miraculously, none of us was hit. The plane was punctured all over with small holes, and the instrument panel was smashed. It was difficult for the pilot to control the plane, but she had to land because we had no parachutes. As we approached for the landing, the German pilot circled and came back to shoot us down. There was nothing to be done but try to get the plane on the ground. It happened that a formation of our fighters appeared, passing overhead, and the German turned back toward his own lines. That is what saved us.

After the war I remained in the military, and I retired at the age of fifty-five in the rank of lieutenant-colonel after thirty-two years.

Senior Lieutenant Yevgeniya Zhigulenko,
pilot, commander of the formation
Hero of the Soviet Union

Yevgeniya Zhigulenko,
46th regiment.
Photograph by Khaldei

I was born in the Kuban region. My relatives come from Norway, and my grandfather was the captain of a vessel. For some faults he was dismissed from the navy, and later on he immigrated to Russia and settled in the Kuban region. My original name, my maiden name, is Azarova. The name Zhigulenko I have now stuck to me quite accidently. If you are aware of the events that went on in Russia in the early post-revolutionary years, with the Civil War between the Reds and the Whites—Russians killing Russians—trying to prove by means of blood whose power was stronger, then you know that the massacre was nearly impossible to escape. My father did not want to be involved in the Civil War. He managed to get a passport that had belonged to a man, Zhigulenko by name. According to those papers Zhigulenko was a physically disabled man, not to be recruited to the army. Thus my father survived, and from then on the family had this name. It is traditional in this country for a woman to change her last name when she marries, so I knew I wouldn't have that name when I married. But in the end it has happened that I've been wearing that name all my life! I feel pity for my original name—I wish I could have it back. I feel so much that we all have our roots manifested in this way.

Since my childhood I have been a freedom-loving Cossack girl riding a horse along the Kuban steppes. My spirit has always been emancipated, unconquered, and proud. Nothing passes by me unnoticed—that is a part of my Cossack nature also. Suddenly, out of nowhere, a strong desire to fly was born in my flesh. In my teens, when at school, I joined a glider club. I was full of dreams and romanticism; another wild desire dazzling in my mind was that I wanted to be an actress. I had drama classes, and we staged several performances in my native town. I even had a pseudonym just as an actor does, and I named myself Lola Bredis.

In the course of my life this childish craziness came true, and I became a movie director. Many years after the war I went to film school in Moscow. I have made two feature films, and in the second I had a small part as an actress.

Back to my youth: when I finished secondary school I moved to Moscow and entered college, but I couldn't completely quit my secret dream of flying. I was spellbound by the mystery of flight. I thought of it as my integration with the universe. At night, I went to Tushino Airfield for night flying in the glider school; in the day, I attended college. I devoted my spare time to music classes at the Moscow Conservatory. You can see now how gigantic my perspective was—how tempting was my life unfolding, how it swirled around me in its wild dance!

On June 22, 1941, I was returning to my college hostel room, full of joy and life, and I sensed something tense in the air. The war—the war has started, the girls told me. I had only a vague knowledge about war, from books, mass media, and propaganda. Now it was a reality to live with. I made up my mind to go to the front.

My path to the front was a comedy. My friend Nina and I had no profession when the war broke out, no skill applicable to the front. We devised a plan. We dug out a telephone number of a colonel in the airforce headquarters in Moscow, and we called him. We spoke to him mysteriously and never revealed our secret on the phone. We said we could tell him our secret only in private. We persistently dialed his office telephone number for a week. We drove him crazy for the whole week, so he surrendered. He signed for us a pass to his office in the airforce headquarters. We entered that huge, concrete building, and going down its long corridors we promised each other that we would never leave the office until they let us go to the front.

I opened the door of the colonel's office and announced, "Comrade Colonel, if you try to get rid of us we will sleep here, we will not leave, we will stay here forever!" He looked at us in horror; his mouth dropped open. We sensed he thought us two crazies. Then he sternly said to us, "What is your case?" We answered that until they let us go to the front, we would not leave. He burst out laughing. "You girls should have told me about it at once! Marina Raskova is forming female flying regiments; she is to be here in a few minutes, and you may personally talk with her."

She arrived so alive and so miraculously beautiful—we were spellbound. We stood breathless, so great was our emotion. She smiled at us; she was well aware of her enigmatic beauty. We murmured affirmatively when she asked if we wanted to join the regiments. She gave us passes to the Zhukovsky Academy, where the regiments were being assembled. Thus my girlfriend and I joined the regiment.

At the training field in Engels, I was assigned as a navigator. Those assigned as pilots had many more hours in the air than I. All of us who were navigators looked upon ourselves as a very elite group because our backgrounds were of colleges and universities. We were well-read, intellectually minded, had good manners, and never heard or said dirty words.

I was assigned to the 588th Air Regiment, and after training we were sent to the front. I flew as navigator with pilot Polina Makogon, who was only twenty-five; but I, being nineteen, considered her to be quite old. Our flights together made me believe everyone was born under her own star, lucky or tragic; but we are all destined to our own fate, a fate impossible to change no matter what the circumstances. My flights as a navigator with Polina substantiated this observation. There were three episodes, the first being in the Caucasus, where our airfield was located in a vast, hilly land. The runway abruptly ended in a steep precipice, but ordinarily it was long enough for the aircraft to take off and land. We took off on a mission, and the wheels had just left the ground when the engine coughed and died. The plane returned to earth, and we were rushing toward the precipice. The Po-2 aircraft were without brakes, and by a miracle we stopped just ten steps from the abyss. We gasped with relief; it was my first experience when I sensed mortality in the air.

We were assigned to bomb a bridge that the Germans were constructing from the left bank of the Mozdok River. On the right bank were our troops. From above, at an altitude of 1,200 meters, it is difficult at night to discern what is below. The small bridge seemed a thin thread. To hit it a pilot had to concentrate all her energy and vision, and more than that, to know exactly her speed, altitude, and course for a full minute before the bomb was dropped. When the target became discernible and was under the wing of the aircraft, I cried to the pilot to hold to the left because we were drifting with the wind. Our bombs missed the target.

The antiaircraft guns were firing, and the searchlights lit up the sky around us. I was sweating and could feel a strip of sweat rolling down my back. We turned from the target, giving way to following aircraft. In the turn we fell into a stall and were nearing a crash, but she managed to recover. Later on, when I myself piloted the aircraft, I understood why she lost control over the target. There is a superhuman psychic overstrain when you are blinded by the searchlights and deafened by the explosions of antiaircraft shells and fire all around you. Your concentration over the target is so intense that it results in a complete loss of your whereabouts—a disorientation. You cannot tell the sky from the ground. Many of our crews crashed in that way.

Another proof in support of my theory of destiny: our aircraft was hit by enemy fire in the Caucasian foothills, and we were descending into a forced landing. In the pitch blackness I could discern a hill on the right side and called out to the pilot to stay to the left, otherwise we would crash into the hill. I was not sure she had heard me, so I decided to flare the area to see the landscape, although for us to use a flare in that way was strictly forbidden—the enemy could spot us. But our lives were at stake, so I violated the order; I had a strong urge to live. In the light of the flare Polina could see the hill; she made a quick turn to the left, and we escaped the crash.

Soon after that episode I was made a pilot, and a younger and less skilled navigator was assigned to fly with Polina. They were flying back from a mission and collided with another aircraft in the air. Both crews crashed and perished. With me, my pilot escaped death three times; with another navigator, she perished. I don't associate her death with any unskillfulness of the navigator. Now that I am so closely studying occult sciences and astrology, I think my pilot was destined to die so young. But I was her silver cord—the thread that

held her to survive. As soon as that invisible connection was torn off
between us, she perished.

In the regiment we had a shortage of pilots, and so navigators were
retrained to become pilots and ground personnel to become navigators. My advantage was that I already knew how to fly, so I became a
pilot. By the end of the war I had a greater number of combat hours
than most of the air crews. I managed to outstrip them because I have
very long legs! There was an order in the regiment that the first pilot
to get into the cockpit and start the engine was to be the first to take
off; I was always the first because I ran faster!

We all volunteered to go to the front and strove to fulfill the most
combat missions, even beyond our physical capacity. We longed to
see the end of that horrible war, to liberate our fair motherland. We,
young girls of the flying regiments, did our best to contribute to the
defeat of the enemy and victory for our suffering people.

But life remains life, and we, as military pilots, still remained
young girls. We dreamed of our grooms, marriages, children, and a
future happy, peaceful life. We thought to meet our future mates at
the front. But our 46th regiment was unique, for it was purely female.
There wasn't even a shabby male mechanic to rest a glance on. Nevertheless, after a night of combat we never forgot to curl our hair.
Some girls thought it unpatriotic to look attractive. I argued that we
should. I said, "Imagine that I have a forced landing at a male fighter
airdrome. Soldiers are rushing to my aircraft because they know that
the crew is female. I, absolutely dashing, slide out of the cockpit and
take off my helmet, and my golden, curly hair streams down my
shoulders. Everyone is awed by my dazzling beauty. They all desperately fall in love with me."

The Soviet army began advancing into the Crimean Peninsula. Our
mission was to keep enemy bombers from taking off from their airfield
by bombing the airstrip every few minutes. My assignment was to map
a course for the regiment and to drop firebombs, which produced a
series of small fires indicating the location of their airdrome for the
other crews to follow. In order not to lose our orientation, we had to
flare the area. The instant the flare lit the area, we were over their
cement landing strip. My navigator then suggested that we fly on five
kilometers to the fascist weapon storage area and bomb it.

We dropped bombs and set the building on fire. For the next several
seconds the silence was frightening, because I knew very well the
enemy would react and smash us to pieces. I was all nerves and fear,
and my teeth clenched. Then the guns all fired along with search-

lights. I smelled gas in the cockpit—the fuel line was hit! When I saw the storage building flaming above me and the moon below me, I knew we had entered a stall. I recovered instinctively. The plane was shaking, losing flying speed and altitude. I headed toward the waters of the strait, and I remembered that there was an auxiliary field somewhere in the hills.

I called to my navigator to give me directions, but there was no reaction. I turned in my seat and to my horror found no navigator. I began sweating at the thought that I had lost my navigator while we were stalling upside down. I could not stand that thought—I had no right to come back to the regiment without her. The altitude of the aircraft was dropping down and down; then the altimeter showed no height at all.

I found myself whispering to my mama to help me. Ahead of me were the banks of the strait. I felt the wheels sliding on the water; then they hit and stuck in the sand. I had made it just to the water's edge. Then I heard my navigator's voice. "What the hell!" I was crazy with relief and happiness. I turned and leaned over her; she was stuck in the cockpit with one leg pierced through the cabin floor. She was alive, she was safe!

While we were stalling, her seat had fallen to the bottom of the cabin, and her leg had stuck into the broken floor. When she took off her helmet, I saw a huge bump on her forehead; she had hurt her head when we crashed. The infantrymen were running to our wrecked plane. She, who had miraculously escaped death, was now grieving over her forehead because she wanted to look attractive! Life took over from the war—we all wanted to love and be loved. She cried with dismay, "Look how many grooms are around, and who is going to marry me with this huge bump on my forehead?" I burst out laughing, but it was a hysterical laughter. Thus I relieved myself of that intensity of fear and tension.

Many of our crews were killed in the war, and we had to cope with this as best we could. The way I felt then was that I wanted the old times of my happy youth to return, and I idealistically visualized it. But at the bottom of my heart the feelings were more complex and complete. Seeing and hearing those massacred or herded into concentration camps as slave labor intensified and hardened our will and desire for revenge.

All my life I've been living with a vision that has become the main theme in both my feature films: a small boy, helpless and desperate in his misfortune. He is not a fruit of my fantasy—he is a real person. In my films he is a symbol of the great Russian tragedy of the millions of homeless, orphaned children.

I met this child on one of my missions. We were flying back to our regiment at dawn, and in the outskirts of a Belorussian village I saw something very tiny, a black spot—but it was something alive. When we landed I saw a small boy all alone in the deserted village. My first impulse was to give him all the rations each pilot carries in her emergency sack: candies, a bar of chocolate, sugared milk. I grabbed it from the cabin and flew to the child, spreading my arms like wings, hoping to see a smile on the face of that tiny creature whom I could make happy for at least a few moments. But in front of me was a skinny, frozen face with enormous green eyes. And in them no glimpse of joy. "Aunty, are you going to the front?" he asked me, and in his voice was a weak hope. "My daddy is at the front. Find him, please. My mama is dying there in the trench. If you find him, she won't die. . . ."

So you see, we couldn't help flying in combat, and we did our best for those tiny human beings so they would never have to suffer anymore—it was a genuine truth of heart.

Junior Lieutenant Olga Yerokhina-Averjanova, mechanic of armament

I was born in 1924. Now I am a retired medical doctor. When the war broke out I was finishing secondary school; I was seventeen. I had a discussion at home with my mother and father, and we decided that I should go to the front to defend the motherland. It was a home council. Moreover, I was the leader of the Communist League organization at school. I lived in the Caucasus in the city of Stavropol.

At first they didn't want to take me into the army because I was so young and didn't have any technical background. But later I was allowed to join the army, and I was admitted into the military school of junior airforce staff. I studied there for three months and was then admitted to the 63rd Air Regiment, a male regiment, which flew the Boston-29 aircraft. I was a mechanic of armament.

In 1943 Bershanskaya, commander of the 46th Guards Bomber Regiment, selected me as a reinforcement for her regiment. It was easier to serve in the male regiment in the physical sense that the heavy duties were performed by the men. But from the point of view of human relationships, it was much better in the women's regiment. When we were on duty we called each other and members of the command and staff by their rank, very officially; and then in the mess or barracks, we called each other informally, addressing each other by our first names. This made friendships and relationships, and it was all due to Bershanskaya, our commander, because she was a marvelous person.

We had a terrible accident in the Caucasus, when four of our aircraft crashed into each other. Two of them were awaiting permission to land at night after a mission, and they were circling and circling because nearby were German fighters, and they couldn't allow them to land. Two others were taking off on a combat mission, so in that darkness they ran into each other and crashed. Only one person survived while seven perished. Some of those could have survived, but they hadn't been provided with parachutes. When they hit the ground some of them were still alive and were crying out for someone to save them because their aircraft were on fire. No one could help them. They couldn't escape from the cockpits, and nobody could come close to the planes because of the fires. They exploded, one after another. Only one managed to escape from the cockpit, and she was permanently crippled.

After each combat night we were allowed to sleep three or four hours before a new duty day. But on the night of a crash we never slept, never left the airfield. We waited until dawn, believing in miracles, asking God to save our girls, waiting for them to return. Many of them did not come back, but sometimes when the planes were missing after a mission they really did return. They were shot down and made emergency landings, returning sometimes two or three days later. They were considered to have perished, but happily they turned out to be alive and safe. Each loss was a great grief to us.

The aircraft carried different types of bombs. One small one made a crackling sound when it hit, and it was very frightening to those on the ground. The biggest complication to our duty was that we had to work at night loading the bombs, and we used torches. If the batteries gave out, we were forced to load the bombs by feeling with our hands where to attach them to the aircraft.

Once when we were stationed in Poland, a male engineer of the air division came to check our work. He decided to teach us how to handle all the equipment and fuses and how to fix everything on the aircraft—he wanted to show us his manly skills. He took an explosive device in his hands that was ready to explode, and when I saw what was happening, I jumped up and threw it away from his hands. At that moment the device exploded, and a piece of shell penetrated his head. He was cut from his eyebrow along his cheek.

We had some nights that we called our maximum nights. These were nights when the air crews made from 12 to 18 missions. Irina Sebrova was a leader in the competition to complete missions; she had 1,008 combat missions, and I worked on the aircraft of her formation. Near the end of the war I was promoted to junior lieutenant.

Our regiment received attention and much publicity during the war, and we were promoted more frequently than the male regiments. The men didn't believe that women could do any good at the front; they thought that it was not the female job to fly combat or serve in the army. Later on, when we had proven ourselves, they respected us.

Hygienically, it was a hardship. We didn't have enough soap or water. Sometimes we used water from puddles to wash ourselves. In one area the water was very salty, so we would melt snow. Our staff would say that we had to always remember that we were women and take care of ourselves.

First we fought in the Caucasus, then in the Crimea, then on the Belorussian front. The women of our regiments would never wish a war to come to anyone—to kill or be killed. All of us wanted to be peaceful, friendly, kind, open, the way we are now in 1990.

Junior Lieutenant Mariya Tepikina-Popova,
pilot, deputy squadron commander

I was born in 1917 in the Urals near the town of Sverdlovsk, and I came to aviation accidentally. I went to teachers' college, and when I was a third-year student, the Komsomol leader of our college suggested that I should enter a pilots' school in Bataisk. He chose me because I was an athlete at school. I was afraid to be trained as a pilot; I didn't know if I could do it. I had planned to be a teacher, but the Komsomol leader persuaded me. From 1936 to 1939 I attended that aviation pilots' school. I was nineteen when I entered pilot training.

When I graduated I flew as a pilot with Aeroflot, our national airline. I had been flying with the airline for two years when the war broke out. I married during this period, and my husband was a pilot, too. When the war started, he was drafted into the army air forces and was shot down and killed in 1941. In October, 1941, right after my husband perished, I was transferred to the town of Dzhanbul with my baby son. I worked there as an instructor until 1943, and there I also buried my son. You can understand my sentiments when I tell you that I couldn't stay in the rear anymore because I lost both of those dear to me, but they wouldn't let me go to the front until 1943. I cried for three days before the commander of the pilot training school allowed me to leave.

I went to Moscow to military headquarters. They wanted me to join the 125th Dive Bomber Regiment flying the Pe-2, because I had by then over 900 flying hours. Before then I never even knew that there were women's regiments! Then I heard that Bershanskaya commanded the 46th Guards Bomber Regiment, and because I knew her, I asked to be assigned to her regiment as a reinforcement pilot.

While I was being interviewed at headquarters, a personnel officer saw my last name and asked if I was related to the political officer of the same name, who was assigned to the same training school where I had been a pilot. I knew that the political officer had been taken and imprisoned as an enemy of the republic in 1937. I thought quickly how I would best answer, because I was not related to him. But in those times you had to answer in such a way as to completely deny any knowledge of him, or the consequences could be quite unpredictable and could include prison. So I answered that I kept my distance from the command and staff of the school and didn't know him. The personnel officer understood my evasive response and replied, "Oh, since he was my best friend, and you are a Tepikina too, I'll let you join the 46th regiment."

I joined the regiment in August, 1943, and I flew my first combat mission a week later. I learned to see in the dark and to determine our target visually. It took practice to recognize objects in the darkness. On summer nights we flew five or so combat missions, and in winter we flew ten and up to fifteen missions. When we returned to reload the plane with bombs and fuel, the navigator would go in and report on the mission just completed. The pilot would stay in the cockpit, and I often dozed while this was going on.

Once when we had been heavily shelled by antiaircraft fire and were walking together toward the command headquarters to report that fact, we turned to look at each other. We burst out laughing, because we were covered with black soot from the explosion of the shells so close to us in the air! And so we remained alive.

I had three forced landings during the war. Once we were assigned a mission in the Crimean area of the Black Sea where our troops were making a landing on the seacoast. There was a very powerful searchlight used by the Germans to spotlight our troops, and then they would shoot at them. I asked our commander if I could blow up the searchlight and got her permission. We succeeded in gliding in quietly with our engine throttled back and then blew it up. But when I opened the throttle to regain our altitude, the engine would not increase power but continued to idle. I didn't want to land in the sea, so I decided to glide to the coast. Then I quite clearly saw the road that led from the coast to our auxiliary airfield, and although I had only 160 meters of altitude, I did manage to glide over the low hills and make it back to the field.

Another time I was on a mission in the Kerch region, and before I crossed the front lines I noticed that the oil pressure had dropped to zero. I knew that in a few minutes the engine would burn up, so I turned back. Below me I saw the signaling lights of an auxiliary airfield and the responding lights of a partisan aircraft, and I descended to land. When we had to make an emergency landing, it was best and safest to drop the bombs before landing. But if we could not see an open area when we were on our side of the front lines, we did not drop them for fear of killing our own troops. In this case I could not drop the bombs, and so I landed ahead of the partisan aircraft, leaving him to circle the field again, because I had a load of bombs. The officer in charge of the airfield started cursing me as I taxied in, calling me every dirty name he knew, because I had cut off the other plane in the landing pattern. Also, he didn't want a loaded bomber landing there. Then, as I drew near him, he recognized me as a fellow pilot from our civil flying days.

What I feared most was flying toward the searchlights and the antiaircraft guns and worrying about the disposition of the guns relative to the target. After dropping the bombs the emotional strain receded, and when we hit the target we cheered. Even my navigator was clapping her hands and beating her feet on the floor, and we forgot about our fear.

Once I was flying a mission, and with forty-five seconds remaining before dropping our bombs, we were caught first by one searchlight and then by some twenty more searchlights. We dropped the bombs, and then I managed to escape by opening the throttle and diving at a speed of up to 170 kilometers per hour. Our maximum diving speed was supposed to be 150. We flew out over the Black Sea at a very low altitude, and then we flew back to our field. When we arrived, nobody expected to ever see us again, because they saw us in all those searchlights and did not think we could escape them. The most amazing thing was that our plane was not even hit on that mission. We were met at the airdrome with hurrahs from the other crews.

I remember when we had our airdrome on the banks of the Neman River, and the Germans, on the other bank, were firing every morning at the girls going to the toilets. To avoid needless losses, our commander asked the ground forces if they could stop that firing. About thirty troops crossed the river and were then subjected to heavy fire from the Germans. A soldier swam back across the river and asked our commander to help save them because they were suffering losses! Our commander sent one aircraft to bomb that area from a height of 900 meters, and they missed. So then I was sent on the same mission with Rufina, my navigator. We flew in at 500 meters and hit the target. Upon our return to the airdrome, there were shouts of hurrah by the whole regiment. We had saved the girls.

On the way back from that mission, we saw a group of fascist soldiers lying in the wheat two kilometers from our field. When we reported it, we were asked to fly over that place and drop a flare to indicate where the Germans were. The navigator said we could not drop a flare because it would burn the wheat field. I circled and dove at the German position three times, down to five meters so our troops could find them. Our soldiers encircled them, and they were captured.

I made 640 combat missions, and I was awarded four orders. I married again in 1945—I married a pilot, and we had a wedding party there in the regiment. Our regiment was released in October, 1945. In 1947 I managed to get a position as a copilot in civil aviation, flying cargo aircraft. I flew only one year, and then the doctors refused to let me fly anymore.

Senior Sergeant Nina Yegorova-Arefjeva,
mechanic of armament

I come from Yaroslavl, a town on the Volga River. I only managed to finish secondary school, and the very next day the war broke out. When I first heard that Marina Raskova was forming the regiment, my first impulse was not to try to join the regiment but to go to the front.

When I joined the army, I was first sent to a military school to take a ground course in aircraft armament. That was in the Caucasus, seventy kilometers from Tbilisi, the capital of Georgia. The class ahead of me had been studying armament for three years before the war, and we were to study for only three months! Ours was a female class: only women. We studied twelve hours a day. Only the command and staff and instructors were men. We hardly slept.

We didn't have any textbooks, and we had to listen and take notes. There was a great shortage of paper in the country, as there is now, and we had to take newspapers and write between the lines for our notes. Further, we not only had to study twelve hours a day but also perform our duties: get up for alarms at night, and at times go to collective farms to help pick and collect the crops. We lived in wooden houses with twenty-four of us in one very small house. We slept in tiers with upper and lower berths.

Our military school was a secret because of the war, and at night we were not allowed to switch on a light. When we had an alarm at night, we had to search in the dark for our clothes. Then we were lined up and marched around, for discipline.

I was assigned to a male fighter regiment after training. We were all distributed to different regiments. Some of the women were sent to the female regiments, but I was not. Later on Bershanskaya, the commander of the 46th Guards Bomber Regiment, chose me as a replacement in her regiment. I found the conditions there much more favorable. Everyone was so nice and open. The Germans called the crews night witches. They liked to sleep at night, and our aircraft made the Germans' life not so easy; they disturbed their sleep. Sometimes, when our planes were throttled back gliding in over the target, the Germans would cry out, "Night witches!", and our crews could hear them.

Captain Larisa Litvinova-Rozanova,
pilot, commander of the formation
Hero of the Soviet Union

I was born in Kiev in 1918. I started flying when I was twenty, and in 1939 I finished glider school; then on to the pilots' school at Kherson, where I became a pilot instructor.

I joined the women's regiment when it was formed in October, 1941. When I was training at Kherson I had an additional number of hours in ground school and became a navigator as well as a pilot. So six of us who had that additional training as navigators became the navigators of the three regiments. I also trained women to become navigators for our regiment. I did not want to be a navigator, I wanted to continue as a pilot, but I had to do it.

In 1942, when we were at the front and had fought for about a year, they decided to form a third squadron of the regiment. I went to the regimental commander and asked to be a pilot. And so I became a pilot again and was named commander of the formation. I was a pilot for a year and seven months.

When Yevgeniya Rudneva, the navigator of the squadron, was killed, I was again ordered to be a navigator. And to the very last day of the war, I lingered as a navigator. All in all I made 816 combat missions; as a pilot, more than 500. No pilot wants to be a navigator! We all wanted to help the motherland; we were all afraid and knew it was dangerous, but still we did not want to show our weakness. We were mere girls; there were no men at all in our regiment, and we got along very well without them. Each combat mission we were face to face with death.

We flew our missions with the pilot in the front cockpit and the navigator in the rear one. We never flew in formation; we took off at intervals to specific targets such as railroad stations or German field headquarters—places the Germans were trying to protect. They placed antiaircraft guns and powerful searchlights around these places to safeguard them. We always flew at night because our small biplanes were very slow and vulnerable. They were made of wood and fabric, and if they were hit by tracer bullets or antiaircraft guns, it would set them on fire. We had no parachutes, and if your plane caught on fire you usually couldn't survive.

On one mission I was the fourth to take off. By that time I was thought to be an experienced pilot, and I flew with a young, new navigator that night. She was formerly a gunner but retrained to be a navigator, and this was one of her first missions. Our target was a fifteen-minute flight from the airdrome.

Halfway to the target I could see four searchlights turn on. It didn't impress me greatly because I was used to them turning on every night. I explained to the navigator what it could mean. I could also see a white spot caught by the searchlights, but in a few seconds that white spot turned into red. I knew quite well what that meant: an aircraft was burning. I calculated it was the first plane that took off from our airdrome. The strangest thing was that no antiaircraft shells were exploding in the air; the antiaircraft guns were silent, but still it was set on fire. I felt so miserable seeing our aircraft falling down, uncontrollable and in flames. The burning plane had hardly touched the ground when the four searchlights were switched on again and caught the second of our aircraft. Usually as we approached the target there was a sea of fire from the antiaircraft guns, and now for the second time the guns were silent. Do you know how I felt at that moment? A bitter tickling in my throat, incapable of breathing. Goosebumps were jumping along my back, and I could hardly feel my feet—they were as if made of cotton-wool. We saw the second plane set on fire too, and I saw in the sky the smoke trail of a fighter. I realized that a German fighter had shot down our two aircraft.

We were approaching the front line, and I realized that in a few minutes I too would be a target for the fighter. I also knew our plane was vulnerable to fighters and that we could hardly escape death. My legs wooden, my teeth clenched. Our velocity was 100 kilometers per hour and his was 500. I was so frightened I couldn't even think of escape. We were across the front line when we saw the third of our aircraft shot down, and I was the fourth. I was to be over the target in two minutes.

Then, as you know, in most tragic and desperate situations your brain begins calculating, and I found my way out quickly. I decided to approach the target from a very low altitude. I throttled back so the engine was idling and we were gliding. We dove down, and I flew over the target at an altitude of 500 meters. While we were gliding over the target I could see the third plane on fire, turning over and over in the air, somersaulting down, the flares exploding one after another in the cockpits. We realized that our friends were dying.

My navigator whispered to me, as though the Germans could hear us, that we were now over the target and were ready to drop our bombs. Normally we would drop the bombs, make a turn while we were still over the target, and pick up a heading to fly home. I decided we should fly on in order to shorten our exposure over the search-lights and to the German fighter. We should then turn back and fly straight over the target, drop our bombs, and be gone. So I told my navigator not to drop the bombs until we were back over the target.

We had been told never to drop our bombs at a lower altitude than 400 meters so that we would not be caught in the explosion. We continued to glide and make our turn, and our altitude was lower than 300 meters. I couldn't even think about the altitude at that moment. The only idea that was burning in my mind was to drop the bombs and quickly head for home—not to be shot down by the fighter. When we dropped them our plane was so shaken by the aero-dynamic blow from the bombs exploding that I thought we would split into pieces. Instantly the searchlights shot into the air trying to catch us, but I glided noiselessly until the altitude decreased to 100 meters. Only then did I start the engine, when we were away from the target. The engine roared as if warning us that we could be caught by the searchlights. I turned my head back, and what I saw shook me with grief. Another of our aircraft was burning and falling, the fifth over the target and the fourth to be shot down.

From all aspects it was a terrible night. The Germans had never before used the combination of antiaircraft guns, searchlights, and fighters to attack us, and our crews were not prepared to face these tactics. Even now I cannot understand why the pilot of the fifth plane didn't realize what I was doing and follow me. I reflected a lot on that and came to the conclusion that to complete her duty was foremost in her mind. She knew she was destined to die, but she didn't change her course and flew on to the target to be killed.

When the extent of the tragedy was realized, all further flights were canceled for the night. That night we lost eight girls in ten minutes. For our whole wartime experience it was our worst, most horrible, tragic night. For the next few nights the Soviet fighter regiments cleared the air for us, and only then could we renew our missions.

In the spring of 1943 a comic-tragic episode happened in my flying career. All the roads were so slushy that no trucks could get through to our airdrome. The airplanes couldn't fly because they couldn't take off. Our main airfield was usually situated forty kilometers from the front, our auxiliary field twenty kilometers from the front. Our routine was that when going on a mission, half of our planes would take off from the main airfield and the others from our auxiliary one.

This night, the twenty aircraft from our auxiliary airfield completed their mission and returned to the field. But because it was sleeting the roads were impassable, and the trucks couldn't get to the field to bring us fuel. So those of us at the auxiliary field were stuck there for three days. On the fourth day we received a message that cargo aircraft from Moscow with food supplies had landed 200 kilometers from us. At the auxiliary field we had been without food for four days. With this message, we received an order to fly to that location and bring the supplies to the regiment.

We gathered fuel from all the planes, enough for eight aircraft, and laid log flooring to help them take off. We wheeled the planes through the mud and slush to that flooring, almost carrying them in our hands. Finally we were ready to take off for that destination. We were to fly that mission without our navigators. It was going to be a difficult flight because it was a 400-kilometer round trip to the cargo planes and back.

We flew to the cargo planes, loaded our planes with food supplies, and then flew to our regiment at a very low altitude of about 200 meters. Only at this low altitude in the daytime could we avoid being shot down by enemy fighters.

During that day I made three flights and covered 1,200 kilometers. When we were at last supplied with fuel and ammunition after flying all day long, we were assigned a night combat mission. I didn't take into consideration that I had already become exhausted by the long daytime flights and that exhaustion had taken a toll on my eyesight, brain, thinking process, and nerves. The moment we took off I was almost snoozing away. By then nearly all the navigators could easily fly the aircraft, and my navigator suggested that she fly while I took a little nap on the way to the target. So I dozed off while the navigator flew.

I thought I had slept but one minute when my navigator shook me by my shoulder, pleading with me to wake up. We were over the target. When I opened my eyes, I seized the control stick and saw lights of enemy aircraft directly in front of me. I began maneuvering to escape them, throwing the aircraft back and forth, performing some incredible maneuvers, and then I lost spatial orientation. Our plane began falling out of control. My navigator shouted at me, "Larisa, wake up, what are you doing? There are no fighters; these are the searchlights!" She even fought with me to pull the control stick out of my hands because we had already fallen about 1,000 meters. I personally couldn't tell the earth from the sky. When I at last regained real consciousness, we were 600 meters above the ground. Only then did I recognize the earth. It's a funny story to tell about that night, but at the time I felt only fear.

Each mission was a constant overstrain. We inhaled the gunpowder, choking and coughing, unable to breathe, from the antiaircraft gunfire bursting around us. It sometimes lasted fifteen minutes until we completely escaped the searchlights. When you leave behind the area of the target, the sea of antiaircraft fire, and the searchlights, the next instant you start shivering—your feet and knees start jumping—and you cannot talk at all because you are wheezing in your throat. This was a normal reaction after each flight. In a few minutes you recover.

When we flew five nights with maximum missions, we lost appetites and sleep in our reaction to the overstrain. We usually returned from the missions in early morning, had breakfast, and went to bed. But if we flew many missions at night we couldn't fall asleep in the morning. And even if we couldn't sleep we still had to fly again that next night, and pilots sometimes fell asleep during a mission. We even had a kind of agreement between the pilot and the navigator that one of us would sleep going to the target and the other returning to the airfield. I have a feeling that there were times when both the pilot and navigator dozed off for a minute or so because of exhaustion.

Sometimes I even forgot whether I was flying toward the target or back from the target. At those times we had to peer under the wings to see if the bombs were attached in order to know whether we were going or returning! Our doctor gave us pills nicknamed Coca-Cola to keep us awake, and sometimes we took so many of them that we couldn't fall asleep at all when we lay down to sleep.

I was twice shot down. The first time was when our regiment was flying from one airfield to another. I was flying as a navigator with Serafima Amosova as pilot, and we were first to take off to find a location for a new airdrome. Then we would signal the other aircraft to land. This day we were attacked by a German Messerschmitt. He fired at us and made a few holes in the fuselage and wings. We made a forced landing, and he attacked us two more times on the ground. We jumped out of the cockpits and ran in different directions to hide from the bullets. After he attacked us three times he flew away. Although the plane had a number of holes in it, we took off and found a new airdrome for our regiment.

Another time, on a night mission over the town of Kerch, I was flying as pilot. Our plane was hit by an antiaircraft shell that stuck into the engine, and the engine quit. When we were hit, our altitude was 1,600 meters. But because the terrain was hilly, I had to think hard about a place to land. We didn't know our exact location, whether we were over Soviet or German territory. My navigator shot signaling rockets into the air, and I could see clearly both the compass showing that we were heading toward German-held territory and the altimeter showing that we were very close to the ground, about 5 meters high. We were not on the coast but in the mountains! I had only a few seconds to turn back from that heading and to level the aircraft. I knocked down two telegraph posts with the wing, landed, and rolled into a deep trench. We were 400 meters from the German front line.

But when we landed we didn't know if we were in Soviet or German territory, so we climbed out of our cockpits and decided we would reconnoiter. If we heard Russian voices we would go on to headquarters and report, and if we heard German voices we would use our pistols and simultaneously shoot and kill each other in order not to be captured by the Germans. We knew that the Germans tortured Soviet women pilots brutally, and our greatest fear was to be captured by them. We were more afraid to be imprisoned than to die. We lay on the ground and waited to hear some signs of life. After a while we heard voices speaking in Russian saying, "Where are you?"

Our regiment lost thirty girls, both pilots and navigators, during the war. On the ground we lost three: one from cancer, one from a bombing, and the third from diphtheria. In quantity, we lost almost the whole flying personnel of the regiment and kept up our strength with replacements. These replacements came in part from male regiments where there happened to be one woman pilot who would be transferred to our regiment.

Initially our regiment was to consist of two squadrons, but when we were awarded the title of "Guards" regiment, a great honor, we were allowed a third squadron. We requested permission to form a fourth squadron, which was to be a training squadron, because we trained all our own personnel. We were allowed to do this, and in fact this squadron also flew some combat missions. The commander of the air army personally forbade our commander, Bershanskaya, from flying combat missions, but I think she flew about forty missions. In our regiment there were twenty-three Heroes of the Soviet Union, of which five were honored posthumously. Eleven received that title at the front and the remainder in 1946.

After the war, when I was traveling on the train with my husband, we stopped at a very small station, and some officers brought a newspaper onto the train. In it was a decree of the Soviet government that said I had been awarded the Hero of the Soviet Union medal, the Gold Star. Where it was really celebrated was on that train with my husband when he was going on a business trip to Moscow. We were supposed to be given an apartment and ten square meters of extra living area. These privileges were introduced at the fiftieth anniversary of Soviet power. Those who first were awarded the Gold Star during the war were given 25,000 rubles. Once a year we can go to a sanitorium free of charge. Upon retirement honorees are given a personal pension. But the people in the Soviet Union have hated all the special privileges given to high-ranking Soviet officials, and so in 1992 all these privileges will be canceled for everybody.

Senior Lieutenant Zoya Parfyonova,
pilot, deputy commander of the squadron
Hero of the Soviet Union

I was born in 1920 in the Chuvash region of the Russian Republic, and I graduated from secondary school, finishing only seven grades. Then I was trained to be a nurse. While I was working as a nurse I decided that I would fly, so I worked at a glider school as a nurse and trained to fly at the same time; first on a glider and then on a powered aircraft, the U-2 biplane. Both flew off the same airdrome. I graduated from that school with excellent grades, and they wanted me to instruct there, so I remained as a flight instructor and trained one group of pilots.

When the war broke out, our school became a military pilot training school, and I was drafted into the army with the rank of sergeant. All the male instructors were sent to the front, and we women wanted to go too, but we were told that we must stay there and teach cadets to fly. But when Marina Raskova appealed to the women pilots to join her regiment, the chief of our school could not restrain me from doing that. I was then transferred to the women's regiment to train for combat.

Because we had only flown in the daytime, they trained us to fly at night. Then I was assigned to the 588th Air Regiment, which later became the 46th Guards Bomber Regiment. When we arrived at the front, the first night mission was flown by our commanders, so we were all sitting on the airfield waiting for them to return. When they returned, we discovered that our own squadron commander had not come back but was killed that very first night. She was our commander and friend, and we could not help but cry. The next night the whole regiment was assigned a combat mission.

I don't want to hide anything; I want to say we experienced many feelings and emotions—fear, joy, love, sorrow—as we faced very hard experiences. Sometimes when we successfully completed a mission we even sang and danced there at the airfield because life is life, and we were young.

In 1945 we were on our last combat mission, one of eleven crews, and it took place in eastern Prussia. It was February; the weather was severe and the roads impassable, and it was impossible to bring needed armament up to our troops. Our assignment was to drop cargo to our infantry and artillery, and our regiment and a male regiment were assigned the same mission.

It was a nightmare to make that mission. I had to go without my navigator because the cockpit was overloaded with armament. The plane was very heavily loaded, really overloaded, with cargo underneath where we usually carried bombs. It was also a daylight mission. None of the other aircraft completed that mission because the weather conditions were severe with the visibility zero—I was the only one. I made the flight at a very low altitude, following the railroad tracks. It was snowing very hard.

We had been told that when we arrived at the appointed place we should circle a few times until our troops signaled to us, and then we could land. I was able to land there because my plane was equipped with skis rather than wheels. Well, I made several circles at that place, and no one appeared to signal me; no one was there. So I flew on for four or five minutes and saw a crowd of people and a tank. I was flying so low that I was afraid the wing would touch the ground when I banked to turn. Suddenly I could see the German markings on the tank, and they had elevated the gun and started shooting at me. German infantrymen began firing at me, the airplane was hit all over like a sieve, and I was wounded in the leg. I made a 180-degree turn and flew away from them. The aircraft was shaking and difficult to fly because of the damage to it. In three minutes I saw our Soviet troops on the ground waving to me, and I landed to deliver the cargo. They told me they had seen me in the air and had shot flares to signal me, but I didn't see them because of the poor visibility. They were grateful for the supplies and also for the information I gave them about the disposition of the enemy.

In spite of my wound and the damage to the plane I had to return to my unit, so I took off for my airdrome. I made it back, but I lost consciousness from loss of blood as I was approaching to land, and the airplane fell out of control the last three or four meters. They lifted me from the cockpit and took me to the hospital. That was my 701st combat mission and the first time I was wounded.

Earlier in the war I had an experience near the town of Kerch in the Crimea. While we were on a mission the Germans were firing at us, and a piece of shrapnel got into the engine. It quit, so we had to make an emergency landing in the darkness, but we landed successfully. The next morning we came to our plane and found we had stopped just before a very deep shell hole.

In the Crimean area the Germans started using a type of shell that when fired had red, green, and white tracers. It then split into many bunches of what we called flowers, numerous smaller projectiles. We feared to be caught by these innumerable "flowers."

I never worried about the condition of my aircraft when I took off for a mission. My mechanics thoroughly prepared my plane, and I never experienced any mechanical problems with it, the armament, or the engine. This Gold Star of Hero of the Soviet Union is not only my star; I share it with all my technical staff and the mechanics. It is because of them that I remained alive. My navigator also became a Hero of the Soviet Union. I flew a total of 715 combat missions during the war.

I have two daughters, one a doctor and one an engineer, and I have a granddaughter and two grandsons.

Senior Lieutenant Irina Sebrova,
pilot, wing commander
Hero of the Soviet Union

Nataliya Meklin (*left*), Hero of the Soviet Union, and Irina Sebrova, Hero of the Soviet Union, 46th regiment

I was born in a very poor family. There were six children, and our parents couldn't give us a higher education. After five grades at school, I went to trade school to become a worker. I took technical courses and became a locksmith. I worked in a factory producing boxes for post offices for four years. Meanwhile I finished courses in nursing and in Voroshilov gunnery.

There were almost all women working at our factory. Some repair shops had men working also, and I was in that group. The director of the plant was a very active man. Once an idea struck him, and he said, "Let us present an aircraft to the sports club." So we got the money from the workers at the factory, and the aero club bought an aircraft with our money. After this there were four people from the factory allowed to enter the flying courses, and I decided, why not fly! At this point I made the decision to fly and live with aviation.

I kept on working and flying. I finished the program and assisted in teaching the young pilots, and soon I was sent to study at the Kherson Flying School to get a diploma as a pilot. At that time there were many women—young girls—studying at this training center, and we felt the war was just here before our doors. So I became a flight instructor, and I was sent to Moscow to teach flying. It became my profession in 1938–39. I had been working as a flight instructor for three and one-half years before the war, and I taught more than fifty pilots.

After the war started our flying school was evacuated to central

Russia. There were rumors that Marina Raskova, our famous pilot, was to form female regiments, and three of us decided to join. When we came to the director of the flying club he said at first that we couldn't leave; there was a shortage of instructors. But finally he signed the papers, and we joined the female regiment.

Before we went into training at Engels, Raskova had a talk with each of us individually. She told us to think twice before going to the front because it was a very severe thing to do. None could be persuaded not to go, and we all joined the regiment. We left Moscow on a train late at night, and we each took with us a mattress and pillow. We started our night-bomber training in the U-2 plane. The Germans called it the corn aircraft because it had been used in agriculture spreading chemicals before the war.

In 1942 we flew to the front, and our first station was in the Ukraine. The first combat night came, and the first mission was flown by the commander of the regiment, Yevdokiya Bershanskaya, with the regimental navigator, squadron commanders, and their navigators. Unfortunately, on this first night we lost one crew. Only then did we really realize we were at the front. No jokes, no kidding, this was a very serious job; now we understood what a difficult job we were to do.

Yekaterina Ryabova was my navigator on our first mission. We approached the target and dropped our bombs, and there was no shooting or firing. I was very disappointed that no one was trying to shoot us, but these were only the flowers, as we say in Russia, and the berries will be later. The combat missions had started, and night after night we flew missions. Then we had to retreat; it was 1942, and the Germans approached the Stalingrad area. We had to change our positions almost every night.

Finally we were stationed in the Grozny area. We had a very warm reception when we arrived there in the northern Caucasus, and this was the first village where the villagers said, "Don't leave us alone with the enemy." When we were retreating down to the south of the country, people asked us please not to fly off and leave them alone. We were stationed in that village for half of a year.

In January, 1943, the Soviet army started its offensive in the Stalingrad area. During this period, for the first time in the war, we stepped on ground that had been liberated by the army. Until then we had been retreating. After some missions in the Ukraine area, we changed our airdromes to the banks of the Sea of Azov. We were bombing the so-called Blue Line on the Kerch Peninsula. It was difficult

Yekaterina Ryabova (*left*) and
Nadezhda Popova, 46th regiment

because there were strong German positions. Most of their military fortifications were concentrated on this line. In this area we lost our best pilot, Dusya Nosal. We were all competing with her as to who could make the most flights in one night. One night before our flights we were talking, and there was a command to take our seats in the cockpit. She was the first to take off; I was the second. I followed her, and we bombed the target. The air situation was very grave, because there were lots of German aircraft in the area, and we tried to maneuver to escape their fire. When we came back to our airdrome I asked if everything was all right with our regiment. They said, "No, Dusya Nosal was hit in the temple with a bullet, and the navigator landed the plane with her dead in the cockpit." Soon after, her navigator, Irina Kashirina, also perished in battle.

We flew to the Crimea, and the Soviet forces started their offensive. We were assigned to the 8th Air Army, but in the Crimea we were assigned to a male air division. When the situation changed for the better, the marshal of the airforce army said, "Give me back my female regiment," and the commander said, "No, I could give you two male regiments instead."

But finally we went back under Marshal Vershinin's command again, and we were given the Gold Star of Heroes of the Soviet Union. The ceremony took place in Germany in a very large officers' club. The first three women who became Heroes of the Soviet Union were awarded this title at the beginning of 1944, and then a second group of nine received the award, some of them living and some dead. The documents had been sent to the Kremlin, but it took a very long time for them to come through. The other pilots didn't envy the pilots who got the Gold Star. In this combat fraternity envy was impossible, because you knew that the next night they could be shot down. Even now many Heroes of the Soviet Union don't think too much about themselves and their deeds. I don't like to show my medal; I wear it on very rare occasions. It depends on your personality. I was in the second group to be awarded this medal. There was then a third group, and some others were awarded in 1946.

On one of my flights my plane was shot down. I landed on a field with barbed wire in the Kerch area of the Crimea, in a small territory that had been liberated by this time. I landed there but nosed up. We got out of the cockpit, and a car approached us. They asked if we were wounded, and we said no. Then they said, "Leave the plane; dawn cracks, and you must go to the ferry to be delivered to the big land." So we got to the ferry and came to the captain, and he let us go with him across the straits.

We were wearing our flying suits and jackets and life vests for swimming because our mission was out over the straits, and it was there that we were shot down. We only just made it to land on that small liberated area. So we were lucky. When we stepped onto this ship there were lots of wounded, and the dead were covered with fabric. We felt ourselves a little awkward because we were safe and sound. Before we arrived at the other bank of the straits we heard the sound of aircraft engines—German aircraft. Everyone who could walk ran to the shore, and the Germans began bombing the boat. We went to the trenches and waited for them to stop. When we returned to our unit, they embraced us; they were happy to see us alive.

In Poland I had a flight assignment to bomb the city of Danzig, with strong fascist fortifications. Suddenly, when I was approaching the target, I noticed that the oil pressure was close to zero. A dilemma arose of proceeding to the target or returning to base. I looked at the engine temperature gauge and it was normal, so I decided there was something wrong with the oil meter. When we were crossing the front line there was some firing from the Germans, and they hit the aircraft. We dropped all the bombs on the target, but I was looking at the instruments. Strong antiaircraft fire shelled us over the target, because this was a strong German fortress. I made a turn and started flying back, and I saw that the engine temperature was increasing. The engine was overheating, and it was a long way back to our lines. I decided to fly higher, so I climbed about 400 meters higher than usual, and it saved me. The engine stopped, and the front line was far ahead—far in front of me. I started gliding and saw that the ground forces were firing, but I just managed to fly over the front line. I made an emergency landing in the dark; I could see the land itself but no landscape. There were no lights, and landing was like walking around with closed eyes. I couldn't see anything except that there was ground underneath us and not water. At this moment I wanted to cry, "Mama, oh bless me, let me make a soft landing." We did make a very soft landing, and there was oil leaking, and the plane was covered with oil. It was a miracle—there were lots of miracles during the war for many people.

After we stopped, we spent about one minute in the cockpit just to listen to the situation. Behind us there was shooting. We got out of the cockpit, leaving our chutes because they were heavy, and started off to the forest, because we decided the front line was on a parallel road. We started walking and took out our pistols. While we were walking I suddenly stopped my navigator—there was a small hill of hay with two people lying behind it. We were afraid to approach them, so we stood watching. No movement. We would have liked to hide in the hay, but we went to the forest out of fear that those two could be fascists. We heard a horseman coming toward us through the forest. We didn't know whether he was Russian or German; we decided not to stop the rider. After some time a car approached. We heard Russian being spoken, and we were very excited. The driver of the car told us that he was going to the front line with an emergency message, so he couldn't take us. He told us we should go down this road seven kilometers, so we did, with our pistols drawn, and it was snowing, but we finally came to our unit. We felt sad, for that happened the first flight of the night, and we missed the remainder of the night's missions.

My military rank was senior lieutenant. I flew 1,008 missions with bombs, but my total during the war was 1,100 flights. I had the most flying hours of the regiment.

After the war I worked as a test pilot, testing aircraft that had been worked on and put back together. I was still in the military when I had an accident flying, and I was on the brink of death. In 1948, while I was still in the service, my daughter was born in Poland, in Toruń city. This is the city of love. After this we went back to Russia, and it was the end of my flying career—I quit flying.

Senior Sergeant Matryona Yurodjeva-Samsonova, mechanic of the aircraft

I was born in 1923. In my family there were six children, and our father joined the armed forces right away when the war broke out. When I went to see him off at the train and to say goodbye, I swore to my father that I would also join the army and go to the front. He said, "No, that must not happen; you are the eldest sister in the family." I was determined to go, so I enlisted in one of the regiments. My mother nearly fainted, because she had lost her husband to the army and now her daughter, too.

When Marina Raskova came to Saratov town where I lived, I applied directly to her for admission. She had founded the regiment at Engels, and Saratov is just on the opposite bank of the Volga River. I asked to join the regiment and she took me, but I had to ask several times before she agreed. By that time I was studying in the aviation technical college; I was a second-year student. I was eighteen when the war started.

I studied with the other girls at Engels for six months and was assigned to the 588th Air Regiment, later to become the 46th Guards Bomber Regiment. I worked on planes for various aircrews during the war, but the last two years I maintained the aircraft of Yevgeniya Popova. When she trusted her life into my hands, I did everything on this earth for her, to keep her alive, to keep the aircraft in the best condition. Yevgeniya trusted me so much that she didn't even put her signature on the release form. This form certified that the aircraft was in order, the engine was in order, and the mechanic had fixed the plane for a combat mission quite all right. I asked her why she didn't sign it, and she replied that she knew her life was in my hands, and she trusted me completely.

We were new at being mechanics, and the airplanes were also newly born. Because they didn't have time to completely fix the planes at the plant and because of our insufficient experience, I had to work on the new plane for a long time to make it reliable. You knew your friend was going to fly it in combat, and you did everything, even beyond your physical might and strength, to have it in perfect condition and to save the life of your aircrew.

Our regiment changed its location very frequently because the front was in flux. First it was occupied by the Germans; then we would occupy where they had been. For our type of aircraft, with its slow landing speed, we didn't really need an airfield—it could land on any field. Once, when we settled down on a new field and started operations, I was on duty guarding the regimental banner. Suddenly, we heard a noise: it was Soviet infantry soldiers running out of the forest. When they saw us they said, "Oh, girls, what are you doing here? The Germans are coming, and they will be here any second!" The crews—mechanic, navigator, and pilot—all jumped into the aircraft and flew away. Some left in trucks. But I had the banner to guard and I couldn't leave it, so I was left standing there, guarding the banner.

In wartime the banner is a sacred thing for the soldier of any detachment, any regiment, and you are to safeguard it as your baby. It should be kept alive all the time. If it disappears, it means the regiment cannot exist anymore. It was a sacred duty for any girl to safeguard the banner. We got on a truck with the banner and drove away, but the truck broke down. The three of us jumped from it, and we saw, coming down the slope, tanks and infantry both Soviet and German. So we decided to separate the banner from the pole, bury it somewhere, and remember where it was buried. When spring came we would come back and dig it up, and in this way keep it safe.

The Soviet infantry was retreating, and the Germans were advancing with troops and tanks. Then we saw that the Soviets were coming up to reinforce with their Katushas, the sacred gun of the Soviet Army. The Katusha comprises many ballistic rockets. Katusha—a purely Russian name—is a form of Katherine, like Kateriana, Katusha. Then the Katushas were set up in their stand and fired, and they crushed all the German tanks and the German infantry. It was a mass of metal, human beings, and blood. It saved our troops from retreating, and instead our troops began advancing. Then we carried the banner and began walking, and it took us almost twenty-four hours to rejoin our regiment.

When the war ended, I returned and finished aviation technical college. I was sent to work as an engineer in the capital of one of the central Asian republics. As for the banner, I was so frightened that night and day—it was a nightmare to me—that I completely forgot the names of the girls who were with me, and for twenty years I tried to remember. Finally, when I came to the twentieth-anniversary reunion in Moscow, one of the girls ran up to me and asked if I remembered that day and how we saved the banner. I started crying, because I lived so far away from Moscow and couldn't come to a reunion for those twenty years. Now they both came up to me, those girls I was with that time, and I cried. The banner is now in the Museum of the Military Forces of the USSR, The Museum of Defense.

Senior Lieutenant Nadezhda Popova,
pilot, squadron commander
Hero of the Soviet Union

When I saw an aircraft for the very first time, the pilot landed, got out of the cockpit, came to us children, and asked what village this was. We told him the name of the village, and he said, "Oh, now I know!" He climbed back into the cockpit and flew away, leaving us in the dust of the prop wash. I had thought only gods could fly, and it was amazing to me that a simple man could get in a plane and fly away.

I was born and grew up in the Ukraine, and I loved our music. I was a very emotional girl; I liked to sing and recite poetry. Before seeing this pilot I thought I would become a doctor, but after this I thought maybe I would become a pilot. My parents would say, "You'll become a doctor, you'll take care of us, you'll cure us," but now I had a desire to fly. I believed in signs, and I was afraid to say something aloud. When I would decide to do something I would keep it a secret—only when I had done the thing would I open my mouth and tell everybody about it.

I was in the tenth grade in school when I entered the air club to learn flying, but I didn't tell anyone about it. At sixteen I made both my maiden jump with a parachute and my solo flight. It was fantastic. At that moment I began to believe in myself. This is a very interesting age—at this age you want to do something unusual. My photograph, standing by an airplane in my flying suit, was in a local newspaper. When I came home my parents asked if it was me, and I said it was. They were angry because they didn't know about my flying—it was my secret. I told them I didn't want them to worry about me.

I was sent to the Kherson Flying School and completed that program. The sports club gave me basic knowledge about navigation and the behavior of the aircraft in the air, but the advanced school for pilots lasted for two years. I finished flying school before the war started. I then returned to the sports club and worked as an instructor. I was eighteen.

I was very shocked when in the early days of the war my brother was killed. We were close, and I cried for days and nights. When my mother heard that her son had perished—he was only twenty and had never even kissed a girl—she met me at our house and embraced me and sobbed, "That damned Hitler!"

I saw the German aircraft flying along our roads filled with people who were leaving their homes, firing at them with their machine guns. Seeing this gave me feelings inside that made me want to fight them. During the war our house, in the German-occupied territory, became the fascist police office. They destroyed the apricot trees and the flowers and used our garage to torture our people. They blasted our school, and it was like a terrible storm had invaded our country. The war changed our lives forever.

When the war started, I sent a cable to Moscow asking to be sent to the front. They refused, but then I was drafted into the regiments

Irina Sebrova (*seated, center*) and Nadezhda Popova (*standing*),
46th regiment. Photograph by Khaldei

Marina Raskova was forming. She had become a Hero of the Soviet
Union in 1939. She was a beautiful woman with wide blue eyes and
long hair; she worked at the air academy as a teacher. After our
training she became the commander of the dive bomber regiment.
But before they had made a single combat mission, she perished in
bad weather. In February, 1942, she was buried in Red Square.

We trained at Engels, on the Volga River. After training, our regiment of night bombers was sent to the Ukraine. I was in that regiment from the very first day until the last. We were innocent of life—
our motherland was endangered, and we would fight the Germans.
My first unhappy day was in training when Raskova told us we must
get out of our skirts, put on trousers, and have our hair cut very short.
Many girls were crying because of their braids, but the order was
fulfilled. We came there to learn bombing and firing tactics, code,
navigation, and how to fire machine guns as well as small arms, and
we flew day and night under different conditions. There was a firing
range, and we dropped bombs there.

One night I was the commander of a flying formation on a training
mission to our bombing range. Each plane had a crew of two, the pilot

and a navigator. It began snowing heavily. Two aircraft crashed, and we lost four people that night; these were the first losses in our regiment. One was a very close friend of mine; it was a grave moment. We were very stressed by our flying conditions; we were without instruments to help us orient ourselves. At that time the equipment was very primitive, and inexperienced pilots became disoriented. Some thought it was my fault because I didn't teach well. When I landed near the bombing range I saw Lilya, my friend, lying on the ground under the aircraft. Raskova asked me, "Where are your pilots— dead! Why are you here, and where are they? You are flying together, and why did it happen that you are here and they crashed?" I was flight commander, and they blamed me for not instructing them properly. When something like this happens, they always look for a scapegoat. I was nineteen years old.

Two other pilots came to the commander and explained how this had happened. The other aircraft had taken off after me, and we started practice-bombing that night. My aircraft was first to bomb, and they followed at about one-minute intervals. I dropped my bombs and made a turn toward the airdrome, and so as each plane approached the bomb area, there were no aircraft ahead of them. On the bombing range there was a circle and some lights illuminating it. We each were to bomb the target and then fly on into the darkness, make a turn, and come back to the airdrome. But the pilots of these two aircraft became disoriented and flew into the ground from 600 meters up. It was snowing, and there was no horizon, no up or down, no aircraft leading them. It was a tragic lesson for us.

I made 852 combat missions, and I was a squadron commander. At the front some of the crews crashed and were killed, and reinforcements came every month as replacements. I was shot down several times, my aircraft was burning, and I made some forced landings, but my friends used to say I was born under a lucky star; I was never even wounded.

During the battle at Novorossijsk, a city on the Black Sea, our regiment was located about twenty kilometers from the city, in a resort area behind a low hill. While we were stationed here we fulfilled two combat missions in cooperation with the naval fleet. One day we were invited to the command post, a dugout where we were briefed by the chief of staff of the naval fleet. A part of our navy troops occupied a small territory of the city on the seacoast, and they had sent a radio message that they had no water, ammunition, medical supplies, or food and asked for urgent assistance.

Our aircraft were supplied with containers filled with supplies to drop to our troops. We took off, and my heart was pounding because this was an unusual mission—not to destroy but to save our sailors. I was fond of seamen; I liked the uniforms and thought they looked like knights. The army and air force changed their uniforms with time but not the navy. So I went on this mission like a child with an open heart.

When we approached that area we saw mountains on the right side covered with forest and the sea under us. Of course we had no parachutes or rubber safety boats, only a small safety jacket. We always joked about these jackets, that they would drag you down into the water instead of keep you out of it. We flew at about one thousand meters, and I knew there were antiaircraft guns and spotlights in that area. We had become clever enough to evade them, so I throttled back and dropped the flare to find the target. While I was looking for the place to drop my cargo I came down a little too low, and my navigator called out, "What are you doing—you could hit one of the city towers!" Just then I saw a torch blinking from the roof of a building, and my knees started shaking. I cried to Katya that we would drop the supplies together because if we missed, the cargo could drop into German positions. So then we dropped the cargo. I increased my speed and glided to the edge of the Black Sea.

About that time the antiaircraft guns started, and all the guns were firing. I felt a shell explode near my aircraft; it hit the wing and made a large hole. My controls were sticking, and I was afraid to be shot down over the German positions, so I started maneuvering at an altitude of about one hundred meters over the sea. I managed to fly back to my airdrome and land. Then the colonel who gave us the order to drop supplies climbed up on the wing and thanked us. The sailors had sent a radio message that they got everything. There were bullet holes in the wings, map holder, and even my helmet. But we were not hit. I said, "Thanks to God, everything is all right."

When the war was over, I came to my native town and was met by a brass band. Lots of people threw flowers, and the flowers were put in the car and they filled it. Then we came to the theater, and there were more than two thousand people there. I was a Hero of the Soviet Union, and the town made this a festivity—I was made an honorable citizen of the city. I was asked to tell an episode of the war, and I told them that particular story. Then a man came up and embraced me and said now he knew who saved them, and he thanked me. He was one of the sailors in that unit on the Black Sea that our regiment had saved. He told me that all the sailors had then prayed to God for our lives, to save us from the enemy's wild bullets.

My friend Yevgeniya Rudneva was killed during a mission. When she came to the regiment she became the regimental navigator. She made many flights with me, and one night, when we were in the Crimea, we were given the assignment to bomb Kerch city. That night she was to fly with me, but she said that it was the first night flight of a new pilot, and she would like to bomb with her. The assignment was very dangerous, and there were lots of fascist troops concentrated near the target. When I was approaching my aircraft that night before takeoff I tripped, and I thought it was bad that Yevgeniya was flying with the new pilot—something would happen. I felt this in my heart, and when I looked into the face of that young pilot I saw something unusual, a disturbance.

We took off, and they were flying in front of me. I watched them approach the target and drop their bombs, and then the searchlights were switched on and caught the plane in their web. A burst of fire shelled their aircraft, and it was immediately set on fire. I changed my direction and started dropping my bombs on those gun positions, and the lights started searching for me, but they didn't find me. I saw their aircraft burning, and the flares they carried began exploding. The burning plane crashed while the searchlights continued to hold it in their lights. It was the 645th combat mission of Yevgeniya Rudneva. After her death, she was decorated with the Gold Star of Hero of the Soviet Union. She was the only daughter of her family, and she had never been kissed. She wrote letters to her professor at the university saying she couldn't be a scientist until her fair motherland was liberated from the fascists. She wrote, "There can be no real science in an occupied country." Later, the astronomers named an asteroid after her. She was a senior lieutenant when she perished at twenty-three.

Early in the war, after a bombing by the Germans, you would look down and see horses, people, vehicles, everything mixed. We are very impressionable people, and when you see all these things your brain becomes overloaded with this terror. I remember some nights I would fly eight or ten missions, and when we were fighting in Poland, I made eighteen combat missions in one long winter night. I stayed in the cockpit almost all the time, and I would have some tea while the aircraft was being reloaded. I remember once we received a message from Warsaw saying that the Polish people had started a rebellion and asking for our assistance. We flew many missions over Warsaw, and it was burning and covered with smoke. It was difficult to breathe the air. After those missions I couldn't get out of the cockpit from exhaustion.

I took part in the battles in Belorussia, Poland, and Germany. We finished the war near Berlin, and we bombed the Swinamunde area in the northern and eastern part of Germany. By the time we reached Germany, there were fewer German planes in the air. In 1943, the forces of our aircraft and the German aircraft became equal, and then we gained air superiority. When the war ended, we were in Brandenburg. Our regiment was released, and the flag of our regiment was passed to the air museum in Moscow. In hall thirteen of the museum you can find our flag today.

When we were released there was a meeting of our regiment. The commander read the order, and lots of us began to cry because of what we had been through together. This was October, 1945. We decided to meet after the war on the second of May in a small park across from the Bolshoi Theater. In 1946, we had our first meeting. During the years the veterans began to show up with their husbands and children, but many of them never married. At these meetings we were crying and laughing. And now every year fewer and fewer of our people come. We were very young and our friendship very warm, as it is now.

Senior Sergeant Nina Karasyova-Buzina,
senior mechanic of armament of the squadron

I was born in 1923 in the Tula region in the village of Kluchyovo, and in 1930 the family moved to Moscow. I finished nine grades of secondary school and went to work. There were four children in our family, and we were not well-to-do. Together with my father I was a breadwinner, and I worked two and one-half years in a plant before the war broke out. When the war started, the Komsomol organization of our plant appealed to the young people to voluntarily join the army. I volunteered and was assigned to Marina Raskova's regiment.

In Moscow at the Komsomol headquarters I was interviewed by an army officer and Marina Raskova herself. I was warned that the service I was volunteering for would be very difficult, because I would have to carry heavy bombs to the aircraft, work in freezing conditions, and probably stand in cold water day and night with little rest. I was told I should think it over, and I replied that I had and wanted to join. We were taken to the town of Engels, where we trained. I completed the eight months' course in armament and was sent to the front with the 588th Air Regiment. Initially I had thought I would be a gunner in an aircrew, and I was disappointed to know I would only load the bombs, not drop them.

This work we did was not really women's work, because of the weight of the bombs that we manually attached to the aircraft. At first I was just an armorer, then a mechanic of armament; then I became a senior technician in armament. A technician not only arms the aircraft but has the added responsibility of overseeing the other armament personnel and their work. We attached the fuses to the bombs, which armed them, and only then attached the bombs to the aircraft.

The bombs weighed 25, 32, or 100 kilos each, and we lifted them into place manually. Some nights we lifted 3,000 kilos of bombs. Three of us lifted the bombs, working together. We did our work at night and were not allowed to have any light to work by. So we worked blind, fumbling in darkness for the proper place to attach the bombs. But the missions never had to be delayed because the bombs were not loaded in time. We worked in mud, frost, sleet, and water, and we were always precise in fixing the bombs. We had to work barehanded so that we could feel what we were doing. They issued us gloves, but working in the dark with a locking mechanism forced us to work without them.

We worked all night, then had a two- to three-hour rest and returned to the planes in the morning to examine the bomb racks under the aircraft. The racks were so low to the ground that we had to kneel to examine and attach the bombs. Each aircraft made about ten missions a night. Early in the war each plane carried a maximum of 250 kilos of bombs, but later they could carry 300 kilos.

We slept in dugouts. A dugout is a large underground trench covered with logs and soil. Inside we had plank beds and a fireplace made of an oil drum. At times we even had a window in the dugout. When we had to move often and quickly, we didn't have time to dig but slept outside under the wings of the aircraft.

After the war I married a military pilot. We moved from one place to another so I didn't work, but I raised two sons. There was some question as to whether we mechanics could bear children after the heavy work and the overstraining of our strength during the war, but it didn't affect us. We were very small and slim during the war, and we had bad nutrition, never enough sleep, and very hard work, but no one complained. I never even felt tired.

Junior Lieutenant Raisa Zhitova-Yushina,
pilot, flight commander

I was born in 1921. When I was four or five years old I would ask my mother if I would ever fly, and she would reply, "Yes, from the stove to the floor!" Of course no one believed that I would fly. At seventeen I started flying gliders, and after a year I entered a flying school. When I went to Minsk, in Belorussia, I was nineteen, and I became a pilot at the sports club. Then the war broke out, and I became a flight instructor preparing male pilots. I was only twenty years old.

In the first days of the war, the Germans started bombing all Belorussian cities, including Minsk. At that time I was in the hospital with pleurisy, and I think about five hundred aircraft were in the air bombing our city. In late June I was told that I should leave Minsk, because the Germans were advancing and were about to capture the city. I began walking to the east, and along the way I lost consciousness because of my illness. I was wearing my flying suit and had a map holder and my belt across my chest. I decided if I found an aircraft without a pilot I would fly somewhere. That was my dream.

I was lying in a field, and some people found me and put me in a car. They were driving east on a highway along with military vehicles, and on the sides of the road there were civilians who were fleeing the area. Suddenly I saw three German aircraft approaching the highway, and I cried, "Aircraft!" and jumped off the car and stayed behind. The fascist aircraft were firing their machine guns, and most of the people in the car were killed or wounded. When I jumped off the car I broke my leg. A military vehicle picked me up and delivered me to the hospital in a nearby city.

While I was in the hospital two pilots that I didn't know came to me and asked if I was a pilot, and I replied that I was. They said, "Tonight a train will go to some other area, and if you want you can come with us." It took us about a month to get to Tambov city, in the center of Russia. There I stayed in the hospital because of my broken leg, and when it had healed I was assigned to the flying club. I worked there until 1943 teaching flying to three or four groups.

Then I went to air-force headquarters in Moscow, and they asked how many flying hours I had. I told them more than a thousand. They assigned me to the 46th Guards Bomber Regiment on July 13, 1943. I started in the regiment as a pilot, then a senior pilot, and later as a flight commander.

My first mission was in August, 1943, in the northern Caucasus.

Left to right: Raisa Zhitova-Yushina, pilot; Polina Petkelyova, navigator; Mariya Pinchuk, navigator—46th regiment

The aircraft flew on their missions at three-minute intervals between planes. It was like a conveyor belt: every three minutes an aircraft took off. When we were approaching the field and runway we would cry out, "Refuel, bombs, get ready!" because we were eager to bomb the positions of the Germans. I still had some problems with my leg, and sometimes, because of nerves, I couldn't move one leg. On my last combat mission, on March 30, 1945, when I landed I couldn't move either of my legs. It was a nerve problem, and the central nervous system was paralyzed. I made 535 combat missions during the war.

Once, on a reconnaissance flight with bombs under the wings, the weather was very bad. I couldn't get to the target, so I decided to turn back. When I landed, the ground personnel were holding the wings of my aircraft to stop it from swinging because of the strong wind. Otherwise, it could turn over and blow up. I watched that scene from the cockpit. When I saw all of them rushing away from the plane, I cried out to them, "Why are you running away?" I learned later that I had lost the vane of one of the bombs attached to the wings, which meant that any second my aircraft could have blown up from the slightest movement.

Our squadron commander, Olga Sanfirova, was shot down when a bullet hit the fuel tank and the aircraft caught fire. They landed between the German and Soviet trenches, and when they got out of the cockpit, a Soviet officer called to them and said, "You girls, you go to the right!" because that area was a mine field. But he meant to *his* right, and they went to their right, and Olga stepped on a mine. It exploded and tore off her leg and she was screaming, and the Soviet officer ran out to help her and stepped on a mine. So it ended that they and several soldiers nearby perished, and only her navigator, Rufina Gasheva, survived.

On a bombing mission one night I nearly lost my navigator, Galina Bespalova. The searchlights caught our plane, but I dove and escaped from it. Galina was thrown completely out of the cockpit by this maneuver, but she was caught on the machine gun, and when I leveled off she dropped back down into her cockpit. She was on her first mission and had forgotten to fasten her safety belt. I called to her from my cockpit several times, but she wouldn't respond. This was directly over the target, and she had already dropped the bombs. I returned to our airdrome and didn't know if she were dead or alive, because I was busy dodging projectiles and couldn't look back. When I landed I found Galina alive but so shaken that she couldn't report to the commander about the mission. I was also shaken when I thought I could have lost my navigator above the target. We became friends then and are friends now. We were like sisters in our regiment, and we took care of every member of our family.

In Poland in 1945 we were bombing Königsberg as a snowstorm was approaching, but we persuaded Commander Bershanskaya to let us make one flight. We bombed successfully and then started to return home, but the ground was covered with heavy, heavy snow, and we were flying just above the trees. When we arrived at the area of the airdrome we couldn't find it, because we were flying in a milk of heavy snow. The stress was so intense my legs began to shake, and I knew the plane was turning yet I couldn't do anything to make it fly straight. Then I tried to land at another airdrome, and when we crossed the Vistula River approaching the field, the ground personnel turned on the lights. But I couldn't see the runway; it was impossible—we couldn't land anywhere. Finally I noticed a flat area and I landed, but when I saw a high-voltage mast in front of us, we both started nervously shaking.

We didn't know whether we were on our territory or German-held territory. I stopped the engine so as not to attract attention. In the early morning we looked around and saw a farm, so we took our pistols out and started approaching. Then we fired our pistols to attract someone's attention, but no one responded. As we came closer we heard a cow moo, and we were frightened even more. We returned to our plane, started the engine, and took off. The weather had improved greatly, and we found our Soviet airdrome. Eight of our planes didn't return that night to their home field. One crew crashed, and one lost its landing gear while landing.

We slept in the daytime. When something happened to our aircraft, or we weren't allowed to fly for some reason, we were very upset, because we wanted to fly as many missions as possible. So for us it was a terrible thing not to fly. As we became used to the danger, we didn't think about death or the losses. When we were going to the airfield to fly we sang, and when we were going to our quarters after flying we also sang, that is if the night was good and we had no losses. We had a tradition that when some crew didn't return, their plates and silverware were put out for them in the mess even when we knew they had been shot down. Their places were set for some days in hope that they might return, which in fact sometimes happened.

The men pilots would look for the airdrome of our regiment, and when they saw the linen outside they started doing acrobatics, and they didn't let us sleep in the daytime. When we were returning from a mission, most of our ground troops knew we were women pilots. When I was flying very low I would close the throttle and say, "Hey, brothers how are you?" and they would light their torches. I wanted to encourage them with a voice from the sky.

We used no illumination in our bombing because dropping flares by parachute lit up everything, and the enemy could see our planes and shoot us down. So no lights, no navigation lights. When a new pilot arrived at the regimental airdrome she had orientation flights with an instructor, and their conversation went like this: "You see this? I cannot see it! Do you see this? I cannot see it! This is a road. I cannot see it!" But after three or four flights she would start to see the small differences in the shadings of the terrain and adjust to seeing at night. When we went on bombing missions we were told only the approximate location of the target, and it was our responsibility to find the target, bomb it, and return to our airdrome. I flew about eighteen hundred hours during the war from 1943 to 1945.

In December, 1945, I left the army, and in February, I joined the Ministry of Geology as a pilot. I had a crew, and together we flew looking for minerals, oil, and uranium. I was working on the aeromagnetic picture of the Karelia territory in the northern Karelski Peninsula near Finland, and the mission was to find iron ore deposits. That year we found a rich deposit of iron ore, and I received an award from that republic. On this expedition I married a pilot, and after this we began flying together. I was commander of that detachment in civil aviation.

My husband became a navigator of civil aviation, flying with Aeroflot. I flew under the Ministry of Geology, but we flew from the same airdrome.

I continued to fly until 1951 when I crashed, and my face was scarred and my head was broken. I was flying a Yak-12, a big plane, and the propeller broke, the engine stopped, and I could do nothing about it because our altitude was only seventy meters. I warned the crew that we were going down. We crash-landed between the trees on the slope of a hill, and the plane started burning. I had hit my head and was unconscious. The doors jammed, and the crew, the navigator and the radio operator, managed to pull me out through a small window in the door of the cockpit. There were also some secret devices aboard the aircraft, and they took them out along with some food and chocolate. Then the fuel tanks exploded. We were one hundred kilometers from the nearest village.

When I regained consciousness, I opened my eyes and asked about our plane. I didn't remember anything that happened, and they worried about that. My eyes were all right, and they bandaged my face. We had a map from the plane, and it saved our lives. We walked out of there, and it was a miracle that the other two weren't hurt at all. There is a saying that if you are really lucky, you were born in the placenta. I believed in that saying and asked my mother if I really was born in the placenta, and she said, "Yes, it is true!" Well, we walked about one hundred kilometers. All the villages in that area are located along the rivers and waterways, and we finally came to a village. So my flying career ended that year.

I have two daughters: one is a doctor, and one is an engineer. My husband crashed and died in 1956. He was the navigator of a Tupolev-114 on an international flight, a technical flight to the Congo, and while taking off something happened. There was a mist and they couldn't see anything, but you know there is this Russian tradition to rely on a miracle, hoping that something will help us survive when everything is against it. So they would say, "All right, God will help us," and take off. There were two crews on that aircraft, because it took thirteen hours to fly to the Congo nonstop. When the plane took off it crashed. One crew was in the tail part, which broke in half, and all in the tail lived; all in the front of the plane died. My husband was in the front crew cabin and he died.

Senior Lieutenant Alexandra Akimova,
navigator of the squadron

I was born in a very common family. My father was a worker, and there were four children in the family besides myself. My father even participated in the First World War, and both he and my uncle were in the Civil War. All my mother's relatives from the old times were determined Communists, and I was born, educated, and brought up in that atmosphere, in the ideas that were proclaimed by Marx and Lenin. My mother was a housewife because there were many children to be looked after, and my father was a schoolteacher. He went to college to learn to be a teacher right after the revolution. We lived in the Moscow region, not far from the city. Later on he graduated from Moscow University and became principal of the school.

After finishing school I entered the Moscow Pedagogical Lenin Institute. While I was a first-year student war broke out. Even before the war started we could feel the strain in the atmosphere, and we took an active part in defense work. There was an appeal to all the young students in the colleges to acquire some knowledge or profession that could be of use to the country if war did break out. So I trained as a military nurse at the same time I was attending college.

After the Germans invaded our country there was an appeal for young girls to be drafted into the female regiments. I was then eighteen, and I decided to join an air regiment. The number of those who could join was very limited, but I had the advantage of being a member of the Komsomol Committee of the institute.

The navigators in the female regiments were recruited from the colleges or higher educational establishments, and I became a navigator. Our education allowed us to more quickly master the aviation techniques. I had never flown an aircraft, but I had made parachute jumps.

In May, 1942, our regiment, then designated the 588th Air Regiment, was sent to the front. Ours was the only purely female regiment. I was an officer in the regiment from the very first day to the day of victory.

In the Kerch area there was a place that was known as Black Death. Over that area my pilot, Katya Peskaryova, and I were shot down. We lost control of the aircraft when it was hit by antiaircraft fire. We had already released our bombs and were then caught in the searchlight. I shot off a flare and the pilot could see the landmarks, but we couldn't find a landing place. I shot off a second flare and we could see, but the ground was very uneven with hills and bomb craters. We landed in that rough area, and the plane veered to one side and nosed into the ground. I had slight facial injuries, but the pilot's leg was caught by the fuel tank. Soviet soldiers from a fighter regiment came to rescue us and took us to a trench where we spent two nights, because it was right on the front line.

In Poland, in early spring, 1945, the visibility was bad, and most of our crews were grounded. Several of us, however, were allowed to go on a mission. After dropping our bombs we couldn't find our airfield because of the weather, and we landed in a field near a forest. It was sleeting, and the ground was very muddy. Some young people ran up to our plane, and we didn't feel very much at ease because they spoke a foreign language, but fortunately it was Polish. We had to wait till morning to take off, when the ground would be frozen; it was impossible to taxi or take off in the deep mud. We asked the boys to guard the plane, and we were taken into the village.

In each settlement there is a head man called *staros*. We stayed at his house all night and negotiated our departure the next day, asking that they help us with the plane. We didn't want to sleep, so we asked the young men guarding the plane to join us in our pilots' rations of vodka, biscuits, and milk. The next morning the ground was frozen, and we took off.

Another time, in 1944, on the Belorussian front along the Neman River, there was a very brisk advance of our troops. We were stationed near a small settlement with very wide streets, and we made them our runways. Suddenly, at night, there was an order for us to get into our planes and train the machine guns in the direction of the front lines—some of the Germans had broken through. We were to shoot at the Germans from the aircraft on the ground. We stayed in our planes all night and fired at the enemy. The next day at dawn we could plainly see the Germans who had broken through. They were nearby, behind the house where our aircraft were stationed. We were to shoot as much as possible so as not to let the Germans intrude into our territory. There were many small groups of Germans cut off from their army by our fast-moving troops. These were a part of them.

Again, in Belorussia, we were stationed in one of the villages, and after dinner we went into the woods to pick strawberries. The commander of the front called our unit because one small German group had broken out, and we were to look for them. We took off on a reconnaissance flight and saw smoke coming out of a small woods, and we also saw some German troops. In another small woods there were Soviets. At that point I was scared. Now I could see how very close the fascists were to our regiment. Then we were ordered on a strafing mission. We could see the Germans very clearly, and I fired at them with my machine gun. They scattered—some of them firing at us, some of them running. Aircraft from one of our male regiments were circling with us, and one of their planes was shot down. We did not want to kill, but we were in the regiment to fight and free our motherland.

When we saw the captured Germans, in spitè of the fact that they were the enemy and had committed such atrocities in our country, we couldn't look at them without a throbbing of the heart. They were miserable figures in shabby clothes, absolutely starving, thin and weak, and we experienced a kind of pity even for the enemy. If I had been given a pistol at that moment and a command to fire at them, I could not have done so.

The very nature of a woman rejects the idea of fighting. A woman is born to give birth to children, to nurture. Flying combat missions is against our nature; only the tragedy of our country made us join the army, to help our country, to help our people.

Russia, for the whole period of its existence, has been an object of assault. At the cornerstones of our history, women were together with men—they stood beside the men. To be in the army in crucial periods is one thing, but to want to be in the military is not quite natural for a woman.

I think American women have the idea of romanticism connected with being in the military, and it leads them to want to be a part of it. That is probably because they have not fought a battle in their own country for a hundred years and don't know the nature of war. If the women of the world united, war would never happen!

Senior Lieutenant Mariya Akilina,
pilot

I was born in 1919 in the town of Ryazan. There were seven children in the family. I don't remember my father; he was drafted into the Red Army right after the revolution and was killed in the Civil War when I was two months old. It was very difficult for my mother to raise us all. She was a cashier at one of the plants and didn't have the means to give us everything we needed, but my aunt was married and childless, so they adopted me.

When I was in secondary school, three of us were selected to attend a parachute training school to learn to jump. While I was in the parachute school I learned to fly gliders. I was sent on to the parachute center to continue my training, and when I finished I became an instructor. I was in lots of aviation parades where we jumped in groups to show our skill. These parades were held at the Tushino Airdrome near Moscow, and government officials, including Stalin, were usually present. At that time the government was appealing to the younger generation with slogans urging, "To the tractors! To the aircraft! To the collective farms! To the plants!" in order that they master the new fields of industry.

In the 1930s aviation was in its glory; young people wanted to become aviators. They were all striving to fly. While I was a parachute instructor, I attended an air club. It was an obligation of a parachute instructor to be able to fly an aircraft. Then I became a flight instructor. I taught one class of cadets; then I married and had two children.

My husband was a military pilot flying bombers. When the war broke out, he flew away to the front that same night. The three of us who had gone to parachute jump school together went to the Military Commissariat and asked to join the army. I was accepted because I had by then made 109 air jumps. I was assigned to a special male airforce regiment training landing forces. I joined the flying squadron making reconnaissance flights. These flights were to be made both day and night, but I flew in the day because I had so few night flying hours. I was assigned to fly the Po-2. It was easy to fly, but it was also defenseless.

On my first actual combat reconnaissance, I was sent to the front at Vitebsk and could clearly see the German advancement. I counted the number of enemy tanks at seventy-nine. They were so occupied with moving on toward Moscow that they did not even fire a shot at my plane.

Later I began flying night missions. On these missions I flew parachutists into areas of German occupation for the purpose of intelligence gathering. I also brought supplies in to the partisans. We flew deep into the German rear areas, and at night it was difficult to maintain our orientation. There were no landmarks to help me in the winter, when everything was covered with snow. When I came to the partisans' area they would signal where to drop the supplies or where to land, whichever was required on that mission. Landing was a special problem because the partisans were in the forests, the space was so short to land in, and there was always a threat that the Germans would appear. The partisans would burn two or three fires to show us the landing place. The German antireconnaissance personnel built fires of their own to trick us into landing there, instead of the partisan landing site. It was difficult for us to know if the lighted fires were ours or theirs, and there were cases where our planes landed where the Germans had built fires.

Such an incident happened to me on the Volkhov front. I was flying behind two aircraft that landed on the false German landing strip and were captured. I landed and was taxiing toward those two planes when I heard a Russian voice shouting, "Fascists! Fascists! Fly away!" I opened the throttle and took off across the runway, climbing up and hitting the tops of the trees. When I came to the partisan runway, I could see a lot of leaves and sticks caught in the landing gear of my plane. While this episode was taking place I had no fear, but when I landed safely at the partisan landing strip I began to shake, and it took a long time to calm down.

One night four of our planes were assigned a combat mission to drop bombs on a German fortification near the town of Mozhajsk. We were circling to drop our bombs and lost one aircraft and crew because the Germans had massed antiaircraft guns to protect the area, and we were under heavy fire. As I turned to fly back to our airdrome, I could see the flashes of antiaircraft bombs around me but couldn't hear them because of the roar of the engine. Suddenly my engine quit, and in its silence I could hear everything. I was shocked at first and didn't know what had happened to the engine. I looked down and saw that the whole floor of the cockpit had been blown away by a shell.

My altitude was about eleven hundred meters, so I decided to try to glide to the Soviet territory, which in fact I did. When the distance between the aircraft and the earth was about one hundred meters the right wing of the aircraft fell off, and the plane crashed to the ground. At that moment my thought was of my children; I couldn't reconcile my thoughts knowing that they would grow up without me. It was winter, and there was a heavy wind building up high drifts of snow. When our plane crashed I lost consciousness. The aircraft had fallen straight into a high snowdrift.

Some hours later I regained consciousness, crawled out of what remained of the plane, and tried to understand what had happened to my navigator and my aircraft. I fumbled with my right hand and found a body under the snow. It was my navigator, dead and frozen. I tried to stand up and immediately fainted. When I again regained consciousness, I knew I must move some way. I couldn't walk, but I dragged my body from one bush to another. I couldn't go far because I was so wounded. Early in the morning a Soviet reconnaissance unit found me and took me to a medical station. When they unbuttoned my flying suit and removed my helmet, they realized for the first time that I was a young woman of twenty-two. They sent me to a nearby military hospital in Moscow.

I was operated on and remained in the hospital for four months. My jaw was smashed, and all my lower teeth had to be extracted. My feet were also badly crushed. Even now I walk with difficulty. Other pilots in the hospital came to see me because they had heard that a young girl pilot had crashed at the front and had been brought to the hospital as a sack of bones. All my ribs were broken and my spine injured. I lay in bed covered with bandages and encased in plaster. The surgeon wanted me discharged from the army, and I wanted to return to flying. He wouldn't allow that and said that I must learn to walk with crutches.

While I was in the hospital a letter came to the regiment informing me that my two children, ages two and five, had been killed in a bombing. The regimental commander decided not tell me until I recovered, because the news would be too much for me in my poor condition. He came to the hospital to take me back to the regiment, not wanting me to go home and discover the death of my children. Back at the regiment the doctor worked with me to train my legs to walk again. She forced me to exercise my legs and feet, and the pain was terrible. At times I would call her a fascist, and she said that someday I would thank her for her strict regime. In time, as I progressed, I worked in the regimental office as a clerk. Sometimes I would get into the cockpit of a plane and found I could work the controls with my hands, but it was nearly impossible to use my feet on the rudder pedals.

One day the whole squadron was to go out on a daylight mission, and they were short two crews. The regimental commander asked the squadron commander if there were two more crews, because we were flying day and night. These crews had to be formed from the pilots and navigators who had been injured and had just returned from the hospital. I asked the commander if he would let me pilot one of the planes, and he didn't want to, but he couldn't find another replacement, so I flew the mission. Within two weeks I flew a number of missions, and then a medical board approved my flying.

About the time we were liberating the Baltic area, at the end of 1944, the regiment received orders that women who were flying in male regiments must be transferred to female regiments as reinforcements. I was transferred to the 46th Guards Bomber Regiment. I was glad to be in a female regiment. It was easier for me because, well, men are men and women are women; I was more comfortable. On the eve of the victory parade in Moscow I was finally told that both my children and my husband had been killed in the war.

After the war I flew in civil aviation until 1964. I crop dusted and flew in the medical squadron until I retired. I adopted two children—two boys—one my nephew, and one an orphan from the siege of Leningrad. I never remarried.

Three
The 125th Guards Bomber Regiment

Introduction

The 587th Bomber Regiment was honored during the war by being designated a "Guards" regiment and officially became the 125th M. M. Raskova Borisov Guards Bomber Regiment. The aircraft flown by the regiment was considered to be the most complex of the Soviet-made aircraft in World War II. The Petlyakov Pe-2, a twin-engine, twin-tail dive bomber, was powered by two 1,100 HP liquid-cooled engines for a maximum speed of 336 MPH at 16,400 feet. The bomb load was specified as 1,000 kg, but the more experienced women pilots regularly carried 1,200 kg. The landing speed was quite fast, and the airfields were not well constructed and at times were nothing more than potato fields. The small forward compartment of the plane was difficult to exit, with the pilot and navigator riding back-to-back. The aircraft carried a crew of three: pilot, navigator-bombardier, and a tail-gunner in a separate rear compartment. Less competent and less experienced pilots were known to be afraid of this unforgiving aircraft, while skilled pilots loved it.

Combat missions were flown in a "V" formation. This was considered best for the bombers, because their machine-gun field of fire overlapped, giving them mutual protection from enemy fighters. If a bomber was forced to drop out of this protective formation for any reason, it became instant prey for enemy aircraft.

All of the pilots and navigators in the regiment were women, while some of the tail-gunners were men. The bombers were escorted by fighter aircraft and protected by them against enemy attack. Earlier in the war the German Luftwaffe fighters, with their overwhelming superiority, often broke through the Soviet fighter protection and engaged the bombers directly.

The first commander of the regiment was Major Marina Raskova. When she was killed Lieutenant-Colonel V. V. Markov, a male commander with extensive combat experience, was assigned to the regi-

Petlyakov Pe-2 aircraft on a mission,
125th regiment

ment. Although no statistics were available, ground personnel included a number of men, mainly mechanics with advanced skills in maintaining this complex aircraft. There was no antifreeze available for the aircraft early in the war. Each engine was drained of water and oil in the winter, whenever an aircraft was on the ground for any length of time, to keep it from freezing. The regiment comprised two squadrons with ten aircraft in each squadron.

When the war ended, Markov married a navigator from the regiment. Retired from the air force as a lieutenant-general, Markov requested an interview—such was his pride in the regiment. General Markov died in 1992.

Five aircrews—a total of fifteen women of the regiment—perished in the war, and five women became Heroes of the Soviet Union.

Captain Valentina Savitskaya-Kravchenko,
navigator of the regiment (vsk)

Lieutenant-Colonel Valentin Markov,
pilot, commander of the regiment (vm)

vsk: This idea of forming three regiments appeared in September, 1941. The antifascist meeting took place in Moscow, and Marina Raskova, a trained navigator, Hero of the Soviet Union, and later a pilot, called upon all the women who could fly to join the army. In October, 1941, many women pilots and other women involved in aviation started arriving in Moscow. Originally one regiment was planned, but instead Raskova formed three regiments. Even then many women had to go home because there weren't enough positions for them. We

Valentin Markov, commander,
125th regiment

were taken to an airfield at Engels, on the Volga River, for training. The 586th Fighter Regiment was sent to the front in the Yak-1 plane in April, 1942. In June, 1942, the women in the newly formed 588th Air Regiment were sent on their first combat mission. Our regiment, the 587th, received the Pe-2 dive bomber, a new twin-engine, very complex aircraft, in August and September of 1942. In January, 1943, we were sent to the front near Stalingrad. There was a shortage of this aircraft, and initially the planes were sent to combat regiments already at the front, so there was a delay in receiving ours. Raskova had insisted that all the women's regiments fly only aircraft made in the Soviet Union.

Marina Raskova, who had chosen to lead our regiment as its commander, perished with her crew while trying to land her plane in very bad weather on January 4, 1943. She was then thirty-one years old, and she had a thirteen-year-old daughter. She hit the high bank of the Volga River while approaching the airfield at the Stalingrad front and crashed. Marina never lived to fly a combat mission.

VM: I was appointed regimental commander at thirty-three, and I was a major. At the end of the war I was a lieutenant-colonel. I finished my military career as a lieutenant-general of the air force.

VSK: The regiment started its combat missions in February, 1943, after more training at the front. The Pe-2 was very heavy and difficult to control while taking off and landing. It could carry up to a ton of bombs. We flew off of fields with no paved runways; these were potato fields. The navigator, who sat behind the pilot facing the rear, would turn in her seat and push on the pilot's back to give her the added pressure to raise the tail of the plane and shorten the takeoff distance.

When we were dive bombing we could carry only the bombs under the wings. At Engels there were too many pilots and not enough navigators. I was a pilot who was taught to be a navigator. The women who were chosen to fly the dive bomber were the most experienced pilots with a minimum of 700 flying hours.

VM: At the time I was chosen to command the female regiment I commanded a male regiment. I had been shot down and wounded and was hospitalized. When I was told that I was to lead a female regiment, the order was like a cold shower to me—I was shocked! The man who recommended me for this position approached me carefully, from a distance. He asked if I knew about the death of Raskova, and when I said I did, he asked what I would think of commanding this regiment. I couldn't visualize how I could command women during war, flying bombers. I knew the aircraft and knew how difficult it was even for male pilots to fly. I couldn't imagine how women could manage it.

I was told I would be given every assistance from Moscow. In fact these were sheer words, only declarations. How could they help me from Moscow, such a great distance from Stalingrad! I didn't believe their promises and asked them to appoint some other pilot, but I was told the order had already been issued and signed. When I left the office, angry and pale, and told my friends waiting for me at the door that I'd been appointed the female regimental commander, their hair rose in surprise and indignation. They believed I would have to go through hell in that regiment. By my nature and character I am very disciplined, and knew that there was nothing to do but agree.

VSK: We women wouldn't even hear of a man coming to command our regiment!

VM: A hundred questions arose in my mind: what should I do as their commander? I knew women's nature very well, and I knew because of their caprice and susceptibility to offense it would not be an easy job to rule them. As their commander I was to fly with them in combat, and to fulfill a combat mission demanded strict discipline on the pilot's part. This was why I hesitated. I also didn't know what the attitude of the women would be toward me. Marina Raskova was their beloved commander; they were so fond of her and wanted to follow her example. I made a decision to be a just, strict, and demanding commander, irrespective of the fact that all these personnel were female. When I came to the regiment they didn't like me.

vsк: Behind his back we called him "bayonet." He was so strict and straight.

vм: They called me so also because I constantly put my principles of strict discipline into their heads, teaching them how to do this and that, seeing to the exact accomplishment of my orders, to their uniforms, boots, and brass. But their antipathy against me did not last long. I arrived at the regiment on February 2 or 3. The regiment had made only a few combat missions beginning at Stalingrad.

The main combat training was at the northern Caucasian front in April, 1943. In that area there was strong resistance from the German air forces, and at that point the experience of the women in combat began improving. They flew at very low altitudes following the terrain, dropping bombs from an altitude of one and one-half kilometers or lower. When we were bombing all the artillery were firing at us: submachine guns from the ground, anti-aircraft artillery, and ground artillery; it was very dangerous. We had very heavy dogfights in the air. All in all, we were heavily attacked by the Germans.

The field airdromes were not more than forty-five to fifty kilometers from the front line. The aircraft could fly about two and one-half hours without refueling. Their speed was 400 kilometers per hour with a range of about one thousand kilometers. During a day we usually made two or three flights. It took the ground personnel two hours to prepare the planes for the mission: to fuel, rearm, and patch holes if necessary. The aircraft was metal, and the loads when we dove were great. On the front edge of the wing there were dive brakes used on dive bombing missions.

After I made a lot of combat missions with this regiment I saw the attitude toward me become softer and more respectful, and by the summer of 1943 we had become real, true combat friends. Many people helped me to fulfill my mission and to train the personnel. Especially helpful were the head of the liaison service, a woman who graduated from the military academy before the war; the engineer of the regiment, responsible for armament; and the squadron commander, Timofeyeva, who had a husband, who was also at the front, and two children. She had joined the army even though she might not have been drafted. Our regimental doctor, a woman, also gave me knowledge of female problems. So I knew everything about the situation in my regiment. Of course there is a specific approach to the command of a female regiment, some peculiar features. You should be delicate when you are treating with the women; you should use your ears like radars.

vsk: A lot of girls fell in love with him; he was very handsome.

vm: The regiment was receiving combat assignments from the air force division. We had two squadrons in our regiment of ten aircraft each, with approximately twenty-one or twenty-two planes in the regiment. As a rule a mission was assigned to one squadron or to a regiment as a whole, but at times an air-bomb division would make a mass bombing. Ours was a regiment of front bomber aviation, and the targets were at the front line of the enemy positions. Manpower firing; strong points; concentrations of armament, tanks, and artillery formations; airfields; railroad lines; stations; bridges; and seaports (at the end of the war) were our main targets.

At the beginning of the war there were more pilots and crews than bombers, and on many occasions I chose who to assign to a mission. There were fixed crews, with no changing of crew members from one bomber to another. As a rule a squadron also operated in the same way. I flew with the regiment when we were assigned a mission. Valentina was my navigator. The female crews competed with other crews and counted their combat missions. And on occasions when I chose some crews but not others, they attacked me, were cross with me—why she but not me! Each mission was a risk to their lives, because all the fire from air and ground was concentrated on the bombers. In spite of all this, the women were striving to go on these missions.

We lost five crews. These were combat losses: five crews, three women in each. But there were many occasions when the crews made forced landings: in swamps, shot down, or jumping with parachutes. Not all the crew would get out sometimes. In one such case the squadron was attacked by many German Focke Wulf–190s, and one of our planes was shot down, burning, and the pilot gave the command to her crew to jump. The tragedy was that when the navigator was jumping her parachute caught on the barrel of the machine gun. She was outside the plane, but the harness was caught and she couldn't free herself. The pilot was trying to help the navigator slide off the barrel of the gun, and she worked the controls to swing her free. The navigator was freed from the plane, opened her parachute, and almost immediately touched the ground. The pilot perished in the crash. This is one example of friendship, mutual support, and bravery. There were some men in our regiment. Some were gunners, but the pilots and navigators were all women. The majority of the ground personnel were also women.

vsk: There were seventy-five women flying in our regiment. Five of them became Heroes of the Soviet Union.

vm: The women in my regiment were self-disciplined, careful, and obedient to orders; they respected the truth and fair treatment toward them. They never whimpered and never complained and were very courageous. If I compare my experience of commanding the male and female regiments, to some extent at the end of the war it was easier for me to command this female regiment. They had the strong spirit of a collective unit, which is still clearly manifested on our reunion day. Fifty years have passed since the war ended, but all these years we've been having our reunions on May 2 in front of the Bolshoi Theater. Most of us are old and sick, but it is our sacred day. We leave our business and illness aside and come there to see each other.

During the war there was no difference between this regiment and any male regiments. We lived in dugouts, as did the other regiments, and flew on the same missions, not more or less dangerous. It's hard to fancy how difficult the conditions were for these women. There should be two toilets at least, for men and women. We had only one! All the crews had almost the same number of combat missions. Almost all of these women were shot down, and after hospitalization, they came back to the regiment and flew bravely. But only after the war were they awarded the title of Hero of the Soviet Union. This bureaucratic machine takes time. And from the present viewpoint, I can see that very few of my girls were awarded that highest title. If I could turn time back, I would have promoted many more of them for that award. Now I have a very grave sentiment about that because many of them deserved it.

vsk: During the war the Germans knew about our regiment, but there were no newsmen or cameramen at our regiment. At the night bomber regiment there were a lot of them from the press. Nobody wrote about our regiment during the war. For the Soviet people it was like a secret regiment, carrying out secret assignments. Only at the victory parade in Moscow did the country learn about our existence. I didn't know anything about American women pilots during the war.

vm: I knew that there were American women pilots who flew planes to Alaska.

vm and vsk: Now the situation has changed, and we know a little more about you, and you know a little more about us.

VSK: I was appointed at Engels to be the squadron navigator. The Pe-2 bomber is not very convenient for the navigator. The design of the navigator's space, we cannot call it cabin, was poor. In front of the navigator there was the armor-protected seat of the pilot, behind the navigator the machine-gun ring, and in the floor there was a small window. There was one machine gun. The pilot had a cannon and a machine gun to fire. The pilot and navigator sat in one cabin, and the gunner was behind us in a separate compartment. We used maps printed before the war. Everything was perfect on them, but many cities were destroyed, so it looked different. The flooring of the fuselage in our compartment was made of clear plastic. When I could not see the landmarks I took off my parachute and peered around the pilot, to the right and left side, looking. I dropped the bombs, which were released by buttons. We used an optical sight, into which we put the altitude and speed of the aircraft.

There were no radio transmitters on the Pe-2 until later in the war. In the fall of 1943 our unit was honored by being named a "Guards" regiment, and our regimental name and number was changed from the 587th Bomber Regiment to the 125th Guards Bomber Regiment. The regiment was also named after Marina Raskova, at our request.

When we were flying, my duty was to navigate the aircraft to the target and to find our route. He, as commander and pilot, could not see other aircraft flying behind us. He would ask me, "Where is this pilot, and where is that one?" and I would say, "Everything is all right, they're following us." He was thinking more about the crews than about the target! After we had been flying with him for some time we called him not "bayonet" but "Daddy." I was twenty-five at that time and he was thirty-three, and now we still call him Daddy.

VM: Now we live in a little-improved world. You (in the United States) know more about us, and let God help us add to our mutual knowledge, to become more easy and less tense.

Senior Lieutenant Antonina Bondareva-Spitsina, *pilot*

I come from the Ural region, from a working family; my father worked at a metallurgical plant in the Urals. Our family consisted of six children. When I was little everyone started talking about aviation, an outburst of aviation, and it became more and more popular. We lived in a small village, and a plane, at that time even a glider, was a small miracle.

I was in sixth grade when a biplane landed. Everybody rushed to see what it was like, what it looked like, what it really was in real life. When I saw that plane my heart began beating fast, and I fell in love with the aircraft at first sight. Later on the pilot who brought the aircraft to the village founded a glider club nearby, and when I was sixteen, I enrolled in the club. In our region they admitted eighteen students, and only two were girls. I was the only daughter in my family, with five brothers, and my mother didn't even let me go to the club until I completed all household tasks and duties. My father was very much against my flying, but I did it anyway. Each time I left to go to the glider school my father would say, "Don't come back, you may not come back, I won't let you in!" Strange as it seems, my mother was not against it—she let me go. I was healthy, robust, and active, and my mother said I was meant to be a boy but turned out to be a girl.

I graduated from the glider school at sixteen. We had to make five parachute jumps before we were allowed to go to flying school. This was not a physical test but one to show whether you were brave enough to fly a plane. I quickly went on to powered aircraft, flying the U-2. When I became an instructor, I was nearly eighteen. Then I taught cadets. I was just under eighteen, and they were seventeen. And I didn't even have a passport of the country yet! You had to be at least eighteen to have a passport. I even had to add a year to my age in order to be assigned the rank of instructor-pilot.

When the war broke out I wanted to volunteer to be in Raskova's regiment, but I wasn't allowed to leave the school. The male instructors had left for the front, and I had to instruct the cadets. Only in 1943, when the women's regiments suffered losses, did I go to the front as a reinforcement.

I joined the 587th, later to be the 125th Guards Bomber Regiment. I, by this time, had 2,000 flying hours. Then I was trained to fly the Pe-2 dive bomber. My middle brother was also a pilot in the war, and my elder brother perished during the war. He was a paratrooper, a member of a sea landing force, and was killed. We received only a notice that he was killed in battle; we do not know the place of his grave. During the war we were each provided with a cylinder that we spun open, and we inserted into it a piece of paper with our identification on it. The official name for our air arm, which was a part of the Soviet army, was the USSR Army Air Force.

On one mission, just as we dropped the bombs, I felt something go wrong with our aircraft. The dive brakes had fallen, and I did not know that. The aircraft began chattering, and it started going down. The sea was below us and we remained alone, because the accom-

125th regiment in front of their PE-2 aircraft. *Standing, sixth from left:*
Antonina Bondareva-Spitsina; *seventh from left:*
Yevgeniya Gurulyeva-Smirnova; *far right:* Galina Brok-Beltsova

panying fighters went on with the squadron. I was searching for a place to land, and then I was caught by two fascist fighters who began shooting at us from different angles. I tried to maneuver, but I couldn't; the plane wouldn't respond. It was like a cat-and-mouse game; they didn't hit any of us, but the shells came very close. Suddenly they disappeared, and I learned later that two of our fighters came to rescue us and shot down the Germans. I finally landed on the airfield, but it took all my muscles, strength, and might—everything that I had—to make it, because it was pulling the nose down toward the earth. God saved us, and no one was hurt. The aircraft was so shot up that it took a month to repair.

One of the most horrible episodes came on a mission when I sensed that there was petrol in the cabin. I bent my head down to see what was happening and saw a hole in the fuel tank, and just then a great shell flew through the cabin over my head. Only because my head was bent down did I survive. My navigator (Brok-Beltsova) was nearly hit also, and she was so frightened that even after the mission her mouth was screwed up in a funny way. It was her nerves; she had seen the shell go over, and her face remained distorted for some time. War is war, and life is life.

While we were waiting for our combat mission to be assigned we would sit on our parachutes, and between the parachutes and our back we had a tiny cloth that we were knitting between flights. When we were assigned a mission, we put it back between our body and the parachute and went off to combat.

At the end of the war, when the women were released, I continued serving in the air force. There were only three women pilots in my unit who wished to remain in the active air force; we were retrained to fly the Tu-2 aircraft and were assigned to a male regiment. I flew until 1950, when I quit flying. I often have dreams about aircraft—of flying. It is my favorite dream.

War friendship is stronger than that between relatives, and we still know about everybody. We take care of each other and help in any way we can, and on great holidays I have received at least seventy letters from my friends!

Lieutenant Yevgeniya Gurulyeva-Smirnova, navigator

I was born on December 24, 1922. Aviation is my fate. I came to it because it was predestined. I loved the sky since early childhood.

I came from Siberia, very far away behind the Urals, to apply to the army headquarters to be drafted into the army. We were all united by the sentiment of defending our beloved motherland from the enemy. I know how the Americans love their land, and we Russians love our land, too. You can understand our patriotic feelings. I know that in America you are heterogeneous just as we are, but you are friendly with each other, you support each other, you are one whole nation. I like your president; I like your people.

I started flying in a glider school and made my first flight when I was sixteen years old. I continued on to pilot-instructor school; then I flew in an auxiliary medical regiment until I came to the 125th regiment as a reinforcement. My assignment was to be a navigator. I did not have a lot of flying hours, but I was a very good pilot.

I was wounded—very few from our regiment were wounded. We were bombing tanks in Lithuania, and there was heavy antiaircraft fire. A shell exploded directly under our aircraft when we were over the target. I had a burning pain in my body, as if a fire were burning inside. I hit against the metal navigator's seat and fell to the floor. I was semiconscious, and my blood covered the floor of the cockpit

Yevgeniya Gurulyeva-Smirnova,
125th regiment

with a shell splinter of about twenty-five centimeters stuck into my thigh. The pilot's seat was protected with armor plate, but the navigator's seat was not.

I knew I had to drop the bombs, so I reached up and found the liquid ammonia, put it to my face, and became fully conscious. Then I dropped the bombs and photographed the target as was required to indicate we had fulfilled the mission. We returned to our airfield and landed safely. By then I was motionless, and they had to throw me out of the cockpit as though I were a sack of coal. I was carried to a military hospital where I was operated on, and I was in the hospital for three months. I came back to the regiment and made a few training flights before returning to active service in the summer of 1944.

We moved from one airfield to another. When it was warm enough, we covered the wing of our plane with a tarpaulin and slept under it, especially in the spring and fall when it was too wet to sleep in a dugout. It was very cold and wet in the Smolensk region where we slept in dugouts. When we returned from our missions we couldn't rest or even dry our things because the floor was covered with water and mud. Our linens, pillows, mattresses, blankets—everything was wet through. Sometimes we left our boots in front of the open fire to dry overnight, and when we awakened, instead of dry we found them burned. Those mornings we had nothing to put on our feet when we heard the alert signal.

By the time I arrived at the regiment the whole squadron to which I was assigned had been killed, and we were all replacements. Only in 1944 did we make our first combat missions. There were eight of us from our squadron who became very good friends and swore that our friendship would endure to the last day of our lives. We are still friends and call each other and see each other, but unfortunately many of us have already died.

No other country in the world let women fly combat, but Stalin proclaimed that our women could do everything, could withstand anything! It was a kind of propaganda to show that Soviet women were equal to men and could fulfill any task, to show how mighty and strong we were. Women could not only bring babies into being but could build hydroelectric plants, fly aircraft, and destroy the enemy. Even if Stalin hadn't let the girls fly we would have volunteered by the thousands for the army.

Our regiment had two squadrons of nine aircraft each. We had very good air cover; not only Russian but also French fighters provided us with protection when on bombing missions. When the German fighter planes came up to try to stop the bombers, our fighter aircraft would engage them.

I only saw one of our aircraft shot down. It started to fall, and only the tail-gunner managed to parachute out. We were instructed on how to jump from our plane if necessary: by jumping vertically to our flight path, with our feet pointed to the ground and our back against the wind. We were to jump through the lower hatch, feet first. The tail-gunner left her position, dropping through the lower hatch also.

The Pe-2 had one bad feature: its landing speed was quite fast, and that contributed to a number of crashes. We had fewer casualties in our regiment than the men did flying the same type of aircraft; I think we were more exact in our flying.

What I feared most on flying missions was being captured by the fascists. We also were afraid of being punished for not fulfilling a combat mission. We couldn't turn around and go back without completing the mission. If we didn't complete our assignment, we could be imprisoned. We didn't think we would be imprisoned but only punished within the regiment. Nowadays people don't pay much attention to trifles, but in our time, in Stalinist days, we were punished.

Today we speak about repression and about labor camps in our country. We say it was a great injustice for the people to be imprisoned by their own government if they spoke out against the system, but at that time we didn't think so. My grandfather was imprisoned after the revolution and sent to a labor camp in Siberia for protesting against Soviet rule. He cursed all the Soviets in his village. Before the revolution he was a rich peasant in spite of the fact that he had a large family. He worked hard, but the Soviets dispossessed him of everything. They tried to force him to join the collective farm and he wouldn't. So he was punished. At that time, when I was young and in school, I thought it was just punishment because he didn't support the system.

I married after the war, and I have only one child. He hasn't any children, and I am not a happy grandmother. My husband died seven years ago.

Sergeant-Major Yevgeniya Zapolnova-Ageyeva, mechanic of armament

My native city is Moscow; I was born there. When the war started I was studying at the Moscow Aviation Institute. We were all patriots and wanted to volunteer. I heard of the three female regiments being formed by Raskova, and I immediately applied and was admitted to the regiment. My knowledge of aviation was theoretical because I had no practical knowledge or flying experience before the war. I became a mechanic.

Our planes usually flew three raids a day, and the interval between raids was one hour. Within that time we had to fix the bombs, load the guns, and prepare for flight. The flight could not be delayed even for one minute, because it was all coordinated with fighter regiments that escorted the bombers. It was very intense. In Stalingrad, in very cold weather with temperatures down to forty-two degrees below zero centigrade, the skin on our hands froze and stuck to the metal, and our hands were black from frostbite. In the Kuban region, in the south of our country, there was unbearable heat, and there we burned our hands on the metal.

When Raskova, who had become commander of our regiment after our training at Engels, perished ferrying a plane to the front, we had a ceremony at the regiment, a deep mourning. In Russia we have a good tradition to pay tribute to the dead after the body is buried. We all assemble in a hall somewhere to say the kindest and most honorable words about the dead person. Then we have a funeral. We were all filled with grief, and it was the greatest loss for us. Russian people are superstitious, and we believe in some signs. We have a sign here in Russia: if a dog is howling for a long time, weeping and sobbing, a misfortune is sure to happen—something terrible. Before Raskova perished a dog was howling for several days, and we asked ourselves, "What is going to happen? What wrong is going to happen?" and she died. Well, again, signs are signs, and life is life.

On the eve of the New Year we have a tradition foretelling our fortune for the coming year. At the regiment we wrote some small notes, saying for everybody what kind of a year it was going to be, and we put them under the pillows. Everyone thrust her hand under the pillow, took out the message, and read it out loud. Raskova read that she was going to have a happy year, but it turned out to be quite the contrary. That year she perished; she was thirty-one years old. She was born in 1912 and was killed in 1943. She left an orphan daughter, Tanya, who had to live with her grandmother.

I returned to the institute after the war, but I had missed four years and had forgotten a lot. My father had perished at the front, and I was not physically well, so I quit and later married.

Sergeant Antonina Khokhlova Dubkova, tail-gunner

Members of the 125th regiment

Some Soviet pilots flew over our regimental airfield at zero altitude. Then we saw that something was dropped from the plane. Our commander was very strict and said, "That is forbidden, and the pilot must be punished." Well, of course it might have created an accident. Then he sent a technician to find what was dropped. What he brought back was a big teddy bear. I don't know where they procured it, but there was a notice pinned to the bear that said: "Dear young girls, we just learned we are escorting you. Don't you get frightened; we'll do everything to defend you, fight for you with the last drop of our blood. Thank you!" That was a gift from the sky. These were the fighters who escorted our bombers. Every bomber flight going out on missions is supposed to have fighter escorts.

I was a sergeant and an aircrew machine gunner. At first I was the only woman machine gunner in the whole regiment. All the other gunners were men, because physically it was very difficult. I used to do gymnastics, ride horses, and row a scull, too, so I had a lot of strength. I asked Marina Raskova to let me fly. At first they wanted to make me a weapons mechanic. Then I asked her, and she liked me and I liked her, and she said, "Well, I will take you in my plane once and see what you look like." She couldn't tell very well without doing that. We flew, and it was enough for her that I didn't throw up on my first flight. Then she said I should take up the studies for two or three months, and that should be enough for me.

The real effort was to recharge the machine gun, to pull the lever when it took sixty kilograms, and I had to do it with my left arm. I could never do it on the ground because it was very hard, but in the air it was one, two, and it was recharged! I squatted with the parachute behind my back, one machine gun behind me, another fixed machine gun that faced down and back. The latter gun was heavier, and it required the recharging. The lighter machine gun could be lifted out from one side and remounted on the other side, depending where the attack was coming from. I was in a separate compartment farther back than the pilot and navigator. It had a small canopy, so that you could see in all directions. I had communication with the pilot on an intercom. We were shot down two or three times. There was a narrow escape, and, you know, we might not have had the pleasure of seeing each other now.

Well, we were shot down in the Kuban region, and there were more German planes there than we had fighter aircraft to escort us on missions. It was very hard for Soviet pilots at that time. I don't remember if we had any escort when we saw German Messerschmitts approaching us. Of course we started firing; we were frightened, and these were our first missions. We were saved, more thanks to the weather. We got into a big, stormy cloud, and the Messerschmitt lost us. But before he lost sight of us he fired a round, and we saw that one of our engines was burning and the fuel was gushing out. My pilot was very skilled, and she managed to land the plane in a small meadow about two kilometers behind our lines. We had an agreement between us that if there were a forced landing, the one who feels better, who is conscious, not wounded, helps the others. It was especially necessary to help the pilot and the navigator to get out of that very small cabin.

After we landed my pilot, Yekaterina Musatova-Fedotova, called, "Tosha, Tosha!" I had with me an instrument, like a small axe or crowbar, to pry open their canopy, but I had breathed in so much dispersed fuel that I was like a drunken person. There was a pounding noise, and four-letter words, and shouting to get out quick and help us! That sobered me a little. Even now I can't breathe in exhaust gases, and I can't stand the sight of petrol. Well, I got them out, and luckily the plane didn't blow up and begin to burn.

The most interesting thing that I remember since then is that I communicated by radio with somebody in the ground forces and told them of our despair and our situation. So on the ground we were waiting for help, and then we saw some soldiers, infantry soldiers, crawling up to us. But we saw that they were our soldiers, and what do you think they came with? Big green leaves, and these leaves were full of strawberries! Probably they heard us talking and knew we were women, the gift sent to them from the sky. That was the first nice thing during the war—red strawberries, beautiful strawberries in green leaves!

We survived the war because of our regimental commander. All through the flights he was addressing his navigator, asking, "How are the girls?" He chose the routes so that we evaded the ground attacks of the anti-aircraft guns and also the German fighters; he knew the situation very well. He told us always to stick together. Of course the anti-aircraft fire couldn't be helped, and the first salvo generally got someone. We began to maneuver all together, the nine of us or the eighteen of us. Well, they couldn't adjust to our maneuvering and missed us, but the fighters looked for an opportunity, for a plane to part from the group so that they could easily shoot it down. When the group stuck together there were nine planes: nine gunners with machine guns, nine navigators with their machine guns, plus the guns of the pilots.

The second time we were shot down was on the western front, but I shot down one plane, too! I didn't know I shot it down, but the ground forces saw everything, and then we had the photographing that begins when you fire. They saw it was shot down; the bullets were tracer bullets, so our soldiers could see where they came from. One of the planes of a male regiment was burning; our plane was hit, but we weren't burning. The fuel tubes all shattered, and the fuel again was streaming out. Then Katyusha, our pilot, saw a little clearing surrounded by the forest on all sides, and she managed to land the plane safely.

The other plane that was on fire was flown by the men's crew. Probably they were conceited young boys not very well trained— they couldn't make it the last one hundred meters to that open space where we landed. They crashed in the forest and burned before our eyes. Because there was no one else around, we had to pick up their remains: one arm, one leg, all smoked and roasted. I thought I would never look at any meat after that. Well, life is life. So we collected the remains of that crew, all three of them, torn apart. No heads, all apart. We gathered them together. There was a parachute intact, so we ripped the parachute apart, covered the remains, and buried them.

The third time we were not shot down, but one of the engines cut off as we were taking off. The height was only one hundred meters, and we were loaded with bombs. Luckily for us there was a field in front of us, so I quickly switched on the radio and said, "Forced landing, forced landing!" so that the ground personnel knew where we were. We made a belly landing, and very soon the crew of technicians and engineers arrived. When they looked under the wings and saw the bombs they nearly fainted—the engineer was a woman, too. One of the explosive devices that attached to the bomb was pushed out and got split up, so it was live. It was by a micron or the hundredth part of a millimeter that the yoke did not detach from the capsule with the explosive. Well, that's probably luck. But when they arrived they thought that I was crazy from sheer fright, because they found me sitting on the fuselage, powdering my face. We had landed on a freshly plowed field and the earth was dry, and there was so much dust you couldn't see anything. So I sat astride the fuselage, my legs down in my cabin, and I thought, I must do something with this dust, so I began brushing it off. They thought, Tosha is gone!

Either you have no time to be frightened or you have to act very quickly, but somehow it's not a helpless fright. You have to act, you have to do something, you have to save your life—not only your life but the lives of your friends. Fright is natural and fear is natural for everybody, but it wasn't freezing—a fright that makes you helpless.

I am frightened now (1990). I don't know what will become of my fair country. I don't know what is going to happen to our country, with the lack of even the barest necessities.

It's not just the lack of things, it's just the sheer stupidity and sabotage! The harvest, they plowed it down; probably they have always been doing it. Throughout the years, when the chief of the Regional Party Department comes to inspect the fields and finds that by a certain date the crops haven't been harvested, he punishes everybody. So what the *kolkhozinks* (farmers) do is to plow it under and say everything is harvested.

Everybody has thought about this, but there is no one to think what to do. No one can do anything here. We are all helpless for some reason. These people are no fools, and even I am no fool. I can tell them what should be, but how to achieve this? It doesn't work because of the resistance, because of the party leaders, and Gorbachev himself—I think he doesn't know what to do. To take the power away from the party you have to begin shooting them. I don't know whether Gorbachev is right or not. I think so far he may be right, because if he starts shooting them, there will start an overall shooting, a civil war. A civil war is something—it will be just a massacre of everybody, by everybody. As I read in a book, everyone is in an excellent state of preparedness to bite or to kill everybody else. And the people are nice, the people are nice. I don't know the psychology of it.

I was a student here in Moscow at the language institute before the war, so I got through two years, four terms; then the war broke out, and I made a break in studies. After the war, in May, 1945, I came back and had two more years at the military institute.

I hated Stalin throughout my life, beginning with the murder of Kirov. I was fifteen then, in sixth grade, and I said, "That's Stalin's deed!" Then there came Kujbishev and Gorky and all the nice men, from my point of view, and I hated Stalin when the war started. Molotov declared, "For our country, for the motherland, for Stalin." I was a coxswain at the rudder of the men's crew, a sculling crew, when we heard the declaration of war. So we came back, landed, put the boat away, and all went to the Military Commissariat to enroll—eight boys and myself. I told the boys when I heard this broadcast that said "for our country, for the motherland, for Stalin" that the motherland is all right, but why should I fight for Stalin? He's a man—let him fight for himself! There was no traitor among the eight boys, no traitor. I might have been shot.

A second time I also might have been shot but was only punished very severely: they didn't let me fly for several months. One of our mechanics liked to paint. He was rather an old man, about forty—we were so young, and we thought he was so old. Our plane was beautiful—it was streamlined; especially when it flew low, you couldn't turn away your eyes from it—like English is beautiful. I like English, and I liked my plane. I like the way English sounds when Mrs. Thatcher begins to speak, or Bush, or Reagan, anyone—I just begin to melt down! Well, on one side of the plane he painted a swallow in flight, and on the other side he wrote, For the Country, for Stalin. So I took the paint and the brush and I smeared it. Then he painted something else very quickly, but there were no traitors, no traitors. I said, "No, I don't want to fight for Stalin!" I was not brave, I was lucky; like all fools I was lucky. If someone had turned me in, of course I would have been shot, shot on the spot.

I graduated in languages from the military institute, and I taught there; I was a senior lieutenant then. I ought to have been something more, but I was so undisciplined. I got out of the service in 1954. After the war I married, and we have one son.

It wasn't the phenomenon itself, the girls being called up and volunteering into the army: it was the spirit, the spirit not of fighting for some person but of fighting for the freedom of the country from those German fascists.

NOTE: After the war Antonina married the brother of her crew navigator, Klara Dubkova. This was the only interview conducted completely in English.

Captain Mariya Dolina,
pilot, deputy commander of the squadron
Hero of the Soviet Union

One of my sons is a pilot; the other is the captain of a ship. I was a flight instructor before the war. In comparison to my comrades-in-arms, the women who dreamed of becoming pilots, I never hoped to be one because I grew up in a very poor family that experienced great hardships. I am a Ukrainian by origin, but I was born in Siberia in the Omsk region. My father, a peasant who had experienced great suffering in the Ukraine, went to Siberia to work on the land, and I was born there on December 18, 1920. There were ten children in our family, and I was the oldest. My father lost both legs and couldn't do much, so I had to labor for the whole family. In 1934 we returned to the Ukraine.

My mother had asked me to quit school because my father couldn't support the family, so I left school and went to work in a plant. At the same time I began attending a glider school. I really came into aviation by chance. Mother didn't want me to attend the glider school because I had to labor. She said that she had asked me to quit secondary school to help the family, and now that I was attending glider school, who was going to work? The head of the glider school came to my mother and asked that I be allowed to continue, because there were fourteen of us, and I was the only girl. Our group of cadets was to be sent to a military flying school to continue flight training. No matter how much my parents objected, I knew from the moment I

Mariya Dolina, 125th regiment

first got into the plane that I was born there in the air, and it became my main purpose in life—to fly. And it was also the matter of my ambition, too, because I wanted to achieve something in life. I was eager to get an education. Because I had to quit secondary school, I thought of acquiring a good profession in aviation.

I graduated from the Kherson military aviation school as a lieutenant in the reserve air force. I became a professional pilot, an instructor, and I was teaching at Dnepropetrovsk Flying School when the Great Patriotic War started. On the eve of the war, we had received some new sports aircraft, U-2s, and yet we sat there waiting, but there was no call to activate us. The male pilots from our school were taken to the front. The fascists were advancing rapidly, and at any moment our area could be occupied by the enemy. I couldn't even think of surrendering to the enemy, but I had never dreamed of fighting, either. According to Tolstoy, war and women are things that don't go together—they exist apart. But when I witnessed all the atrocities of 1941, the death of my friends and relatives, peaceful civilians, I wanted to help liberate my people from the enemy. I want you to underline in red that it was the cherished dream of the girls to liberate the land, but none of us wanted to fight—to kill.

My flying club was stationed with the 66th Fighter Division of the air army, and we women wanted to voluntarily join it. Finally the commander agreed to take us—we would all retreat together. There were one other pilot, a girl navigator, and myself. We were ordered to ferry our aircraft at night across the Dnieper River. Before we left we were assigned to set on fire all the petrol and to explode the hangars where the planes were kept. I was to ferry three aircraft to the field where the division was moving. We set the hangars on fire and also the house we had built with our own hands, where we had lived so happily. When I flew over that night the river was burning with oil, and everything on the ground was burning. It felt as though even the air was on fire. The next morning I was enlisted into the air division, and I became a military pilot in one of its regiments.

I flew 200 missions with that regiment. I was assigned to special missions, such as ferrying important people and the wounded. My plane was very small, and although it was hit it was not shot down. The German fighters tried from time to time to shoot it down, and I would maneuver. The U-2 was a slow biplane, and the fighters' velocity was so much greater that I could fly very low to the ground and make turns so that they didn't hit me. It was difficult for the enemy fighter, for he quickly overshot me—God saved me!

The morning Raskova came to the staff of the southern front to select women for her regiment, I was the only woman there. Raskova said I must join the women's regiment. I said, "No, I don't want to go, this is now my family, my regiment; how could I?" I cried bitterly at losing my friends. She showed me Stalin's order saying that all the women should be in her regiment. Raskova was a strong-willed and strong-hearted personality. I was transferred to the training base at Engels, where I was assigned to fly the Pe-2 dive bomber.

A most difficult flight took place in 1942 at the northern Caucasian front. It happened in the village of Krimskaya, where the military situation was very complicated. This village was first liberated by the Soviet army, and then was recaptured by the Germans, and again liberated by the Soviets, and again captured; this went on twice or thrice a day. The combat going on in this area was quite severe.

On June 2, our forces managed to free the village. The weather conditions were very bad, with low clouds at about nine hundred meters. Nine aircraft were assigned to fly that mission, to try to destroy the enemy fortifications in that village by bombing. Yevgeniya Timofeyeva, deputy commander of our regiment, led our nine bombers. On this mission my left engine was hit by enemy fire and quit, and I began lagging behind in the flight. We were alone at the target, because the other aircraft had already bombed. We had to fly there and bomb without a fighter escort, because our fighters had started a dogfight with enemy fighters. The German planes attacked us, and we had to fight alone; of our nine bombers, five were shot down. My aircraft was set on fire while fighting with the Messerschmitts. Our squadron shot down four of the enemy fighters by ourselves. So we simultaneously bombed and shot down the four aircraft. Two were shot down by other formations and two by the formation that I led. Afterward my tail gunner was given a gift, a bonus of 1,000 rubles for shooting down a German aircraft.

When the fight was over I was trailing behind, and my formation stayed back with my plane because they didn't want to leave us alone. Although the plane was shot up, it was not on fire until the German planes, seeing that my formation was alone, returned and fired on us again, and my engine caught fire. It was only because of my friend Tonya Skoblikova that we remained alive. One aircraft from my formation went ahead to our airfield, and our two planes were left alone. So Tonya held off all the German fighters with machine-gun fire to protect and save us. Then Tonya's plane was hit, and she had to leave and land on one of the fighter airfields.

I proceeded alone, and our plane was attacked again by a German fighter. The right engine was hit and caught fire also. By that time my navigator and tail gunner had run out of bullets, so they started shooting flares instead. Then the German fighter came around and flew right up next to me, and I could see his face. He showed his teeth, and he looked so ugly. His face was freckled, and I remember his face until now. He was ferociously smiling at me, his face distorted with hostility, and he showed me his fingers, gesturing one, two. I didn't know what it meant, and later on, when I was in the military hospital, I asked a fighter pilot what he was signaling. I was told he was asking, "How would you like me to shoot you down, in one attack or two?" Then he left, apparently thinking that because both engines were now on fire, our aircraft was done for. As we descended Galina Dzhunkovskaya, my navigator, pulled my goggles down over my eyes. She realized that I needed to see to land, and smoke was beginning to enter the cockpit. The goggles saved my face and eyes when the fire entered the cabin. I sustained burns only on my chest. We made a belly landing, and our gunner pulled us out of the cockpit, because Galina and I were already being burned. We were beginning to burn in the cabin.

Our gunner was a man, and he saved our lives. He was wounded in the leg and sustained other injuries from the rough landing. The canopy was jammed, and he succeeded in prying it open and saving us. We beat the canopy with our hands and heads, trying to force it open. I was in shock. We landed just two kilometers from the front line. When he pulled us from the cabin, we fell on the ground, and the grass around us was burning—it was about one meter high in the summer—and we had to roll about to put the fire out around us and on us.

The artillery men saw us land, picked us up, and took us to a military hospital. There I fainted. I had a spinal compression injury from the shock of landing and was hospitalized for a month before returning to duty. Now (1991) I must have surgery on my spine because of that injury. No one could believe we were still alive because they saw an explosion in the air, our two engines were on fire, and they saw no parachutes. So, at our regiment, they thought we had perished. We were too low to jump when we were set on fire, and the wind was blowing in the direction of the fascist troops. If we could have jumped, we would have drifted across the front line.

Another time I was shot down on the northern Caucasian front. I had received an order to leave the aircraft and parachute down, but I loved the plane and wanted to land it, and I did. The controls were disabled, and I landed using the engines for control. The dive brakes were also damaged and had fallen down.

On another occasion, one engine was set on fire, and I landed the plane with the one remaining engine. When I was on final approach to our field all the systems quit, and the other engine quit, but I managed to land and save the airplane. Every flight in the Pe-2 was a game with death, a very dangerous game. That was why in the air force there was a certain lore that if a pilot or navigator made seventy missions in a Pe-2, they were awarded the medal of Hero of the Soviet Union. I made seventy-two combat missions in that aircraft; I was born under a lucky star! All in all I flew 2,800 hours.

Once we were stationed at an airdrome that had a male air regiment, the 124th, nearby. About half of our regiment made happy marriages with members of that regiment. My first marriage was with a navigator from that regiment, who died in 1972. My mechanic of armament in our own regiment divorced about that time, and we married. We had been through the hardships of war together so we knew each other well, and we started a new family. My friends told us that two broken hearts had been united.

In Operation Bagration we suffered very great losses and severe battles. After fulfilling these combat missions we were awarded various orders, medals, special streamers, and certificates. For that operation I was awarded the Order of Combat Red Banner. For all combat during the war, I was awarded two Orders of Red Banner, one Order of Lenin, and the Hero of the Soviet Union.

When we had successfully freed Borisov town, our regiment was titled Borisovski Regiment. After that operation the girls asked me to throw a streamer out of my plane, on which they had written an inscription: "To the Inhabitants of the Town of Borisov with Military Regards, from Women Pilots of the Borisovski Regiment" with the signature of Mariya Dolina. They had made the streamer out of ten military towels sewn together. I didn't know how to throw the streamer out of the plane, because I was a little afraid of Markov, our regimental commander. I decided that at a very low altitude, I would say there was something wrong with my engine and that we were going to land at the Borisov airdrome. Markov said all right. So I lagged behind and made a circle over the town, and it was burning, all afire; it looked like Stalingrad had looked. Besides the streamer itself, we penned a letter to the Borisov Party Council. The letter said that we wished the inhabitants to restore the city, to flourish, continue peacetime jobs, and help people survive, while we continued our job at the front. We threw the streamer out, and the city people carried it into their museum and kept it there, and now it is in the Minsk Museum.

After we dropped the streamer and returned to our formation the gunner reported to Commander Markov that there was nothing wrong with our engine, and he realized that it was a hooligan trick. When we landed he arrested me and put me for fifteen days in the guardhouse. But I only stayed there two days because they needed pilots. Markov entered the guardhouse and told me that there was no time for sitting and relaxing, I must work and fly.

It is distressing even now to speak about the war, because we lost forty-seven of our girls. And war is not a female profession, but we were defending the liberty and freedom of our country. Those who remain alive must live long and remember those who perished and should relate the experience to the younger generation. The feeling of all these women in our regiments who remain alive, and of all the people that had to undergo the hardships of the war, is that all people should work for the peaceful existence of all the countries so that war does not come to any land. We are not a militant nation, and we had to bear twenty million losses, so we call on all the people of the world not to let that happen again.

Presently, I am in the Presidium of the Republican Council of the Veterans in War. On May 9, 1990, I was asked to talk in front of our President Gorbachev on behalf of the Ukrainian veterans.

Sergeant Anna Kirilina,
mechanic of armament

Before the war I was a textile worker, and I was keen on parachute jumping; I jumped out of sheer sport. When I was jumping I got a strange, unpleasant feeling inside, but there were boys there too, and I didn't want to show fear in front of the boys! So I didn't show it, and I jumped several times. When war broke out I went to volunteer for the armed forces, but nothing happened. There was a shortage of labor at the plant, and that might have been the reason. Then, suddenly, I was called and admitted to the air regiments being formed by Raskova.

All our hardships started at Stalingrad. I had to affix 1,000 kilos of bombs to the aircraft—I alone. The bombs came in boxes totally unprepared. I had to affix ten bombs to the plane, and each bomb weighed 100 kilos. We had a special metallic cable that lifted the bomb, and then we attached it to the aircraft with our hands. I also prepared the bombs for explosion.

Then I had to prepare the machine guns. It was in winter, a severe, frosty winter. I had to do my work with bare hands, and my hands froze; my right hand was completely frozen. I bandaged it and tried to hide it; otherwise I could be sent back, and I didn't want to be sent to the rear. Later on the hand came alive again, but for some time it remained dead; I couldn't feel it at all.

Our underground dugouts were heated by a very small fireplace called a *burzhujk*, made from an oil drum. After the revolution there was a class of people called bourgeoisie, who were known to live in much better conditions than the peasantry, workers, and average people. They had more wealth, more luxuries, like this fireplace that during the war was considered to be a luxury—it was our luxury. And that's why people called it *burzhujk*, derived from the word *bourgeoisie.*

We had no place to wash our hands or our linen. We lived in dugouts with no water to wash, and when we had any it was cold. When we received the detonators and explosive elements, they were in special metallic boxes, very small boxes. After we emptied them we used the boxes for heating water. When you live in a primitive, ugly domicile, you try to make it comfortable and cozy even if you are not there except for short periods. Just when it would become somewhat inhabitable we would move to another location, leave everything behind, and start anew at a different airfield.

Wartime is wartime, and war is not a labor for women. We didn't even feel what was happening because we were so physically overstrained. But the war made us not friends but relatives. It made us sisters—dear, dear creatures to each other. On the day of our reunion we say, I go to meet my sisters, because for the four years of war, we all went through and experienced so much that sometimes it seems impossible for a human creature to know it in her whole lifetime.

Certainly there was love and friendship. When I went to the front I had a fiancé—an engagement—and we agreed that when we returned home, we would marry. Moreover, I belonged to an orthodox church, and I never violated the rules of the church. If I swore my fiancé to be my beloved man, I could not betray him. I remained loyal to him through all the years of war, and after the war we came home and married. I had to conceal my beliefs for a long time because I would have been persecuted, but now I can speak frankly about that.

I was a devoted textile worker. As a pilot loves her aircraft, I loved my instrument very much, and when I returned to the plant, entered the room, and saw my textile instrument standing there, I rushed up to it. I was extremely happy that I had returned to peaceful labor. After the war and those bombings, those sleepless nights, the happiest moment of my life was when I entered the plant and realized the war had come to an end! I now still work at the same plant, and fortunately I'm healthy and I go on laboring.

Junior Lieutenant Antonina Pugachova-Makarova, navigator

125th Regiment Pe-2 crew preparing for a flight

I was born in 1924. When I was a child I dreamed of becoming a pilot, but because I was short, I was not allowed to join the air force. When the war started I was in the ninth grade in school.

In 1942 I joined the army. I was sent to the military aviation school in Moscow, where a battalion of girls were studying meteorology and other aviation sciences. Shortly before graduation, the school received an order to select the best-trained girls and send them to the regiment of Marina Raskova. Only ten were selected, and we all did our best to be among them. I was afraid that my short height would be against me. Before the final test I put thick pieces of paper in my high boots to make me look taller, and I was put on the list to go.

We were sent to Yoshkar-Ola to be trained as navigators. We trained in the TB-3 dive bomber. It could dive and drop bombs, and it would shake, rattle, and jump. We were told to bring some buckets along with us because we weren't used to flying, and all of us were leaning over the buckets being sick. We also trained in parachute jumping. I jumped twice, which was required in our training.

After training, the commanders selected nine of us to go to the front. I was very happy that my dream came true. We then started training in crews: navigator, pilot, and gunner. My crew commander was Tamara Rusakova, who was a very fine pilot and a very strict commander. She made us clean the aircraft after every flight, and only then did we have the right to leave the airdrome. When there was snow on the ground we had to make a hangar out of the snow to protect the plane. Everyone else would have left the field, but we would still be working.

The 587th regiment had lost the equivalent of a squadron soon after the war started and needed replacements. In March, 1944, we were sent to the front. We found the atmosphere in the regiment to be intelligent, strict, and just. Commander Markov liked order; he was a very clever and educated man and a gifted pilot. We all tried to do our best to please him and do our duty in as excellent a way as possible. Among ourselves we called him *Baty*, which is a familiar form of papa. It was because of Tamara and Valentin Markov that my flying career ended so meaningfully. He had an incredible, magnetic influence on all of us.

At the front our airdrome was near Smolensk. During our first combat missions, we were flying in formation and escorted by fighters. It was nothing like I had expected. I thought we would be endlessly attacked by Germans and firing at them. I fancied to see explosions of aircraft, shells, bombs, and flames here and there, and bullets tracing like wildfire in the sky. In reality there were no German aircraft, and everything appeared very simple: to fly, drop bombs, and go home. We could see the explosions of antiaircraft shells. There was black smoke, and then it disappeared. It seems to me that God saved us, and we felt calm and believed that nothing would happen to us. There was that feeling that God watched over us. Usually when we flew missions there were twenty-seven aircraft, and I could not tell if I was a good navigator because we were in a formation and followed the lead plane.

But many of our missions were difficult, and we lost a lot of our combat friends. The worst thing was to see the bomber of my friends being shot down: there is smoke and fire, and it is going down, and you are flying, and you can't do anything to help them. When we were bombing Libava city on the Baltic Sea it was especially dangerous. Each of our planes had five machine guns to defend it, and we had fighter cover. When there were only a few German fighters in our area, our fighters started dogfights with them, and our gunners had nothing to do. But when there were lots of German fighters, we had to help protect ourselves, using our own machine guns. When I became a navigator in the Pe-2, I felt I had an advantage. Tall navigators had to sit, but because of my height I could stand up and see very well. In the aircraft the fumes of the fuel bothered me like an allergy, and sometimes I felt that I was going to lose consciousness.

Our regiment was given the honor of becoming a "Guards" regiment, and in that ceremony we changed from being the 587th Bomber Regiment to the 125th Guards Bomber Regiment. We were awarded two combat orders.

Life goes on. All of us enjoyed the days when we could have a bath. There was a truck with a large box on top, and each week or so this truck arrived at our regiment, and we could have a bath in cold water. It was like a holiday for us. We especially wanted a bath after a combat mission, but that was often impossible. When we were stationed near a village the people there would sometimes invite us to their homes, and we could bathe there. We liked to sleep on clean sheets. There is an old Russian tradition that before going into battle you should wash all your linen and clothes and put them on; we knew that any day we could crash and be killed. This is our old, old tradition, and if our logistics personnel could not bring us clean towels and linen, we washed them ourselves.

Just after the war I returned to civilian life. I realized that I had only nine years of school and that sooner or later I would have to continue my education. I went back and finished secondary school, then teachers' college, and later on a pedagogical institute. All these years I've been teaching in a secondary school and in other higher educational institutions.

We have a saying that if you like to climb mountains, they will kill you; and if you are devoted to flying, the aircraft will kill you. My pilot, Tamara, continued to fly, and on a flight above the Baltic Sea something happened to her plane, and she crashed and died.

In the Kremlin after award ceremony of Hero of the Soviet Union Gold Star medals. *Bottom row:* Klavdiya Fomichova (*left*), Nadezhda Fedutenko (*center*). *Top row:* Mariya Dolina (*third from left*) and Antonina Zubkova (*far right*), 125th regiment

Sergeant Antonina Lepilina,
mechanic of armament

I was born in Moscow in the family of a confectioner. My mother was most of the time a housewife. Upon finishing eight grades of a secondary school—there are normally eleven grades—I went to work in an aviation plant as a controller, checking parts for the aircraft. When the war started and I heard Raskova was forming the women's regiments, I went to Komsomol headquarters and asked to be drafted there. I was accepted as a mechanic of armament to her regiment.

The pilot of my aircraft was Mariya Dolina, and my most anxious moments were while waiting for my aircrew to return from a mission. Both my pilot and her navigator, Galina Dzhunkovskaya, were awarded the Gold Star of Hero of the Soviet Union. Everyone in my crew survived the war, and we finished the war together. In the Caucasus region my crew was one of four shot down, and it was the first time that our aircraft did not return from a mission. I cannot even describe my emotional experience at the thought that my friends might have perished.

They were shot down on a mission when both engines and fuel tanks were hit by enemy fire, and Mariya Dolina managed to belly-land the aircraft. When she did, the cockpit hatch jammed, and the girls couldn't get out. By this time the cockpit already was full of smoke. It was the tail gunner who saved their lives. He got out of his cockpit, crawled along the fuselage, forced the canopy open, dragged them out of the cockpit, and rushed them away from the aircraft. They were no more than fifty meters from the plane when it blew up.

Another time they didn't return from a mission that day, but the next day they were flown back to our airdrome in another aircraft. I had watched our navigator, Galina, while she was in the presence of Commander Markov and guessed that they had feelings for each other. It was just an undercurrent, because they didn't act in any way but properly, ever. But when the girls were brought back burned and injured, Valentin Markov himself carried Galina out of the plane and over to the vehicle to bring them to the regiment. Then we all knew his feelings for her. They were married after the war.

Lieutenant Yelena Kulkova-Malutina,
senior pilot

I was born in Leningrad in 1917, the year of the revolution. While I was still in school, I attended glider school. I was seventeen years old. When I graduated I entered a pilot's school of civil aviation, which I completed in three years. I was then sent to a Urals unit of aviation, and I worked as a pilot in medical aviation. The connections between the Kazan region and the central part of Russia where I worked were bad. The roads were in poor condition, and the only possible way to carry mail and things such as food and sick people was by plane. I flew a U-2 mainly to carry the sick. This unit was called a Unit of Special Activity.

In 1942 I was transferred to the town of Magnitogorsk, where I was an instructor-pilot. I was twenty-three or twenty-four when the war started, and I trained male pilots in a military training school. At that time, just before the war, Soviet aviation was in its glory. There was an outburst of aviation development, and aviation was widely talked about. In our present-day situation, we never talk about cosmic space and exploration. Aviation flourished then. At the school I was the only woman out of eighteen instructors. It was in an open airfield, and there was no place for a ladies' room. Everything was open; to find a place I had to go behind a bush, where I could be seen by everyone, and there were only men. I was so shy and embarrassed that

I didn't even have a gulp of water in order not to go to the ladies' room behind a bush. And the cadets insisted on asking our commander why I didn't ever have breakfast!

Then I was transferred to a group that was preparing to fly in one of Marina Raskova's regiments. The regiments had suffered losses at the front, and they needed crews to take their places. By this time I had 1,500 hours of flying time; that is why, as an experienced pilot, I was trained in the most complex plane, the Pe-2 dive bomber. In our school the nutrition had been very poor: it was wartime. When I went to the regiment the food was so much better that for a period of time I couldn't eat enough—I just ate much food. It took time before I felt full. When I joined the regiment everyone was so friendly, so helpful—they loved each other. Even though I came to the regiment for only the last year and a half, I cherish the friendships I made for all of my life.

On July 24, 1944, when I was on a combat mission, I received a heavy wound in my belly from a fascist shell. We were assigned to bomb a certain target, and the weather was bad, with low clouds. When we made our first try we did not manage to bomb the target, because it was completely covered with clouds. We went back to our airfield and then returned and made a second pass over the target. The enemy artillery was ready for us: they fired at us so much that many planes were set on fire, but there were no planes shot down. My plane was not set on fire, but I was shot and severely wounded. I realized I was wounded, but I didn't feel extreme pain. I told my navigator, who was also named Yelena, that I was wounded and asked what I should do. The navigator said: "We must go on because there is no place to land. We will all crash if we don't go on to a field where we can land!"

We lagged behind our unit, because it was difficult for me to continue flying the aircraft. Fortunately we found the airfield of a fighter regiment, and I managed to land. But very many times while in the air I fainted, and my navigator gave me liquid ammonia to inhale so I would regain consciousness. When I finally landed the plane, I lost consciousness completely. I was carried to the military field hospital but didn't know anything until I awakened surrounded by three thousand wounded. They operated on me, and it turned out to be very serious, as are all wounds in the belly. The girls from the regiment visited me there when they could. I had eleven holes in my rectum. I was transferred to the Moscow Military Hospital, where I stayed for two months, and then returned to my regiment.

I returned and flew combat, even though I was not considered fit to fly. I couldn't stand not to fly, so I finished the war with my comrades-in-arms. I also participated in the victory parade in Red Square. I stayed in the army until 1949.

After the war I also flew the Tu-2. I was a lieutenant. We have three lieutenant ranks: junior lieutenant, lieutenant, and senior lieutenant. When the war ended and our regiment was released, I joined a male regiment. While I was in the regiment I married a pilot, got pregnant, and retired in 1949.

Sergeant Nataliya Alfyorova,
mechanic of armament

I was born in 1921 in the town of Penza, 600 kilometers from Moscow toward the Volga River. My father was a teacher in a higher school, always beyond secondary school. My family moved to Moscow when I was a child. I entered teachers' college there, and I also started in a parachute school. But the year before the war, the government stopped women from engaging in any kind of military sport that could endanger their lives, so I wasn't allowed to finish.

When the war started I heard about the women's air regiments, and my girlfriend and I went where they were interviewing for the three hundred positions in the regiments. There were thousands of girls in line waiting to apply. I was accepted into the 125th Guards Bomber Regiment as a mechanic of armament. We trained from nine in the morning to three in the afternoon and then from six to nine in the evening. When we finished our training, we trained the next group of mechanics.

At the front, one of our difficult jobs was cleaning the machine guns. The guns became very dirty inside, choked with smoke and burned particles. We had to lift them; they weighed sixteen kilograms and were two meters long. We were all so small and thin—what was Raskova thinking about when she chose small girls for such jobs? In the winter, especially, we had to carry the machine guns through the snowdrifts on our shoulders to the dugout to clean them, because it was too cold to properly clean them outside. Everything to do with ammunition was bulky and heavy.

We were given only forty-five minutes to rearm the aircraft after a mission and often worked almost beyond our physical capacity. Soon we devised methods for rearming that were not in our manuals but were necessary in order for us to finish on time. When we loaded the bombs we usually had six girls to carry and attach them to the aircraft.

My first aircrew perished on a mission. I had a very emotional feeling about their deaths. I wondered if I had in some way failed them; perhaps I had not charged the machine guns properly or erred in some duty I was to perform. I lived with that uneasy feeling until the tail-gunner, who had survived, wrote to me from the hospital. He told me that the pilot and navigator had been killed by one shell and that the aircraft and guns were operating properly. It was chance, not something I had done improperly, that had caused their deaths.

Lieutenant Galina Brok-Beltsova,
navigator

Galina Brok-Beltsova, 125th regiment

I was born in 1925 in Moscow, and I finished secondary school there. I was very sports-minded. When the war broke out the government sent out an appeal to the strong, mighty people to join aviation. The boys and girls were tested in a centrifuge and drafted into aviation. We were then trained to be gunners or navigators. Without any boasting I can say we were all mighty, healthy, robust, and patriotic young people. I trained in 1941 and 1942 in a military school. Then I was drafted into the Emergency Aviation Regiment, became a navigator in the Pe-2 dive bomber, and was sent to the front as a replacement. My pilot was Antonina Bondareva-Spitsina. I flew thirty-six missions during the war.

When I was sent to the 125th regiment, I was struck by the skill and competency of the personnel and inspired by being there with a group of young girls whose uniforms were covered with medals and orders. The pilots and navigators were so confident and well-trained, and it was all because of Marina Raskova: she was their ideal, their hero. We all need an ideal, an example to follow. It makes you develop your own energy. The "old ladies," or "aged," as we called the crews that had been with the regiment since the beginning (even though they were only twenty-three or so), taught us not to be afraid but to face the reality and the hardships with courage and to overcome. We learned not to lose our composure but to have the stamina and agility to survive.

On one mission we took off and were flying toward the target, and one of our engines quit. We began lagging behind the formation. A dive bomber never flies to a target alone: it always flies with a squadron, and that squadron is protected by fighter aircraft. If your plane is falling behind the squadron, you are to return to your airdrome. Otherwise the enemy fighters will shoot you down. And now we were alone without fighter cover. The bombs were affixed to the aircraft, and we had no emergency area to drop the bombs, which meant we might be dropping them on our own troops. But we couldn't land with the bombs, either.

We knew they would explode when we landed, because these were not Soviet bombs but captured German bombs. The peculiarity of the German bombs was that they had no mechanism on them to prevent them from exploding if you landed with them still attached to the aircraft, as ours did. So there was no way out but to continue on to the target.

The German antiaircraft guns filled the air around the squadron, which was by then way ahead of us, but our lone aircraft didn't attract their attention at all. We dropped the bombs and turned to fly home. Then we were attacked by two German fighters coming in from different directions. We all did our best with our machine guns, but it was quite useless; the tracer bullets we were firing did not even reach the fascist aircraft. They attacked us from positions from which we couldn't return fire. This was a section between the tail and the wings that could not be covered.

We could see their faces: they were smiling at us and made another circle with their guns firing and terrible smiles on their faces. Antonina thrust the plane abruptly to the right and to the left, weaving and jumping in the air. All of a sudden we heard nothing. Then we saw that the Soviet fighters had come back to help us after they finished escorting the formation back to our airfield. And so the German fighters vanished. No one believed that we would ever return from that mission.

Another time, in east Prussia, they decided that we could carry more bombs if we carried less fuel. As it turned out, we were completely overloaded. A Pe-2 from a male regiment took off just before us, crashed into a hangar, and exploded, not being able to clear the hangar. We were next in line to take off. You have to forbid yourself from thinking that your plane will end up the same way. You concentrate on a successful mission. On takeoff, our pilot held the aircraft on the ground until it had adequate speed, and when it lifted off, it was apparent that we were extremely overloaded. We felt it dragging us back to earth. But we made it; our aircraft cleared the hangar, and we did have a successful mission. It was a victory—not over the German troops but over ourselves. You fight your own cowardliness.

While I was awaiting assignment to the front I had met a male pilot, and we became engaged. After I went to the regiment at the front I received a letter from him every single day. The whole of my squadron read them, because very few of the other girls received letters. They used to say to me, "Galina, it's true love." Later I married him, and the whole squadron was present at our wedding. He came to our regiment to marry me, and it was the happiest episode of my life.

Once we had to land with the bombs still attached to our plane. While we were being fired upon by antiaircraft guns as we approached the target, our plane and another in our squadron collided in the air. Our aircraft became partially uncontrollable. Our pilot made a decision to return to the emergency airfield, a fighter base, to land. As we maneuvered to approach for a landing all the fighters were turning away, because everyone knew we were carrying unexploded bombs. The airfield was very small, and we couldn't brake because it could cause the plane to go on its nose. We landed, and we continued to roll and roll and ran out of smooth runway. There were trenches there, and we nosed into a trench, but it was in sand. The bombs stuck into the sand, and that stopped them from exploding.

There were cases during the war when some Soviet planes did drop bombs on our troops when they had to turn back. That was a very good lesson: for the rest of my life, I swore that if I took up something and was determined to do it, I must do it until the very end. This part of my character led me for all of my life up to the present moment. Only when I fulfill the mission do I feel content.

Now I am a history lecturer in twentieth-century history. And I specialize in the Second World War—The Great Patriotic War. I have a doctor's degree, and I am the head of the History Department at the Moscow Engineering Institute. I am interested in all the changes that have gone on and are going on in the world; I am not old-fashioned. I want to be up-to-date and in a new wave, so to speak. As Saint-Exupéry said, nothing can be valued as highly as man-to-man relationships and understanding.

Major Marta Meriuts,
chief of regimental intercommunications

When I was young I worked in a drugstore, and my dream was to become a pharmacist. Then, in 1929, there was a call from the party and the government for twenty women to be admitted to military colleges to test a woman's ability to survive as cadets. At the time I was told about this opportunity I didn't know what I would do in a military college. At first I thought no, but then I applied and was admitted to the College of Communications—military engineering communications. I had never even seen a soldier at that time and had no idea what I was getting into!

So I became a military cadet. We had to wear a man's uniform: very large, with heavy boots, pants, and jackets. I had long braids down to my knees, and I received an order to cut my braids because we had to look like the male cadets. We girls went to the hairdresser, and he said that he couldn't cut off such gorgeous braids; his hands wouldn't perform such a sacrilege. He gave us scissors and told us to cut off our braids ourselves; only then he would he give us a man's haircut. We had to wear men's underwear and use the same bathing facilities as the men, but at separate times.

All these things were not for a girl's soul. I was eighteen then; we were young, and the male underwear was the worst. After some time they made female uniforms and special underwear for us, and life seemed better. But it was very difficult to study and be with the male cadets, for we were required to take thirty-kilometer marches with all ammunition. When we came to a certain location, we had to set up and establish communication at an exact time. The male cadets didn't even think of us as women. There were ten of us girls in that institute with about a thousand male cadets!

In 1933 I graduated and was sent to the field as a lieutenant. There I met my husband, who was also in the military, and we married and had two children. We were stationed together, assigned to different regiments but on the same base in the Kiev region, when the war began.

In 1941, when the war broke out, I was thirty-two years old and held the rank of senior lieutenant. By then I had been in the armed forces for some time. On the eve of the war I was serving on the staff of a Kiev army regiment. I had taken my eldest son to the Crimean coast—we have such camps for children to have a summer holiday—and had returned to Kiev. I was on duty when the war began.

On August 1, 1941, I was given an order from the commander of the
southwestern airforce group to communicate with an aircraft flying
over us. We were to tell the pilot, carrying an army commander, to
land at our base. I went to the airfield communications and asked the
signal engineer to connect me with that plane. The engineer told me
the radio system was not operational, and the only possibility of
communicating with that aircraft was for me to get into a plane, take
off, fly to the proper altitude, and contact the plane air-to-air. So I got
into an aircraft, and the pilot prepared for takeoff. At that moment
the German dive bombers bombed the airfield and hit our plane. I
was seriously wounded in the head. At that time I was communications officer of the regiment. Our aircraft was among many more
destroyed in that raid, and a lot of people were killed on the airfield.

After I was wounded I was in hospital for three months. When I
recovered I was assigned to Raskova's regiments and became chief of
intercommunications for the three regiments. Later I went in that
capacity with the 587th Bomber Regiment. I was not allowed to fly
after the head wound, and I had lost the sight of my right eye completely. I told this to Raskova, because when we went into combat I
was supposed to fly with the regimental commander. Raskova said
not to worry, one of my deputies could fly with her. I had to leave my
two sons, one five years old and the other three. The children were
given to the orphanage when both my husband and I were drafted to
the front.

In our regiment there were some men in maintenance. There were
very young girls who wanted to be liked by them, and they made
friends and made love. There was one girl who had been a hairdresser
before the war. Once they asked her to curl a girl's hair, and she put a
metal rod into the oven and heated it. Its real purpose was to clean the
guns, and she used it to curl her hair. The temperature was very high,
and it burned her hair; she had wanted so to look nice!

The girls in my ground communications unit worked well in a
very difficult job. We had to reorient for new targets whenever we
moved. We would be told, for example, that spot one should be
bombed, or spot two, and so forth. Later into the flight, we would be
told by the ground forces to tell our aircraft that a different target
must be bombed, because the troops would have advanced.

Not many women in the regiment had children, and they knew I
had to leave my children in the orphanage. When I thought of them, I
sobbed bitterly. Once the army commander came to our regiment and
learned that my children were in the orphanage, and he let me fly to

the orphanage for one hour. Everyone in the regiment gave me small presents for the children, and I went to visit them with a rucksack full of chocolate bars, sweets, and biscuits.

All of us in the regiment were friends and liked each other, and we helped in any way possible. We all had such strong beliefs that our first and foremost task was to liberate the country. And none of us ever fell ill during our work period. Mentally we were overstrained, but physically nobody gave in. Our regiment was highly valued by the commanding staff of the army of the front, and we were awarded, on the banner of our regiment, two military orders. The first was Kutuzov, named for the commander of the army in the First Patriotic War in 1812, a national hero. The second was Suvorov, also a great Russian commander, who climbed over the Alps with the army.

Once, after the war, there was a reception in the Kremlin, and the military commanders of all fronts and armies were present. The girls from the regiment were invited to that reunion. The commander of the front, under whom we fought during the war, asked why we had been asked to this reception and who we were. We had to explain that we were the pilots and the mechanics of the 125th regiment. He had thought it to be a male regiment, and it was a surprise to him to learn about us after the war. Even now very few men can believe that women crews could fly the dive bomber.

I finished the war in the rank of major, and I retired from the military in 1956 as a lieutenant-colonel.

Senior Lieutenant Galina Chapligina-Nikitina, liaison pilot, flight commander

I was in sixth grade when an amphibious plane landed in the lake and then took off from the land. That was when the idea of flying came to my heart. I was among the best Pioneers; that is what we called this group who were like American Scouts. Three of us were allowed to go up in the plane. I remember the pilot, but I don't know what happened to him, because at that time our people disappeared in a very strange manner.

I was born in Leningrad in 1920, and when I was eight months old I lost my parents. I spent my childhood in boardinghouses. Finally I found myself in my mother's sister's family, and I called her mother. When I was finishing high school some pilots came to our school and asked, "Who wants to fly?" Many children raised their hands, of which three were girls, and I was one of them. I was about eighteen, and after school I went to the aviation club to study theory of flight. I

had six lessons at school and four or five hours at the club, and I didn't
have the time to study at both places. I went to a girlfriend, told her of
my difficult situation, and asked her advice. My girlfriend told me
that in Bataisk city there was a flying school with a female squadron,
and I decided to enroll.

Before graduation from high school we filled out the application
for flying school. We had to pass a medical check; then our biogra-
phies were checked to see if any of our relatives were in labor camps
or other places for criminals. Last, we were tested in mathematics
and history. Only five girls from the Leningrad area were admitted,
and only two of us graduated from flying school. It was a civil aviation school until 1939, when it was turned into a military flying
school. At that time the squadrons of male students remained at the
school, and our squadron of female students was transferred to Tambov, where I graduated.

When pilots graduated from the civil flying school they were then
given a job in civil aviation. Three of us were sent to Alma-Ata city in
central Asia, bordering on China. We were happy because this is an
area where the great apples grow, and *Alma-Ata*, in the Kazakh language, means "big apple." We spent three days there and then were
told there were no vacancies. We were instructed to go to Semi-
palatinsk, a city that is now a nuclear site, also in central Asia. We
were twenty years old at this time. What we found was an airdrome
and a two-story building. At night the wolves were howling, and we
were frightened. It was in a desert. There was a small railroad station,
and two trains came there: one in the morning for people to go to
work in a factory, and one in the evening for them to go home. All day
we spent our time at the airport. I arrived there in the fall. There were
lots of handsome pilots, and I made friends with many of them. They
liked me and said the airport was not a proper place to live in a room
with two other girls. They said they would find me a room out in the
city. The pilots and the others who studied there would play soccer,
and I was the goalkeeper.

I would fly to the Chinese border delivering mail. We flew the U-2,
an open-cockpit plane, and we tried to cover our faces as much as
possible. Only our eyes were showing.

In the early part of 1941 I was transferred to Novosibirsk city. The
government issued a decree that our country must have 150,000 pilots! By this time the Second World War had started, and Poland,
Czechoslovakia, and France were all occupied by German troops. The
government understood that our flying schools could not train enough

military pilots, so they sent squadrons to different cities to organize flying clubs for basic training. Later the graduates of these flying clubs were sent on to the military schools to be trained in more sophisticated military aircraft. I trained pilots as a part of this program from 1941 to the beginning of 1942.

In April, 1942, a telegram from Marina Raskova came, ordering that I immediately be sent to Engels to join the women's regiments in training. I had to learn the manuals and military routine, and I remember that our days were very busy. When I arrived, I had 570 flying hours. I was called to Raskova's office, where she told me she wanted me to be her liaison pilot. She had three regiments training under her command, and she needed someone to fly to the various airdromes to fulfill missions for her. My title was chief pilot—like an adjutant would be in a ground army. It was a great honor for me. Then Raskova told me that she would train me to fly the Ut-2, because it was the only such aircraft in the regiments. It was a new plane, and it was for her use. It cruised at 220 kilometers per hour, had two open cockpits, a fixed landing gear, and no armament. It was a very good aerobatic aircraft. I may have been the only woman who flew the Ut-2, because I have never met or heard of another who flew it. When I landed on some field or military airdrome and they saw that I was a woman pilot, they were surprised, because this aircraft looked like a small fighter.

The daughter of Marina Raskova studied at the ballet school in the Bolshoi Theater, and I was sent to evacuate her from Moscow. Raskova sent a letter along with me asking her daughter to please give Galina some milk. She knew that I had in the past flown a number of high-ranking officers, and they had eaten in the plane and offered me nothing. She trusted me and my flying to put her daughter in my hands.

At the front we were stationed near Stalingrad, and we were bombing the German positions there. The living conditions were grave at that time. We were living in the trenches with no water to drink except when we melted snow, and when we had meals in the canteen, which was an old wooden building, we saw the water dripping from the ceiling onto the tables. We joked that we were eating, and the soup was still in our bowls!

After Stalingrad we were sent to central Russia and then to the Kuban area in the northern Caucasus. Once I flew to the airdrome with the airforce commander to initialize the liaison between the many airforce regiments, because there was no ground communication between the regimental airdromes. When I was about to land a German plane passed me, and I could plainly see the black crosses on the wings and the yellow around the crosses. I also saw the pilot, who looked gaunt, and I noticed that he had white hair. I decided not to land, and I pulled up and flew to a nearby small village and began circling the church at an altitude just above the tops of the trees to evade the German aircraft. My plane was defenseless, and it was also difficult to fly because it was extremely sensitive on the controls. The German was following me, and a burst of machine-gun fire hit the surfaces of the plane, but he didn't set it on fire. I even bit my lips until blood came trying to level the aircraft. Then he flew away, and I landed at the airdrome. When I landed a handsome and tall man came to me and asked if I was alive. He asked me in the manner you would ask a man, using a man's vocabulary. I said yes, I was alive, so he knew then that I was a woman. He said, "Oh, all of us were thinking that the German pilot would kill you!"

Because I flew over Soviet territory and there was little threat from ground fire, I flew at as low an altitude as possible; otherwise, I would have been strafed and shot down by German aircraft. Part of my duty was to pick up the remains of our crashed pilots in parachute sacks. Most of the bodies I carried were in pieces. One of our pilots had very beautiful hands; everyone noticed her hands and commented on them. When they loaded her remains into my plane a hand was sticking out of the bag, and I recognized it as her hand.

When I was away on such a duty I was walking along by our front line, and I heard some strange, intermittent, soft whistling sounds. I didn't recognize the sound immediately and turned my attention to listening—then I realized those were bullets! Bullets singing. They were shooting at me.

My flying duties required that I land wherever I was to pick up or deliver someone or something, and I landed on roads or small fields— the nearest place. Once I was told to pick up one of our wounded pilots, Irina Osadze. Irina's aircraft had been hit by an anti-aircraft shell, the shell hit the Plexiglas of the bomber, and pieces of the glass were sticking out of her face and neck. When we arrived at the field hospital the nurse wanted to pull out the pieces, but Irina did it herself. She didn't fear pain.

Another time I flew to another of our pilots, Yelena Kulkova-Malutina, when she was wounded in her belly, and her bowels were perforated in twelve places. I flew to the field hospital with our regimental doctor so he could find out where she had been transferred and to check on her wounds. On our way back I couldn't land on our airdrome because of a heavy fog, and I decided to land elsewhere until the fog cleared. When I climbed up out of the fog a Soviet fighter was right there. He pulled alongside, showed me his navigational chart, and indicated that he did not know where he was. I then showed him where the airdrome was. When he landed he asked who was the pilot of this number twenty-eight aircraft, and he was told Galina. He said that he must find her and kiss her, and when they asked him why, he told them that I had saved his life!

When I was told to fly somewhere I was only given a general idea of where it was; I was to fly there and then find a certain place. I would draw my route on a map and fly there, but it seemed to me that God saved me many times.

Pilots want to play games with the aircraft—to violate the law. Katrina Musatova and I decided to fly to another airdrome where Katrina had a boyfriend, so we carried some turnips and other vegetables, flew over the barracks, and threw the vegetables, bombing them *boom, boom, boom* on the roof. I was a pilot, and now here I was being a navigator-bombardier! We made another pass, and there they were, out there eating the vegetables as we flew over.

In October, 1944, I was invited to join the Airforce Liaison Squadron. In the 125th regiment I was the lone liaison pilot, but in the airforce army there was a whole squadron. I was promised that I would be appointed flight commander in that squadron, but when I arrived, there were ten to fifteen aircraft and the same number of male pilots. Some of them were full of indignation, saying, "Why? Aren't there any good pilots in our squadron so that you decided to appoint this small girl?" I told the commander that I would like to be appointed to the position right now, but first let these male pilots see what kind of a pilot I am. The commander often tested me and sent me with other crews on a mission.

Once I flew with another aircraft and my plane was faster, so I lost him in the bad weather, a mist. You can see the terrain only vertically, but in front of you, you can't see anything. I had to maneuver and make some turns, but finally I came to my destination, and the other pilots were happy to see that I was still alive. They kissed me and hugged me with tears in their eyes.

Then, after all, I was appointed flight commander, and all my subordinates respected me greatly. Finally, I selected the best, the handsomest of the pilots in the squadron, and I married him. Unfortunately, two years ago on Victory Day, May 9, he died. He was only sixty-seven, and he should have lived longer. He had been flying for forty years: twenty-five in military aviation and fifteen in civil aviation. I have two daughters; both of them graduated from institutes, and they have their own families. After my husband's death I moved to my junior daughter's apartment, and we live together.

Sergeant Yekaterina Chujkova,
mechanic of armament

When we are awarded orders or medals in our army, we have a tradition: to drop our orders and medals into a crystal glass filled with vodka and to drink that glass of vodka to the bottom. In the wartime we had to use empty food cans instead of the crystal.

I was born in 1925. When the war broke out I lived in Leningrad and was finishing secondary school. The pupils from senior classes were sent to dig trenches at one of our airfields. When winter came and we were not allowed to dig trenches anymore, we were sent to escort citizens of Leningrad to shelters when the bombing started. We had a special pass that allowed us to escort people in the daytime as well as at night. We also accompanied the militia in searching out traitors who climbed onto the roofs of our plants and factories and indicated with flares where the factories were located so the German aircraft could bomb them.

When the siege of Leningrad began, the ration of bread was 125 grams (about 4.5 ounces) a day. We were starving, and we were physically weak. It was difficult to move. We students were assembled and given a portion of mash made of soup without any fat, any meat, anything. Just boiled water and a piece of brown bread. All of the students were gathered in one place to be given some food in order for us to survive this siege. And that was the way it was in 1942. My sister worked at a plant, and when her plant was evacuated to Moscow, she took me with her.

I arrived in Moscow and reported to the Young Communist League with my documents to be stamped. One woman on that committee asked me if I wanted to go to the front, and I said yes. Marina Raskova's emissary had come to Moscow to select girls for the regiments. She saw me and asked why I wanted to join the regiment, because I was so thin and small that I could hardly move, suffering from the starvation in Leningrad. I told her that in Leningrad I had to survive the siege and that I would put on my weight when in the regiment. The army received much better nutrition than any civilian at that time. Maybe she felt sorry for me—I was accepted to join. At that time my mother and a sister and brother lived near Moscow in the German-occupied territory, my grandmother was still in Leningrad, and my father had perished at the front. One of my other sisters was evacuated to Siberia with the kindergarten where she worked.

When I joined the regiment, it was 1943. At this date the regiment badly needed reinforcement. I was taken right to the front and trained there for a month. I was taught how to arm the bomb with the detonator and to attach it onto the aircraft itself. I trembled when the instructor tested me, because I was still so weak and the bombs weighed so much—I was trembling like a mouse while he stood there watching me affix the bombs to the aircraft. We had all our training right on the airfield, and our model was a real plane.

At night we had to take our turn on guard duty: to take a gun and guard the aircraft. In the winter we had to dig the bombs out of the snow blown by snowstorms, and we found it was much easier to keep the bombs under the plane. Guarding the planes was not a very pleasant duty, for our eyesight was constantly strained. And we had to listen, too, very hard. The shift was two hours on, then two hours off to rest; then another two hours' guard duty. I was frightened to be out there at night, and when I heard a noise in the forest I would call out, "Stop, who's coming? Stop, who's there?" If no one answered I said, "I'm sorry, but I'm going to shoot; excuse me, I'm going to shoot!"

The aircraft were distributed on the sides of the runway at great distances from each other, and my guard post was near the forest. In the distance I saw a figure, then no figure, then a figure again, and I cried, "Stop, who's coming? I'll shoot!" I shot into the air; then I shot at the figure, and it fell down in the snow. It turned out to be a Russian guarding the perimeter who had forgotten the password. He lay in the snow until the information was passed on to the staff, and they came out and found he was one of our soldiers. He was frozen but unhurt!

I was a very good singer, and I was keen on singing. I was in the chorus, and when I was affixing the bombs to the aircraft I would sing out loud, and everybody could hear me. Once, when I was preparing the last plane before the night, I knew it was the last assignment for that day. I was polishing the guns and affixing the bombs, and I took off my boots because it was easier to climb up on the wing without them. The technician of armament came up and said that I was again doing my duties bare-legged. I replied that my boots were so loose it was hard to work in them. According to the army rules I should have been punished for being out of uniform, but I was not because there was no one to replace me. We didn't wear socks, only foot cloths—big, bandagelike cloths. We had to resew our uniforms; they were men's uniforms and didn't fit. In the winter we were cold, and we used a modified oil drum for heat in our dugout. We would go to the forest with an axe and chop wood for ourselves. We did everything for ourselves—washed linens, sewed our clothes, dug our dugouts, chopped our wood—everything.

Near the town of Smolensk they put another engine in the aircraft and had to use a special wood ladder to climb up. We decided to steal the ladder for firewood for our stove. It was very, very cold, and we were afraid of the forest at night, so we chopped up the ladder and carried the small pieces into our dugouts. The next morning we lined up, and the commander of the squadron said that someone had stolen the ladder. She asked who had stolen it and said that the ones who had stolen the ladder should take two steps forward. She repeated that, and the third time, all of the girls in the first squadron took two steps forward! There was a new girl who had just joined the regiment, and she also took two steps forward. The commander asked why she was doing that, and the girl said that she would do what everybody else did. A few days later the same commander came into our dugout and saw that it was very warm, and she said, "Good for you, you found a way to keep warm!" This was the commander of the squadron, Nadezhda Fedutenko, Hero of the Soviet Union.

For our breakfast we had a dry piece of bread. We worked so hard and slept so little and had so little proper food that when I was working the streams of tears ran down my face. The streams ran down while I was cleaning different small devices in the petrol and affixing the bombs to the aircraft at dawn. I never said to myself, What have I come here for? I only thought how difficult it was.

We always saw the planes off on their missions, and we stood on the airfield and watched them return. If the squadron came back in tight formation we were happy. But if they came back one at a time—one aircraft landed, and then another, and another, and another—it meant that they had been attacked by the German fighters. We recognized our own aircraft according to the sound of the engines. We immediately knew that it was our pilot and plane. In the evening, when we exchanged information about each of our planes, we would describe them as we would a close relative. One would say, "My aircraft was the fourth one to return," and another would say, "Mine was ninth to land." We experienced it very intimately. It was the leading topic of our conversation.

Each of our planes had five machine guns. When they got back, if all the bullets had been fired, we had to reload each gun, and it held 270 bullets. It was impossible to carry the box with the bullets into the aircraft, and it was very difficult to load the guns, especially in the pilot's cabin. The cockpit was very small, and the machine gun was directly in front of the pilot, where all the instruments were located. I had to crawl on my knees.

All the girls in our squadron lived in our dugout. In other squadrons they did it differently. And in some places we lived differently: sometimes in houses, sometimes in smaller dugouts.

I was arrested during the war and sent to the guardhouse, and there was hardly a person who was not arrested at some time. Mostly we were arrested for exchanging things with the local peasants. We would exchange our men's underwear for potatoes, pies, milk, and so on. We exchanged what we didn't wear. Once I went to the nearest village with a girlfriend to make an exchange, and on our way we met a commissar from our regiment. She realized what we were doing, and we were arrested for three days and put in the guardhouse. It was no worse than the dugout, and it was warm there, with something to eat and a heap of straw. The other girls would bring us a book and push it through the window. There was a soldier guarding you when you were in the guardhouse; for example, my bosom friend Sasha was standing guard on me with a gun. There wasn't any special detachment to guard us; our girls did it.

Our friendship has been preserved until the present day. Youth is youth. We made pillows out of our foot cloths and embroidered the Pe-2 on them. Everybody embroidered the Pe-2 on their pillows. When it came time for our last farewell at the end of the war, we could not imagine how we could go on living without each other. We made a good family.

Lieutenant Ludmila Popova,
navigator

I was born and raised in Moscow, and my father was a military man up to the 1930s. Then, in October, 1941, he was called back into the military and was killed at the front. I was seventeen. From the moment I found out he had been killed, I was determined to go into the military and avenge his death. When I was old enough to join the army, I was sent to an aviation school and became a navigator. Later, in 1943, I joined the regiment to take the place of those who had perished.

Galina (or Galya) Tenuyeva-Lomanova was my pilot, and she was wounded in combat. Our mission was to bomb a very well-protected target, and we were hit by heavy antiaircraft fire; the aircraft was riddled by bullets. There were holes in the engine and in the nose of the aircraft, and the engine was steaming. Lomanova was wounded in her arm. Then there was a great explosion in the nose of the plane—a shell exploded there. At first there was so much smoke in our cabin I could hardly see, but I felt the aircraft descending. When the smoke dispersed I saw Galya lying unconscious against the control stick. We had already lost 2,000 meters in altitude, and I took her by the shoulders and held her back from the stick. Then she regained consciousness, took the controls, and began flying the plane again. She decided we could make it back for a landing at our own airfield.

When the shell exploded, the glass in the canopy of our compartment was blown out. The wind blew away everything, and the map that I had in my hand flew away also, so I had nothing with which to navigate. Before combat missions, our commander always warned us that we must know the location of places and the terrain of the flying area by heart in order to find our way without the map. We didn't realize what the purpose was for that, and we would talk about those grumbling commanders who always tried to find some fault with us. And then, when I found myself in that situation, I realized how important it really was. I had to bring us back to our airdrome by memory. We managed to stay airborne all the way back to our own regimental airfield. Galya asked me to help her land the aircraft, because she felt she was not capable of doing it alone with only one arm. I helped her with the controls as best I could. When we landed she was sent to the hospital, and I was assigned to another pilot.

My new pilot was Irina Asadze, and she was the pilot I finished the war with. She retired at the end of the war, and in 1946 I also retired from the air force.

When we were in eastern Prussia our gunner was severely wounded in the head. We couldn't help him, because he was in a separate compartment farther back from us. The only thing he managed to say on the intercom was that he was wounded; these were his last words. We had already dropped all our bombs, so we detached from our formation and at maximum speed returned to the nearest airfield. When we were approaching the field we shot two rockets in the air to indicate there was a wounded person on the aircraft. When we landed we saw that he had lost much blood. He couldn't bandage himself because he had lost consciousness. He was taken to the hospital and operated on, and he lost part of his eyesight. We went with him and waited there until after his operation. I was never wounded—God saved me! I flew forty combat missions in the war.

Life is life. Certainly war is a difficult job to do, but it was not confined to gravity. We found time to have fun, to dance and sing, on those nights when we hadn't had any losses. We were young and romantic and had a lot of dreams; thoughts for the future. We came from different parts of our country. There were other Muscovites, and we would get together and imagine the day when we would go home and stroll along the streets. Everyone would look at us and admire us, the streets would be lit, and all would be sunny and shiny with war far behind us. War is not a normal thing for any country, for any state, for any man, and especially for a woman. And war is not the form for settling differences between countries.

Lieutenant Yekaterina Musatova-Fedotova,
pilot, commander of the formation

I started flying in a glider school when I was sixteen, and in 1941 I began working as a pilot-instructor. From the beginning of the war I wrote letters asking to be sent to the front as a volunteer. When at last they let Raskova form the regiments, she sent us all a letter asking how many flying hours we had. Because we all wanted to help our country and go to the front, we added hours to our totals. If we had 100 hours we wrote that we had 700 or 800 hours and were very experienced pilots. The chief of our training school went on holiday, and we took advantage of that and escaped to Engels, because he wouldn't release us from our instructing jobs. Four of us from our school arrived at the women's flight training base at Engels. The regiments had already been trained by that time. Very quickly they also trained us, and we became part of the 587th Bomber Regiment, as it was called at that time. I was nineteen years old.

The Pe-2, the aircraft flown by the 587th regiment, was a fine airplane, probably the best in either the German or Soviet air force. But it was complex and difficult for women to fly, especially small women who were slim and hungry. The control stick was heavy to move, and our arms and legs were so short we had three folded pillows behind our backs. The navigators helped us by pushing on our backs as we pushed on the stick to get the tail up for takeoff.

I was a born pilot. In my flight formation there were three aircraft, and I piloted the lead plane. The experienced pilots carried 1,200 kilos of bombs, and the inexperienced carried 600 kilos. When we were

Klara Dubkova, 125th regiment

assigned a combat mission that was urgent and important, the ground staff carried the regimental banners onto the airfield, and we took off with the accompaniment and rustle of the banners.

Once, when we were preparing for such a mission, I had climbed up only fifty meters on takeoff, and one of the engines quit. We were loaded with 1,200 kilos of bombs; it was a failure of everything. I couldn't turn back to the airfield, because all of the regiment were still taking off. On the right side was a forest, in front was a small village, and beetroot was planted horizontal to our heading. I had but a fraction of a second to decide what to do, so I chose the only course: to belly-land in the beetroot field. So down we went into the field. The aircraft came to a stop, and we were all alive and all right. At that moment the ambulance, fire truck, and people came running. I felt absolutely empty, drained; all I could think was, This is the way pilots crash their aircraft. At this moment Tonya (Antonina Khokhlova), our tail-gunner, got out of the plane, sat on the tail, took a mirror out of her pocket, and began powdering her face. She said to me, "Yekaterina, you dusted my face!" The earth was dry and dusty, and our landing stirred up the dust. Klara Dubkova, my navigator, turned to Tonya and said, "We could have exploded when we landed, and now you are making merry!" Tonya replied that with our commander as pilot that would never have happened. With humor she said to me, "You could have landed at the village where they would feed us with fried potatoes, and now we are hungry!"

Many things go together in this life—ridiculous, funny episodes. Once, because I was on an emergency airfield, I was called to join up with the squadron in the air. I took off and felt the plane dragging to the right, so I gave more power to that engine, climbed up, and joined the formation. Then I saw the rear gunner in the plane ahead of me putting his whole leg out of his window! He was giving me a signal that something was wrong with our plane. I didn't know what was wrong, I only felt it. And because there was no transmission between aircraft, he was trying to show me with gestures and signs. When he put his leg out, I understood that one landing gear had not retracted. When we returned to our airfield after completing the mission, all the other planes were given permission to land except ours. We circled the field, and then we were given the order to parachute out of the plane. I didn't understand why we were to do that, and I decided to land the aircraft on the one gear. I managed to land on the left gear, and then, very slowly, I moved off the runway to clear it for other aircraft. At this time there were cameramen at our field shooting a film about our female regiment, which was to be called *The Wings of the Motherland*. When we landed safely, a lot of people rushed toward the plane, and among them were those cameramen. When I got out of the cockpit, a cameraman came up to me and asked why I spoiled such a good shot, because our plane didn't turn over or crash. He expected us to turn over and to show in the film how we crashed, and now we emerged safely from the cockpit!

Another time we took off on a combat mission and formed up with Markov in the lead, and I felt that one of my engines was slowing down. Markov perceived the situation and slowed down the whole formation. He helped us to stay with the formation throughout the mission and made sure we could keep up. If we dropped back, our fighter escort would go with the formation, and we could be shot down easily by the German fighters. So it was because Markov always tried to take care and see that we were protected that we made it back.

We had to land on a fighter airfield because of the bad engine instead of continue on to our own field. When we made the return flight to our airdrome, I decided to show off to display my skill and ability. On our airfield there was a group of male fighter pilots. They were constantly watching us landing and taking off, so I decided to be the star of the day. I was coming in for a landing and I bounced, so I added power and went around. I thought, Now I will show them how I can land, and I did the same again—I bounced! On the third try I thought, Now I must show them, and I made a very bad landing. I had never done that before; I was so very embarrassed.

I got out of our plane and went to report that we had returned to base, and Markov said, "Girls, have you had a good sleep this night?" I said yes, even though we hadn't, because we had to change some instruments in the plane and then fly back. He answered that we hadn't slept that night, or I could have landed the aircraft as I usually did. He didn't consider us to be ready to fly that day, and he said we could not go on the mission that morning. The three of us stood in front of him and begged to go, and he said no. We sobbed, and he put his fist on his desk and said, "No, I order you to bed to sleep, now go!"

We were shot down again when bullets hit our fuel tank. Our fighters got in a fight with the fascist fighters, and we were left without any escort. There were nine bombers left without escort, and all but one of us was shot down by German fighters. We all made forced landings, and we all survived.

Sergeant Mariya Kaloshina,
mechanic of armament

I was born in 1922, and I came to Raskova's regiment a little later in the war. It was in 1943, because I was only finishing a secondary school in the tenth form when the war started. While finishing school I had a dream to enter the Airforce Academy, but at the beginning of the war it was evacuated to central Asia, so I entered an aviation technical college.

In 1943 I was assigned to the 125th Guards Bomber Regiment and taken to the front. I was then twenty-one years old. I had taken the six-month training course for the regiment, which was easy for me because I had some technical knowledge. At the front I was appointed to be a mechanic for the commander of the formation, Alexandra Krivanova.

To affix the bombs to the aircraft, we stood on our knees and rolled them. When we got used to doing it, we rolled the bombs with our feet, our hands on our hips. There were different types of bombs: the small bombs made to destroy buildings were calledy *Fugaska*. There were other small bombs called *Zazhigalka*, and they were incendiary bombs. During the war, the Germans dropped *Zazhigalkas* on Moscow. I lived in Moscow when the war broke out, and we would stand on the roof of a building, pick up the bombs, and throw them into sand. Then they would stop burning. Children stayed on the roofs during the war to do that.

At Königsberg I had much work to do, because there were constant raids over the fascist territory; we didn't have a spare second. In the daytime we provided the aircraft with bombs, and at night we were on guard duty. We slept for about three hours.

I had to guard three aircraft at night; it was March, and the snow was melting. In March, in Russia, the snow is deep. It only starts melting under the snow, and there are floods of water. I was walking along and water fell into my boots, and it soaked through. My socks and my boots were full of water, and I guarded the aircraft for a long time in that condition. When I returned to our dugout I didn't even feel the pain in the skin and legs, I felt it in my bones—the very stem of my legs. We could never leave our post on guard duty.

Once when the regiment moved we landed on an airfield near Minsk. There was no one at the field when we arrived, and then German crews came out of the forest and saw the airfield occupied by Russian crews, almost all of them women. They were at a loss for words to be taken prisoner by Russian women. All of the habitable dwellings nearby were mined by the Germans, so we had to live under the wings of our aircraft on that airfield.

We were young girls and wanted to look womanlike. We were sick and tired of the men's boots, and once I decided to put on these slippers I knitted for myself. From other people's point of view, it was ridiculous when I appeared in my slippers in uniform!

All of us liked to knit. We liked handicraft work, especially embroidery, and found it to be the most amusing spare-time occupation, except for one girl in our regiment, Belova by name. We used to joke about her and say that if she only started embroidering, the war would soon be over. It happened that she took to embroidering, and the war was really over soon!

After the war I returned to my peaceful profession of radio engineer. I worked for Moscow Radio for twenty years. I was a sound producer, and later on I worked at restoring old records. In 1962 I was awarded the Order of Labor Red Banner, a very honorable award. One year ago (1990) I retired.

Senior Lieutenant Galina Tenuyeva-Lomanova,
pilot, commander of the formation

I was not even sixteen when I decided to join an aero club. It was usual to be a Komsomol member in order to join a glider club, but I was not. So I went to a Young Communist League committee asking to be admitted into the Komsomol, and then I joined the aero club. Later I became an instructor in the same club. The only time I ever jumped with a parachute was while instructing there. I was given no instruction, and I broke my leg when I landed!

When the war broke out I stayed on as a military flight instructor with the rank of sergeant. By this time I was already married and had given birth to a daughter. My husband was also a military pilot—a fighter pilot. Later we both went to the front; I to Raskova's regiment, and he to a male regiment. He perished at the front in 1943.

Our military school was evacuated to another area, and I took my mother, father, and daughter with me. It was such a mess in the early part of the war. Some military schools were released, some moved, and there seemed to be no logic in it. Then our school was unexpectedly released: the pilots transferred to the infantry, and the instructor-pilots went to a male air regiment.

I went to Saratov to pick up the orders for the male regiment at the headquarters of the Volga front, and there I met Raskova. She asked me why I was with a male regiment and said that I should join her regiment. We were real patriots, and we loved our country and our heroes. Raskova was well-known throughout our country and throughout the world. She was a national hero, an attractive and beautiful creature whom I admired in all respects, so I agreed to fly in her regiment.

At Engels I was trained to fly the Pe-2 dive bomber. Raskova, who was to command the dive bomber regiment, was by profession a navigator and had to be retrained as a pilot in order to lead us in combat. She was first trained on the SB-2, a twin-engine, three-place aircraft, and then trained herself in the Pe-2. She had few hours up to that time as a pilot; most of her hours in the air had been as a navigator. The Pe-2 was the most complicated aircraft of the war period and required more than a little skill to fly.

When our regiment was to fly on to the front, two of our aircraft had engines operating improperly. Mine was one of them. So while the rest of our second squadron flew to Stalingrad, we stayed where we were. At that time Raskova was in Moscow, and she knew that we were in Kirzhach while they were repairing our aircraft. So on her way from Moscow to the front, she flew to Kirzhach to join up with us and lead us to the Stalingrad front. But the weather conditions were very bad, so it was not a nonstop flight. We landed in the settlement of Lopatino, where we saw the New Year in. On January 4, 1943, we took off for the front. We flew in a formation of three aircraft with Raskova piloting the lead plane. Before we took off Raskova gave us an order that we could leave the formation only if an engine quit; we should fly as a formation.

We could have landed along the way as we flew across three airfields, but it was Raskova's order to fly directly to the Stalingrad front without landing except in emergency. The first airfield we flew over had a little snow on it, the second was already overcast, and the third was completely obscured—visibility zero. The flight was very long, the fuel was very short, and we were supposed to land in Razbojshina, but we couldn't because of the weather. I think Raskova might have thought we could land on the Engels airfield, which is located on the banks of the Volga River. One bank of the river is fifty meters higher than the other, and she was looking for a place to land and trying to recognize the landscape. We would go into clouds and out, and in and out of them, and when we saw she was maneuvering, we dropped back a little in our formation and lost Raskova's aircraft in the clouds.

Gubina Ljubov, the pilot in the third aircraft, and I had some training in night flights, and we could orient ourselves by instruments. My navigator and I decided to examine the terrain of the Volga River while in flight, but we could see nothing. So we broke out of formation, and I no longer knew where the other two aircraft were. By then the visibility was so bad that I could hardly see the wings of my own plane! We were descending, and my navigator said, "There is the earth!" As she said it, I pulled back on the stick, the aircraft bumped the ground, we crashed, and the plane was destroyed. All three of our planes crashed. All three crew members perished in Raskova's plane, and all of us survived in the other two planes.

When Raskova's plane crashed into the embankment her head hit against the gun sight, and it split her head in two. When her body was found—she was to be in an open casket—a doctor performed surgery on her and restored her head and face, using a picture. I also hit my head and face. My navigator flew by me in the cabin and struck the instrument panel, and her legs were hurt.

The other crew also saw a small black spot on the earth—it was a bush—so they pulled the nose of their aircraft up just in time to avert flying completely into the ground. Luckily we stopped on the edge of a deep slope. Although we all took off with clear skies, the weather conditions became worse and worse, but Raskova felt she must go on to her regiment. She did not use the good judgment to land while the weather conditions were good enough to do it. She was anxious about her regiment and wanted to get there. After the crash I was without an aircraft and had to return to Engels to await a new one. Major Valentin Markov became the commander of our regiment.

On my first combat mission in Markov's formation I stuck to him very closely. I was afraid to deviate from the course, because after the accident I felt a little fear and nervousness. On this first mission my plane was shelled by antiaircraft guns, and my gunner was mortally wounded. After the shelling ceased, I asked my navigator and tail gunner if they were all right. They both said yes, but I saw the blood spattered on the glass, and when we landed and they removed the gunner from the plane, he was dying.

Yet another time we were shot down when I was making my fifth combat flight. We bombed successfully and were already descending when suddenly we were machine gunned into the left side of the aircraft. It cut through all of our systems and damaged the fuel tank and one engine. The plane had a black tail of engine smoke behind it, and we made an emergency landing at a Russian fighter airdrome. I had the same navigator that was with me when we crashed with Raskova. When we made the emergency landing, we discovered that the landing gear was damaged. The tires burned down completely from braking, and the wheels were twisted. The commander of the fighter squadron based there greeted us in "pure Russian style"—using bad words—thinking it was a male crew. He didn't want us landing there when his fighter aircraft needed to come in to land. When we got out of the cockpit and he saw we were women, he was embarrassed and felt bad about how he greeted us.

Once, when a new engine was installed in my plane, I made several test flights, and I was letting down to land when suddenly I saw a German fighter under my wing. He didn't shoot me, or even try to, and I landed even though he could have shot me down, because on the test flight we were not prepared to defend ourselves. After we landed safely the German fighter strafed our airfield and flew away. But because he had observed the field, the German fascists returned that night and shot up the field and bombed it.

I was wounded once when we were on a combat mission in 1945 bombing the port of Libava. We were flying by the sea, so we had to think of what we would do if we were shot down over the water. We were over the Baltic Sea to bomb the seaport, which was strongly fortified by the Germans. The whole air division was sent to carry out that mission. Our squadron was the last of that gigantic group of Soviet aircraft over the target. The antiaircraft guns were firing at us; one of the shells damaged the left engine, and another shell wounded me in the right arm. I was bleeding and lost consciousness for a short time. Ludmila Popova, my navigator, gave me liquid ammonia to inhale and also bandaged me while I was unconscious; then, together, we held the aircraft controls. For 2,000 meters it descended uncontrolled. I regained control, but the regiment had flown on. We were left alone with a damaged aircraft, and I with a wounded arm. I decided to try to make it back to our home field. We made it, and the navigator signaled with a rocket that the pilot was wounded. When we landed, the right engine no longer ran either, and the aircraft was towed off the runway.

Life is life, and war is war; we were young girls, and we liked to make merry and sing. One of the girls in the regiment had a beautiful voice and often performed at amateur concerts. For such occasions we stitched for her a white silk dress made out of parachute fabric.

I flew up to 1947, when the regiment was released, and then I retired.

Sergeant Nataliya Smirnova,
tail-gunner

I was born in Moscow in 1924. I come from a family of office workers. When the war started our family was evacuated to the town of Gorky, on the Volga River. Our means were limited; I had to help my family, so I worked as a ground radio operator. In 1942 I become an aircraft radio operator. I began flying in civil aviation, but we were all longing to get to the front. I sent my documents to various army offices asking to be drafted to the army, but in vain. When the 125th Guards Bomber Regiment was suffering great losses they remembered my application, and I was sent to the regiment as a reinforcement. It took me only one day to pack my things.

I was a tail gunner and radio operator, and on one mission we were to bomb the port of Libava. In the tail-gunner position, we entered the plane from under the fuselage by way of a small hatch. My position was behind and completely separate from the pilot and navigator cabin. The top machine gun was fired through an opening directly above my head. I never sat but stood facing the tail of the aircraft, with my feet on the lower hatch and my head thrust out of the upper hatch. Libava was a seaport, and severe battles were waged there both on the ground and in the air.

Our navigator called my attention to the area above the port. It was black with smoke coming from the burst of anti-aircraft shells. Our plane was thrown back and forth by the concussion of the explosions; anti-aircraft shells seemed to be exploding beneath us and all around us. One of them exploded directly below my hatch, blowing open the lower hatch and throwing me completely out of the aircraft through the upper hatch. I found myself on top of the fuselage and felt a strong stream of air trying to blow me completely off, because we were flying at a very high speed. I tried to grasp the skin of the aircraft, but it was smooth and I couldn't hold onto it. But suddenly I felt something holding me to the plane. It turned out that my parachute harness had caught on a strap holding the machine gun in place. I still don't know exactly how I got back into the aircraft, but I managed to drag myself back inside. When I found myself again in the cockpit, I shut the lower hatch with my feet, but I couldn't feel them. They seemed boneless, and I had to sit down. I couldn't catch my breath, I couldn't make a sound, and my pilot was calling me on the radio. After a moment or two I pulled myself together and told her that everything was all right.

Another time we were returning from a mission to Pilau and were approaching the airfield when I saw a tail of white steam dragging behind our plane. First I thought it was fuel; then the white color turned into black. My pilot was Tamara Melashvili, and she was very strict. She was also very emotional and easily excited, so I didn't want to upset her until I knew the cause of that steam. My first question was, "What is the fuel pressure?" My second was, "How much fuel do we have left?" Tamara asked why I was constantly asking those questions because everything was all right. But it wasn't. Our aircraft had been hit on the mission and was leaking antifreeze. Our oil line had also been hit by the shell and was leaking under the fuselage. I felt the sleeve of my right arm and my side and found them soaked. We then made an emergency landing.

Four
The 586th Fighter Regiment

Introduction

The 586th Fighter Regiment (Air Defense) was the first of the three regiments to become operational in April, 1942. A defense regiment, its primary duty entailed guarding important targets from incursion by enemy bombers and escorting aircraft of important persons. Thus the mission of this regiment was not to hunt enemy aircraft—to pick a fight—but to guard specific targets from destruction. In this protective stance, when the enemy planes were turned back, they were not pursued. The mission, being defensive in nature, explains why this regiment did not have an outstanding record of enemy kills and thus was never designated as a "Guards" regiment.

The original commander of the regiment, Major Tamara Kazarinova, an experienced military pilot, was recalled very early on in the war because of failing health. Her replacement was a male pilot, Lieutenant-Colonel A. V. Gridnev, who commanded the regiment until the end of the war. Originally there were two squadrons of ten aircraft each, manned only by women pilots. Later an additional squadron of male pilots joined the regiment. Some of the ground personnel were also men, including a number of mechanics, because the fighter aircraft were mechanically quite sophisticated, and the women mechanics had been given only minimal training during the short period before moving to the front.

In September, 1942, eight women pilots with accompanying ground crews were detached from the 586th and temporarily assigned to two all-male regiments during the Battle of Stalingrad. These regiments consisted of pilots known as free fighters, pilots who actively sought out the enemy and engaged them. Three of the women assigned to these regiments perished in combat. Two of them, Lilya Litvyak and Katya Budanova, became aces while flying with the male regiments. Litvyak was credited with twelve kills and two shared kills; Budanova was said to have shot down even more enemy aircraft, although

Left to right: Lilya Litvyak, Yekaterina Budanova, Mariya Kuznetsova, 586th regiment fighter pilots

the exact number was not known. Both of them died in combat in the summer of 1943. The remaining women pilots with their ground crews were later returned to the 586th. Lilya Litvyak, whose remains were not found until 1989, was posthumously awarded her nation's highest award, Hero of the Soviet Union, by then-President Mikhail Gorbachev in 1990.

Early in the war, without radar, fighter aircraft were airborne at all times protecting vital areas. When a radar unit warning of enemy aircraft in the vicinity became operational, it became possible for air defense fighters to remain on ground alert, instead of being airborne and visually searching for enemy aircraft. The term "readiness one" was used to indicate a fighter aircraft at the end of a runway with the pilot in the cockpit, ready to start the engine and take off to intercept the enemy as it approached. The regiment was initially equipped with a Soviet-made Yakovlev (Yak-1) fighter, a single-seat, low-wing aircraft with a liquid-cooled 1,100 HP engine. It had a top speed of about 400 MPH and carried two very small-caliber machine guns. Later the Yak-1 was replaced with more advanced Yak aircraft, equipped with heavy-caliber machine guns and a 20 mm cannon.

The first Yak-1's had a radio receiver only; later, the aircraft were provided with two-way radios. No antifreeze was available for the aircraft early in the war, and it was necessary to drain the engines of water and oil in the winter whenever the planes were on the ground for any length of time to keep the engines from freezing.

The regiment flew 4,419 combat missions, engaged in 125 dog-fights, and shot down thirty-eight enemy aircraft. Ten of the women pilots were killed during the war (including the three killed while assigned to the male regiments), and nine more joined the regiment in 1943 as replacements.

NOTE: Nine women pilots of the 586th regiment were alive in 1990, and all of them were interviewed.

Senior Lieutenant Tamara Pamyatnykh,
pilot, commander of the squadron

Tamara Pamyatnykh (*left*) and Galina Burdina, 586th regiment

I was born in September, 1919. When I was sixteen I attended glider school, and then I went on to the aviation school at Ul-iganovsk to become a flight in-structor. When the war broke out I became a military officer and taught cadets. On October 10, 1941, I was called to Moscow. It was an exciting time, for ev-erything was chaotic, everyone was running away, and there were lots of refugees in the rail-way station. I thought I was to be sent to the rear, but instead I was admitted to Raskova's reg-iment.

We trained at Engels starting in the last days of October, and when Raskova asked us in which regiment we wanted to serve, I said the fighter regiment. We trained in the Yak-1, and later I was appointed commander of the formation.

My first combat mission was

in July, 1942. We were to fly escort for a transport aircraft carrying Voroshilov, a member of the State Defense Committee, to the Stalingrad front. When we arrived and I got out of the cockpit to report, the officer at the airfield looked at me and asked, "Where are the pilots?" I was a lieutenant, and when I told him we girls were the pilots, he didn't believe me. He walked around our three aircraft, saw two more girls there, and he still couldn't believe it! He asked how we were going to fly back, and I told him the same way we came here.

In August, 1942, three of us were assigned a combat mission: to deliver a message to the commanding staff of the army concerning its movement. It took considerable time to fly there, and it was dark before we arrived. None of us had flown the fighters at night; we hadn't been trained in night flying at all. I could see Stalingrad burning, but I couldn't see the front line and feared we might land on an enemy airfield. At that moment the Soviet forces shot a rocket into the air to indicate the location of the airfield. We had no lights turned on, and I was afraid that one of the other two planes would land on top of mine, so I turned on my lights for just a minute, even though I had no permission to do it. Galina Burdina told me that if I hadn't done that she would have landed on top of me! We all landed safely— our first night landings.

On one combat mission with Raisa Surnachevskaya as my wingman, we were assigned to intercept and shoot down a German reconnaissance aircraft. We soon saw not one aircraft but two formations of German bombers totaling forty-two planes. We climbed until our altitude was well above them and dove down firing at the lead aircraft of the formation. Each of us shot down one bomber on our first pass through their formation. Then we turned and approached the formation again and shot down two more bombers. By that time my guns were empty, and I decided to ram one of their bombers with my aircraft. I came so close to the enemy that I could see the face of the pilot. He was a huge man with a very fierce face. I was about to ram him when my plane was hit with gunfire, the wing separated from the aircraft, and I fell into a spin. It was also on fire.

I was being thrown about with so much force that my arms were flailing about, and I couldn't even get hold of the seat belt. I had already opened the canopy. My life flew in front of my eyes. I wanted to jump, but I couldn't open the belt. I didn't feel fear, but I thought I was going to die. At last I got the belt open and I didn't even jump—I was thrown out of the cockpit! I pulled the ring of my parachute, and it opened. When I landed, I started touching myself to see if I had injuries because I thought I had been severely wounded. I had blood on my face, and I felt very ill. My face was hurt, and the blood was running down. When my parachute opened, I was only 150 meters from the ground.

I looked up to the sky and saw that Raisa had circled around and was making another attack on the bombers. I thought, If she makes that attack alone she will never survive. I went to the telegraph station to report to my regiment that my aircraft was down and destroyed. Then I saw Raisa walking across a field, and it was wintertime, and there was snow, and we were in our fur boots. We came together and embraced each other and had the feeling that we had both been given birth again.

But in spite of the fact we were safe and alive, I began worrying that I might be punished because my aircraft was destroyed; I wasn't afraid, but I thought something might happen because of it. Instead, we were decorated! It came over the radio that we had turned back the large formation of German bombers and shot down four of them. We were each awarded the Order of the Red Star. Then the King of England, who read of this event, sent each of us a gold watch through the Soviet Minister of Foreign Affairs. Mine is inscribed: From the Minister of Foreign Affairs to the brave and gallant pilot Lieutenant Tamara Pamyatnykh—from the King of England, George VI.

Once I had an accident in the air. I was assigned the mission of intercepting an enemy reconnaissance plane, and I flew the mission with Galina Burdina. I came in to attack the enemy aircraft and discovered that it was an Airacobra, an American-built Russian plane. At the same time the Airacobra pilot mistook my Yak for the enemy. I didn't fire at him because I recognized him in time, but he came in and started firing at me. The problem was that when you are told by the ground controller that enemy planes are in that area you just assume that one is it, and you start shooting right away, not looking to see what plane it really is. The Airacobra's bullets hit my fuel tank, smashed the instruments, and hit through the armor plate. The wings were shot, and I had to return to my airfield.

When the other pilot mistook me for an enemy plane and I recognized him as a Soviet fighter, I began diving away. He dove after me and then Galina dove after him, for she wanted to save me. He continued firing and hitting my aircraft, and then he flew away. I managed to land on our airfield. When I got out of the cockpit, I saw that there were holes in my jacket where a bullet had gone completely through but hadn't touched me! At first the regimental commander didn't believe me when I told him a Russian Airacobra shot me down, but when they cut open the gas tank they found Russian bullets, and then he knew it was true. That pilot was to be tried by a military tribunal for his mistake, but we applied to the commander of the army with a personal request to set him free because we felt so sorry for the young boy. So he wasn't sentenced and went on flying.

In 1944 I fell in love with a pilot from a male fighter regiment, married, and flew in my husband's regiment for the remainder of the war. In July, 1944, my husband was shot down and imprisoned by the Germans in Buchenwald Concentration Camp, but he survived. When Buchenwald was liberated by the Soviet troops the prisoners were half-dead. When my husband came out into the fresh air he fainted, and he was taken to an American hospital. He was there for twenty days receiving nourishment, and then he was loaded into a Soviet aircraft and brought back. We did not meet until after the end of the war, in Moscow. He remained in the air force for the rest of his career and retired as a colonel. I gave birth to three children, and now we have five grandchildren.

Senior Sergeant Yekaterina Polunina,
senior mechanic of the aircraft

First I was a mechanic of the aircraft for Olga Studenetskaia, the pilot who shot down a Junkers Ju-88 bomber, and who was a deputy squadron commander. I was very surprised when she chose me to be her mechanic; probably it was because she knew I had worked at an aviation test factory. I remember when she was coming in to land and the elevator cable on her Yak broke and she couldn't land, so she opened the throttle, gained altitude, and jumped. When she jumped, the stabilizer hit her in the back as the plane was spinning, and she spent seven months in the hospital. She came back to our unit but she was not allowed to fly anymore, so she went to light aircraft aviation.

Once I was arrested. I had to do some technical work on the aircraft that took some fifty hours, and when I went to the mess to have a bowl of soup, the commander announced a lineup. I was arrested because I wasn't on duty, and I was given ten days in the guardhouse. It was a cabin in which I could only stand still. I couldn't bend, I couldn't lie down, only stand still. The most difficult thing about it was keeping up morale. The most outrageous thing was to go outside the door of the room with a man standing behind me with a gun sticking in my back saying, "Go and have your—whatever you have to do." And I had to do it in his presence. I was doomed to stay there ten days, but I only stayed two, because no aircraft could do without the mechanic. Afterwards I read in the documents of the political staff of the regiment that I was punished because I had not prepared the aircraft for flying. But that was not true—I didn't have to prepare it for flying; I had fifty hours to do some provisional work with the plane.

After the war, all of the women who were mechanics before the war or who were attending school in mechanics or who were faculty members teaching mechanics—all changed careers. None went back to it. They found it was too heavy a work for women.

One night we were having a little rest on the heaps of straw outside on the airfield. The field was not lighted, and we suddenly heard the roaring of an engine in the air and thought it was a German plane. At that moment it turned on its identification lights—forbidden in wartime—and it became clear that the pilot was asking for lights on the runway for landing. And when it landed and we came up to the aircraft, we didn't know who was in the cockpit, a German or a Soviet pilot. If a German pilot, what to do with him: to imprison him or to fire at him? Just then the canopy opened, and a robust young man speaking Russian called us bad names, and said, "Why didn't you give me identification lights on the wind tee for the runway to land on?" He was short of fuel and was on the verge of crashing. We were so happy that he turned out to be a Soviet pilot and not a German one.

One day, at the end of the war on an airfield in Hungary, a sport-type plane came in and landed. As he taxied toward us, I realized he was not a Russian but a foreigner, and he said in German "Kaput" as he got out of the cockpit. I looked then at the wings and at the tail, and I saw the German fascist crosses. I knew I had allowed the landing of a fascist aircraft! In our regiment there was only one person who could speak a foreign language, Nina Slovokhotova, our deputy regimental navigator. She asked him in English who he was, what nationality he was, and he explained he was Hungarian and had arrived by himself to see what had happened to his native town, Budapest. And I, Yekaterina, had allowed him to land.

In 1943, after ten of our pilots died during the war, nine more came to the 586th regiment as replacements. Nine of our pilots are still alive in 1990. The Yak fighter was a sophisticated and difficult plane to maintain, so the senior engineer and squadron engineers were men. But the engineer in avionics and the engineer in armament were women. Not only women served as mechanics but men also. Most of the mechanics have suffered from ill health after the war.

The fighter pilots had to act as their own navigators and gunners, and so they had to have experience and many flying hours. Each regiment had a rear service battalion for fuel, cooks, ammunition service, chemical service, and guard company, and the airforce regiments only had the responsibility for flying missions.

There was no water, so we boiled snow; there was no antifreeze for the planes, so we drained them in winter after each mission and drained the oil and heated it in barrels with a stove underneath. The barrels were on skis like a sleigh, to take to the planes. If a plane made a forced landing, we often towed the sleigh to the aircraft for many, many kilometers. All the mechanics, twenty-two of us, were students of the Moscow Aviation Institute.

Early in the war our regiment had the Yak-1 fighter with two machine guns of 7.62 mm caliber, the same as rifle bullets—very small caliber—so it was necessary to attack about three times to shoot down a plane. In 1942 they replaced them with 12.7 mm machine guns and a 20 mm cannon that fired through the gearbox shaft. The Yak engine, as well as the machine guns, started with compressed air, with a very long tube to the compressor; and if the tubes broke in the air, the pilots couldn't fire their guns. It was difficult to adjust these machine guns so they wouldn't hit the propeller. The guns were called "klicks" because they made that kind of noise. Each gun weighed 20 kilos, and it was heavy to clean and oil in the winter.

The main mission of our air defense regiment was not to shoot down but to chase away enemy aircraft. We started in combat from the banks of the Volga River on to Vienna, Austria, where we were then equipped with Yak-9 fighters. Our aircraft guarded bridges; many river crossings including the Don, the Voronezh, the Dnieper, and the Dniester; industrial centers; railroad centers; and our troops at the front.

The pilots flew 4,419 combat missions and 125 dogfights and shot down thirty-eight enemy aircraft. Few of the places the regiment guarded were destroyed by enemy aviation. Some eight crews from our regiment were assigned to two male fighter squadrons on the Stalingrad front, and they flew in pairs with male pilots as their wingmen because they did not have as much experience.

The wingman's duty was to protect the tail of the lead fighter pilot. When one of the girls, Nechayeva, was protecting the squadron commander who was about to land, three German Me-109s attacked them. She had no fuel, no ammunition, but she covered his aircraft with hers, and everyone there saw her killed. Budanova, another of our pilots sent to the male squadron, perished in July, 1943, but not before she shot down over twenty German aircraft; and Lilya Litvyak, also an ace, died in August, 1943. Five of the eight pilots came back to our regiment. Our pilots would dive as much as seven kilometers in a dogfight, and their blood vessels were damaged.

There are monuments to both Budanova and Litvyak. The mechanics knew their pilots very well. I am the regimental archivist.

Captain Alexandra Makunina,
chief of staff

We moved to Moscow when I was four years old. I was twenty-four when the war started, and we were on an expedition to find mineral deposits in the Ural Mountains. It was not until the fourth day of the war that we found out about it. On August 3 I got to Moscow. On October 10 I joined the army, went to train at Engels, and then on to the front with the 586th Fighter Regiment. It was a difficult time for Moscow itself, as the German troops were very near the capital, and it was being bombed from the air by the fascists.

Most all the women in the regiment had gone to glider school. I, too, had gone to glider school. I was in my first year of postgraduate studies after finishing in the Department of Physical Geography at the university. I flew the gliders and jumped with a parachute. I was looking for adventure, and when the war started my first impulse was to join the partisans on the ground. Being a geographer, I had been on some expeditions looking for deposits, and I also was a mountain climber. I trained with the regiment at Engels where I had navigation courses. My teacher was Marina Raskova, and Raskova herself appointed me to be chief of staff. I was striving to fly, but Marina said to me, "In the regiments I've enough girls who can fly the planes, but to be chief of staff I must be sure you are a person of brains." She would say that the staff was the brain of the regiment. As chief of staff I was the second in command on the ground after the commander of the regiment. The position carried a wide range of responsibilities. I had the responsibility of planning the work of the regiment on the ground, air training, and combat missions. My rank was lieutenant, and I finished the war as a captain.

Besides the staff itself there was a control post responsible for the combat missions, and it was part of my duty to organize its work. Also the women could come to me if they needed something—they could and they did! They could go to town when they were not on duty, get their hair done, meet the fellows, fall in love. When bad news came from home I authorized short-term leaves for them. They used to say, "Who sleeps less than anyone in the regiment—the chief of staff!" It was a strain for me to be of this rank and to serve as a commander, and as a consequence I began fainting. I never slept more than three hours a night, sometimes not at all. When I began fainting I asked to be appointed deputy commander because I couldn't physically stand the overstrain any longer.

When I became the deputy commander my duties were to plan combat missions and training flights—schedule everything. My profession and training as a physical geographer helped me a lot. For example, when the regiment started for another airfield I had all the maps, and I explained to the girls the terrain and topography of the new area.

The women were all volunteers, and it was a fever of patriotism, a necessity for them to do something. I myself could not have acted in any other way; it was proper to be at the front and to do this work. The very notion, the very sense of defending the motherland, was the duty of all the men and the women too. But I don't think women should make combat flights at all; I think a woman should remain a woman. Combat is not for a woman.

I remember when we received military clothing for the girls: jackets, overalls, boots, pants, all male clothing, everything very large. We didn't receive any underwear for women; it was not a normal situation. One of the girls received very, very large boots, and while she was checking the aircraft and getting it ready for a mission, she took off her boots and performed her job bare-legged. At this moment the staff of the regiment was approaching. She realized that it was going to be a uniform violation and she would be punished, so she had to leave her job, jump into the boots, and stand straight in order to report to the staff.

In our regiment the girls were attractive. They were very young and fresh, and nearby was a male regiment. Well, they got acquainted and they loved each other. Once the commander of that male regiment came to our commander and said, "I can give you as many aircraft as you want if you give me five girls [at this point he gave their names]; let's make an exchange!"

It is a fact that girls were arrested for some violations. Sonya Tishurova was keen on dancing, and she even formed a special group of girls who performed national dances in the regiment. She tried to teach the Belorussian national dance to everybody. Once she was arrested for three days for absence without leave, and when a person is arrested they are to take off their belt. She was put in a guardhouse, a room where she could do nothing, just stay there with her meals brought to her, but she still could see through the window that life was going on. Sonya stayed there without a belt on her uniform, and a brass band arrived at the regiment. It grieved her not to attend, because bands almost never came to the front. Besides, there were a lot of male regiments, and she was so popular among all the dancing fans who knew Tishurova was the best at performing the dances. So they came to her rescue and brought her a belt so she could be in uniform. She escaped from that room and came to the dance and then returned to the guardhouse!

High-ranking officials decided who was to be punished and what the punishment would be, but lower ranks could prescribe shorter punishments.

Senior Lieutenant Mariya Kuznetsova,
pilot

I began flying in 1936, when I was eighteen. I was born in a city near Moscow, and my parents were peasants. My father was arrested in 1937. When I started at the aeroclub I had to write in the documents that my father was arrested and imprisoned, and for this reason, because he was considered an enemy of the people, I was expelled several times from this flying course. My friends, however, persuaded the principal of the school to let me finish the courses. My father died during the war.

I became a flight instructor in the Po-2 in a military pilot school and taught there for five years, graduating about sixty pilots. In 1941 I joined the army and was assigned to the 586th Fighter Regiment as a pilot guarding targets like bridges and such.

I took part in the actions at the Stalingrad front, and I was there when the German troops in Stalingrad were surrounded and surrendered. I remained there up to the summer of 1943. They had sent four of us to the Stalingrad front to join a male fighter regiment, and there we met the enemy's every mission. I shot down three enemy aircraft. We suffered great losses of planes and pilots at that time, and because of a shortage of aircraft I didn't fly on every combat mission. Men mostly flew the Yaks. Of four aircraft flying in a formation, one was piloted by a woman—me. I shot down a Ju-87 and a Ju-88, German bombers. At that time German planes were superior in number, and in each battle we either lost an aircraft or a crew. Our fighters attacked the bombers, and the German fighters fought our fighters,

Two pilots before the war: Mariya Kuznetsova (*left*)
and Valentina Volkova-Tikhonova, 586th regiment

and one of our pilots said, "We have to fight the enemy on our own
fair land, and in an alien sky which at present doesn't belong to us."

I was shot down several times, but God saved me. My mother was
a believer, and she prayed to God for my safety. But rumors reached
my parents that I had been killed, and, figuratively, they buried me
twice. Once my propeller blades were hit by bullets, and they skimmed
down the fuselage, just missing the fuel tank. Another day I was
fighting with a German aircraft and didn't notice that I was out of
fuel. The engine stopped, and I dove away from the combat. I felt so
sorry for my aircraft—I didn't want it to crash—I had to spare it. I
knew we were extremely short of planes, so I decided to belly-land,
and I was fortunate that it stopped just short of a very deep trench.

In 1943, because of the shortage of planes, the regiment could only
make six or seven combat missions a day. There were more pilots
than planes. When I was fighting I could see the gunfire and flashes of
shell, and I remember the Germans didn't even let us have dinner!
They knew from reconnaissance flights what time we usually had
our meals, and they would attack the airdrome. Once they knew the
location of our canteen they strafed it. The cook jumped into a trench
but was killed by gunfire. We pilots usually had dinner on the surfaces of the wing of our aircraft, and the food was brought to us there.

In the evening we were given 100 grams of alcohol to relieve the stress. We gave our alcohol to the men, but after heavy losses of our pilots we did drink it. Otherwise we couldn't fall asleep.

One day we were guarding a railroad station near a lake at Stalingrad, and we were given an order to intercept a group of enemy planes coming to bomb this station. Another woman pilot, Belyayeva, and I took off, and when we arrived in that area we saw a group of about ten German bombers, and we started a dogfight. During the maneuvers Belyayeva's plane was shot down, and I kept on fighting. It is our pilots' tradition to do that. We did our best not to let the enemy bomb the objective. Moreover, we shot down two fascist aircraft. The German bombers dropped their bombs in an open field and turned back. You must watch for your friend who has been shot down, and I kept looking for her; she jumped with her parachute and was safe.

Our male regiment flew the Lavochkin-5 aircraft. They were more modern and advanced than our Yak fighters. From the very start the male regimental commander didn't believe we were good pilots. Once he decided to test us and said, "In the afternoon we will have a training dogfight between male crews and you two, so two men and two women compete with each other." Belyayeva and Budanova flew, and the male squadron commander and wing commander took off. When Belyayeva was in her cockpit she said, "I will approach their aircraft from the rear," and she did it, and won the mock attack. They were so carried away by the dogfight that they didn't even notice several German fighters approaching above them, getting ready to attack. The fascist fighters had the advantage because they were above our fighters, who were instructed to land on another airdrome because ours was blocked by the Germans. These two girls proved that in their Yaks they could fight the men in the more sophisticated aircraft—everything depended on skill.

One day I miraculously escaped death. I performed my mission and left the plane with the parachute in the cockpit and went to report. It was early in the spring with the temperature above zero centigrade. The mechanics had to start the engine occasionally to keep it warm in case I needed to fly, and suddenly it burst into flames. The mechanic escaped, but the aircraft burned completely. Probably a hole had been shot in the fuel tank and fuel was leaking, so for the third time I was very lucky.

By this time, in the summer of 1943, the Germans did not send any combat planes to our area, only reconnaissance aircraft. That is why we women pilots flying in the male fighter regiments in Stalingrad were about to be returned to our own regiment, the 586th. One of the girls who had remained with 586th regiment learned that we had fought severe dogfights with the enemy. Out of envy she escaped from the female regiment in the plane of a male pilot who had fallen ill and flew to the male regiment where we served. Her name was Anna Demchenko. She did this without permission and was punished for it.

When I was escorting a cargo Li-2 aircraft—constructed in the Soviet Union using the design of the American C-47—that carried blood from Moscow to the front for the wounded, I asked the pilot to take me home to Moscow, my native city. He didn't want to take me on board the plane. He was superstitious and believed that when a woman is on the plane it may bring misfortune. I shamed him; I had been protecting him for three days on his flights to the Stalingrad front, and he did not want to take me. At last he agreed, and I flew home and spent three days.

I came back to the airdrome and there were no planes at all, because the regiment had moved to another airdrome. But there was a Yak-1 fighter the mechanics were repairing, and after a plane was repaired, it was required that a pilot test fly it. The commander of the airfield ordered me to test it, because I was the only pilot at the airfield. I had a scheme to escape in that plane and catch up with my male regiment. Nobody knew about it except the mechanic. He threw all my belongings into the cockpit the night before, and in the morning I innocently took off, wagged my wings, and flew away. No one knew that I wasn't going to return.

In 1943 General Osipenko decided to assemble the female pilots who had been sent to male regiments back into the 586th regiment, and he ordered us to return. We refused to obey his order because we wanted to fly with our male regiment. Then the general cabled us and ordered the regimental commander to put us to a military tribunal. But we had strong support and protection from the commander, who encouraged us not to return, because, he said, we had not deserted the army. To the contrary, we deserted to the front! Nevertheless we came back to the 586th.

In Romania, when the regiment was released, I married the commander of the air regiment, a major. I know one woman, Yamshikova by name, who flew for thirty years after the war was over. She tested jets.

NOTE: Mariya Kuznetsova died in 1991.

Technical and mechanical staff, 586th regiment,
May, 1945, in Budapest, Hungary

Sergeant Nina Yermakova,
mechanic of armament

I was born in Moscow in 1920. I went to secondary school but only completed seven grades. Then I worked in a factory as a tailor's cutter. I was a very good Komsomol member, and when the war broke out the plant received certificates from the Komsomol headquarters allowing some of us to be enrolled in Marina Raskova's regiments, and I was chosen. On October 10, 1941, we left for Engels where we trained. Then I was assigned to the 586th Fighter Regiment. Before the war I hadn't even been close to an aircraft.

I started and finished the war in the same regiment. We lived as a large family. They called me the best singer in the regiment, and they jokingly named me the USSR Honorable Singer. I even sang solos when our regiment marched. When we were marching the commander of the regiment, Lieutenant Colonel Aleksandr Gridnev, would call out, "Yermakova, sing out!" and I would start the song, and then the rest of the regiment would join me.

After the war I went to an aviation plant and worked as a mechanic of armament because I didn't want to give up aviation. My work was very hard; it was mostly manual labor. I worked there after the war for fifty years, and now I am a pensioner. Because of that hard labor I've got strong hands. I also have a very strong body. I participated in many athletic events when I was young.

Senior Sergeant Valentina Kovalyova-Sergeicheva, mechanic of the aircraft

My father perished in the Civil War of 1919. When my mother found out about my father's death she became very ill. It was the year of my birth, and my father had never seen me. I was carried into the orphanage because my mother couldn't take care of me—she was deathly ill.

In 1924 my mother's sister married and took me from the orphanage and brought me up. In 1933 I finished the secondary school of seven grades and went to a technical school. When I finished that school I was sent to a factory that produced searchlights for the front. When I went to the plant to work, my cherished dream had already formulated in my mind—I wanted to be a pilot. I decided to join the glider school. When I finished the courses I became an instructor pilot.

When we came to serve in the regiments they cut our hair very short and issued us male uniforms—we looked boyish. The commander of the army came to our regiment for an inspection and when he saw what we looked like he thought we looked very ugly. When the command was given to about-face we turned but the boots didn't, because the sizes were much, much larger than our feet; they were men's boots. Afterward he said we should be given smaller boots and skirts. He also allowed us to grow our hair.

In the regiment I became a mechanic. I was full of grief. I wrote to officials and asked them to let me be a pilot, but they said then they would have to train another to be a mechanic, because we needed mechanics. I had done technical work in the plant, and that is why it was appropriate for me to become a mechanic. We would warm the planes at night every two hours to keep them from freezing, and after warming them we covered them with special blankets as if they were children—babies. We wore padded trousers and padded jackets, and one night when we all rushed to warm the planes, everyone put on all their padded things, but I managed to only put on my padded jacket. When I stretched up I realized I was dressed only in underpants, and behind me was a man. He didn't know what to do, whether to look at me or do his job. I realized what was happening and jumped over the truck so as not to embarrass the man.

Galina Butuzova (*left*) and Valentina Kovalyova-Sergeicheva, 586th regiment

I was very disciplined and I liked order. I was never arrested during the war, but the people who provided for the aircraft were arrested routinely. In our dugout we had a *pichka*, a Russian fireplace, a stove. Each crew lived together in one dugout. When it rained we always knew it because the water came in. We would ask the girl next to the entrance how much water had flowed into the dugout, and she would put her hand into the water and say, "No, no, not much yet, sleep quietly, not much yet!" And then when we came to realize that there was so much water in the trench that everything was floating, we would jump up and go out in our underwear to ask the men on the truck with a pumping machine to come and pump out the water so we could go back to sleep.

The first house we stayed in was a house of wood with very thin boards, and the temperature was as low as forty degrees below zero centigrade, and it was dangerous to live in under those cold conditions. We had lower and upper bunks, and on entering the house you could see two containers of water brought into our quarters by the logistics battalion to use for washing ourselves. We washed immediately and very quickly, because the water might freeze before we finished. Those of us living together tidied and cleaned the room daily; one day one girl and the next day another. When we washed the floor, it was so unbearably cold outside that the floor dried only by the fireplace, and the rest of the room was slippery—covered with ice. We had a girl with us who slept with her head to the east, and she always wore a cap on her head at night because it was so cold, and every morning she awoke and the cap on her head was glued to the wall—frozen to the wall. We dried our clothes over the fireplace, hanging them on strings. The heat from the fireplace was so hot that sometimes our clothing burned.

We each were provided with a rucksack; a piece of soap; men's underwear and our padded uniforms, jacket and pants; a blanket; a mattress cover; and a pillow. The pilots were provided for in the same way. Except for our initial training when we were all together, we were not billeted with the officers and pilots. One of our pilots kept a little bit of perfume in the cockpit, and she was punished for that. It was a violation of rules; not even a lipstick in the cockpit.

The first pilot of my aircraft, Irina Olkova, demanded order in our work from beginning to end, and before she got into the cockpit, she personally examined the aircraft. Only after that did she get into the plane. We clashed because she said something went wrong with the aircraft during the flight, and it was my fault that it did not work properly. I invited an engineer to examine the engine and aircraft, and he did. He then declared that it was in perfect order. We had different personalities that didn't work well together, and this pilot had a sort of male character, you know. Then reinforcements came—new pilots—and I was assigned to one of the young pilots, Tamara Voronova, and after the war she married and had four children. I was her mechanic until the end of the war and we became great friends, and to this day we visit each other.

For the last seventy years of this socialist existence we have been used to saying no words about anything at all, to refrain: that is why now we look upon this chance with you as an opportunity to relate our stories.

NOTE: *Yekaterina Polunina, archivist for the regiment, was present and asked to add something to Valentina's story, saying that Valentina would not tell it about herself.*

"Valentina comes from a very famous and outstanding family, the Popkov family, that was repressed during the Stalin period. Her father perished during the Civil War, and the family, the Popkovs, brought her up. After the war it turned into a very tragic situation. Her girlfriends, with whom she had been serving in the army for all those years, couldn't even phone her. All her telephone conversations were monitored. She was pursued by the government because her uncle was repressed during this period and was imprisoned and pronounced to be 'the people's enemy,' and he was rehabilitated only this year [1990]. "Valentina was at the front, which is why she was not imprisoned. All of her family and relatives were imprisoned at that time. She was the only one who survived outside prison. She was dismissed from the plant where she had worked before the war—just because she was alive! She was brought up in the 'family of the enemy,' as they called it, and for that reason she was isolated, totally isolated, from all of her friends. Each of us was warned by the KGB after the war that we could never see her or phone her because she came from a family of an imprisoned enemy of the country, and only one girlfriend called her. Later on they threatened to imprison her friend's husband just because she had been phoning Valentina. She suffered very much.

"Now she is responsible for the work of the regimental council. She writes to everyone in the regiment, she cries for them, she is very sorry for everybody else—but not herself. Life made her keep silent."

Lieutenant Valentina Petrochenkova-Neminushaya, pilot

I was born in a small village near Smolensk, and when I was five years old my family moved to Moscow. While I was in school I heard that some of our women pilots, Grizodubova, Osipenko, and Raskova, made a nonstop flight to the Far East. All the country greeted these brave women in Moscow. After this I decided to become a pilot. I was then under sixteen, and when I went to the aero club I was not allowed to join because of my age. I went to the classes anyway, even though I was not listed as a student. In the spring, when the cadet pilots started flying, I was not allowed to fly. I went with my father to the militia station and asked an officer to give me a new birth certificate with my birth listed as eight months earlier, and he did it! That is the way I started flying.

When I finished the course at the aero club I was not allowed to study at the flying school because I was under eighteen. So I joined the glider school. In the summer of 1940 I took part in a glider all-union competition, and I became a Champion of the Soviet Union by flying seven and one-half hours, maneuvering, looking for the clouds and updrafts, and finally arriving at the destination. Because of that, I was sent to the glider school as an instructor.

When war broke out I was appointed as an instructor in the Po-2.

In 1942 Stalin signed an order that we must prepare forces who would be delivered behind the lines by parachute. Many of my girlfriends from glider school wrote to me from the front that they flew fighter aircraft, and I envied them. I wrote many letters to my command asking to be sent to the front, but I was told I was needed there to train landing-force parachutists. At Kazan city there was a parachute training center, and I was awarded the title of parachutist in February, 1942. We jumped from an altitude of 800 meters, and it was so freezing cold that we hid our hands in the spare parachute and couldn't control our landings. The airfield was icy, and it was so windy that when we landed, the parachute remained full of air. We were sliding away across the icy field with the wind, and only the instructors or bushes could stop us! I was told that when I had prepared sixty men for this airdrop operation they would let me go to the front.

So I was given an airplane, a mechanic, and thirty parachutes. It was my mission to teach those men. There was one incident when one of the men was to jump, and he was frightened and refused to leave the aircraft. Then he caught the rudder cable in his hand, the plane started descending, and I could not control it. He held on tightly, and I tried to calm him down, begged him to release the cable, patted him on the head, even kissed him, and then I beat his hand with the rope, but he held on. I pulled him back into the cockpit with his legs up in the air and finally landed the plane. After this event the man was released from parachute duty.

I finished the training of parachutists and went to Moscow, where they wanted me to fly the Po-2 with the 588th regiment, but I refused and said I only wanted to fly fighters. I was sent to the training center for air defense pilots, and when I reported to the commander, I said that I wished to train in fighters. He said, "No! No women!" and I said to him, "I will go nowhere, I will fly fighters," and I sat in the chair. "All right, you can sit here!" he said, and turned and left the room. I spent all the night in his office, and when he returned in early morning I was still there, sitting on the chair. I said that I would sit there and go nowhere, and he said that there were two hundred men in the center and they lived in the dugout, and where should he put me? Finally they took some plywood and made a small cabin for me in the corner of the dugout.

It was very difficult for me when the flying started. The cadets had about thirty-five flying hours when they came there, and I had about four hundred, and my instructor said there was no use training me like those men because I could fly. Because of my flying hours I was not allowed to fly but sent to duty in the kitchen and other services. The commander said that when the first man could fly the fighter aircraft then I would be the second one.

When flights in the fighter started, all the pilots and mechanics were near the runway. When it was my turn I started taking off, and it looked like a zigzag because my legs were trembling with nervousness, but when I was up and flying everything went well, and I was crying, "Hurrah!" in the cockpit. It was a small plywood aircraft, the main fighter before the war. If a bullet hit the plane it would catch on fire, and a lot of pilots died in it because of that. I made three flights that day and three perfect landings. I reported to the commander, and he told the men they should follow my example and fly as I did. Then I flew the Yak-7 and -9.

We were trained to dogfight in the air, and I was the last of the pilots to complete this training for combat. It was the end of November and it was snowing. We had a dogfight, and as we approached the runway the snow started. The instructor landed and then it was my turn, and I saw a wall of snow with no ground visible. The commander at the field radioed to me: please land your aircraft. We had a wind tee pointing down the runway we should use, but I couldn't see it because both it and the snow were white. So I asked them to please put a car at the beginning of the runway for me to see, and I made two approaches and finally got the plane down, and the commander said I did perfectly. That was my last training flight.

In December, 1943, I arrived at the 586th Fighter Regiment in Kiev. Kiev had been liberated in November, and there was a lot of combat in that area. So I made my first combat flight in December, 1943, to guard the railroad bridge crossing the Dnieper River. Step by step we approached our own borders, and then in Budapest we celebrated victory day.

I was flying an older Yak on a training mission near Budapest when I lost flying speed doing an Immelmann maneuver. It fell into a spin and the wings began shaking, and finally I pulled it out. I was so low and the countryside so hilly that the people on the ground saw what was happening and turned away, because they thought I was going to crash. During that time my whole life flew before my eyes, and I pulled out so low that the aircraft radiator touched the ground, and it bent the blades of the propeller! I landed, taxied, stopped the engine, took off my parachute and went to my quarters pale as death, opened the door, and fell down unconscious. The doctor came to see me, and it was three days before I made my next flight.

I was eager to fly more, but my brother was killed in the war, and when the war ended my mother asked me to come home and not to fly any longer.

In 1946 I married a pilot I met during the war, and he said, "You choose—aviation or me." So I stopped flying. My husband was a test pilot, and we moved many times; he died in 1981. After the war I was the senior test technician at the parachute center. I worked at our space training center, and when there was a program for women to fly in space, I trained them to use parachutes. During the war I flew 250 combat hours, and I left the army in November, 1945.

(Officer, rank not stated) Nina Slovokhotova,
deputy regimental navigator

I am a professor and doctor of science and chemistry doing research in radiation physics and polymeric chemistry. I graduated from Moscow University before the war, and I was a postgraduate student in chemistry when the war started. I was invited by Raskova to be chief of chemical service, but there was no chemical warfare.

In 1943 I was trained as navigator for the regiment. I was then twenty-four. I planned the routes for the pilots, showed them how to escape the anti-aircraft fire, and trained pilots in navigation, but my major responsibility was to work with the radar location station. It was the first model of our radar, and I watched enemy aircraft on the screen and directed our planes to intercept. The area of regimental responsibility for air defense was divided into squares, and I was a guidance officer. I was one of the first radar navigation officers in our country.

When we moved to a new area I would fly with the regimental commander and mark the maps of the area with landmarks for the pilots. I was also responsible for ground information. We had communication with ground forces, a net of air surveillance. As an inspector I would go to the posts of air surveillance centers, where the girls working there were supposed to know the difference between Soviet and German planes.

The first radars were delivered in 1942, but it wasn't until 1943 that a net was formed and we knew how to maintain it. Because pilots flew missions for many hours both day and night when the situation was very intense, we had no time to sleep for four or five days at a time. The radar was set up far from the runways and airdrome, usually three to five kilometers, and it was camouflaged so we were not bombed. We lived underground in dugouts, but later we lived in houses. Early in the war the fighter pilots had only radio receivers, no transmitters, in their aircraft. In 1943, our planes were equipped with two-way radios. There was one episode when a woman pilot sighted an enemy aircraft, and then he dove into the clouds, and the girl burst out crying on the radio, "He escaped, he has escaped!" I would call to the artillery and ask them the altitude of the enemy aircraft, and there was close cooperation between us. The pilots usually thanked me for identifying the fascist planes in the air so they could attack, but sometimes the pilots reproached me for not finding any. After the war, when I was defending my doctoral dissertation, one of the women who had been a famous pilot during the war, Olga Yamshikova, came to the restaurant where we were celebrating and said, "I don't know what kind of chemist she is, I don't care, but she was a very perfect guidance officer during the war!" When the pilots landed after a mission they reported, and I was to write a combat message. They also related the episodes of dogfights to be forwarded. One day our pilots Tamara Pamyatnykh and Raisa Surnachevskaya were in the air, and I informed them that in a certain area there were some German aircraft. They flew there and saw forty-three German bombers flying toward the railroad station they were guarding near Kursk, and the girls attacked the leading aircraft, split the formation, and shot down four planes. The Germans turned back, never bombing the station. It was an important target for the fascists, because a massive concentration of Soviet troops and ammunition had been drawn to that sector to prepare for the Kursk Bulge battle. A British war correspondent saw this dogfight and described it in his press release. The Queen of England made her husband, the King, give each of these girls a gold wristwatch. Tamara Pamyatnykh is a remarkable woman.

When the women pilots were protecting a particular area and there were no enemy planes, they could fly two or three missions in a day. But when there was a dogfight, the maneuvers and steep dives made the blood come from the ears—there was a blood overload. Under these conditions they could only fly one mission; the men could fly more.

Galina Burdina was on duty, readiness one, in the cockpit, and on our field in Hungary was a Romanian squadron, because by that time the Romanians had surrendered and were fighting on our side. One of them saw Galina in the cockpit—she was a very beautiful girl—in her helmet with the curls of hair showing, and the pilot said, "I saw her over Korsun-Shevchenkovski." That was when we were bombing the cargo planes of the Romanians and Germans on an airfield, and one of the pilots was Galina. They flew very low, and this pilot could see a girl with curly hair and a beautiful face in the cockpit, and the pilot said, "I saw a woman pilot when she flew by," and nobody believed him at that time. Then in Hungary at the airdrome he recognized her curly hair, because he had memorized her in those few seconds!

During the battles near Zhitomir town there was a lot of night bombing—fascist raids—and it was very difficult for our fighters to find the target aircraft at night, even though they were guided. At night, when the planes were taking off or landing, the spotlight flashed for just a second to show them the direction, but there were some lights along the runway. We on the ground were fascinated by the view. On the one hand we realized it was dangerous to carry out missions at night, but on the other it was a remarkably spectacular performance. It was as if a huge prehistoric dinosaur were swinging its wings, with burning, gigantic eyes sparkling here and there in complete darkness, only stars twinkling in the sky. The lights along the runway were blue, and they were switched off after landing.

In another instance near Saratov, the Germans tried to bomb a bridge across the Volga. Komyakova shot down one aircraft, and after that no Germans appeared in the sky for some time. Some of the missions were to escort some very important person, for example, Nikita Khrushchev, who was at that time the First Secretary of the Ukrainian Communist Party and a member of the military council of the Ukrainian front. When he was flying from Moscow to Stalingrad, the pilots from my regiment escorted his transport plane. At that time the Germans had air superiority at Stalingrad. The German planes were flying all around our airfields, and in the daytime it was impossible to take off or land. They would fly for about one and one-half hours and then leave to refuel, and other German aircraft didn't arrive right away. The Russian planes would then use this short interval to land and take off. When our pilots took off from this airfield they still had others at their disposal, so if the runway was blocked they flew to another airfield.

When the girls from my regiment were going to fly to Stalingrad, everyone realized they could meet their death there. I remember their faces at that time, beaming with happiness. They were at last to fly to the front to fight the hated enemy, and they were saying, "At last our dream came true." I will remember that forever!

I always keep in touch with my friends—it is for the last day of my life.

Senior Sergeant Anna Shibayeva,
mechanic of armament

I was born in 1917 near Moscow, together with the revolution! I worked at a plant as an expert in medical equipment. When the war broke out I voluntarily joined the army. I knew nothing about aviation before the war. I was selected by Marina Raskova to join the women's regiment as a mechanic of armament. I was trained in Engels with the other girls and then assigned to the 586th Fighter Regiment. I served in that regiment until the very last day of the war, and the pilot of our crew was Zoya Pozhidayeva, and the aircraft was the Yak fighter.

After the war I went back to the plant and retired last year from the same position I held before the war.

My husband was killed in the war. We had no children, I never remarried, and I live alone. But I have very many sisters from my regiment.

Lieutenant Klavdiya Pankratova,
pilot, commander of the formation

I was born in the Crimea in 1916, but later on I moved to the Ukraine. I was admitted to glider school and then graduated as an instructor. Later I entered the Kherson Aviation School and received the rank of lieutenant. I had only excellent marks, and that is why I was given the rank of lieutenant before the war. I graduated in 1938, so I was twenty-two years old. I then began working as an instructor-pilot preparing the cadets for the air forces. The chief of our flying school went to Moscow and learned about Raskova's regiments. He returned and told me that he had lost me to Raskova's regiment, having blurted out that he had a woman instructor in his school. My cherished dream was to become a fighter pilot.

When I joined the 586th Fighter Regiment (Air Defense), my duties were to escort other aircraft and to work in air defense. In about 1943 I became a night fighter. It was difficult because the ground areas were not lighted, the sky was absolutely black, and I flew by intuition. I could see, not very clearly, some black spots in the air and shot at them, and I couldn't even see where I was shooting! There were nights when we had to repulse the attack of the fascist bombers, and the sky was black with aircraft and no lights at all.

I lived with the feeling that I was doomed to live in the air, and when an air attack began, I was eager to fight. One time we were prepared to take off on a mission, and we took off across the runway instead of down the runway. While the first aircraft succeeded in the takeoff, mine flew into the pillbox at the side of the runway, and the plane was destroyed. When it hit the pillbox, it came apart completely and exploded on the ground.

Once a male pilot and I were assigned a mission. We took off in our two fighters and had a battle with German Junkers, Ju-88s, and I shot down one of the bombers while I was fighting. The German aircraft I shot down exploded, and no one got out. I lost contact with my wingman; the weather conditions were very bad, and he just disappeared. When I landed at our airdrome he was there, but he had to land at several places before arriving at our home base because he had lost his orientation. My own map holder was blown away while I was fighting, but I flew back by instinct and memory.

When we took off at night I knew that the only way to survive was to be ice inside, to feel absolutely nothing, to concentrate, to focus only on the mission. To fight at night had to be by intuition, because we could actually see very little. The takeoffs and landings were extremely difficult—no lights, no guidance. When we returned to our field we were allowed for a short time to turn on one landing light. You needed to be psychic or have a sense of the situation to know where the ground and runway were. Before a flight I had to think over everything, every detail of the procedures.

Early on in my flying, in the glider school where I began, I had to compete with the men, but I never felt inferior to a man, never, and I also knew if I were to perform in something I would do it even better than a man!

In the regiment I was the most frank, open, and lively girl. I was always full of humor, the first to be merry, and my sisters in the regiment constantly asked me to sing songs, tell a story, dance, but life changes a personality drastically. Now it's difficult to believe that I was a ringleader in the regiment.

Once four of us were ordered to fly to the Kursk Bulge, to support the ground troops there. There were four aircraft: two commanders of the formation—I was one of them—and two commanders of the squadron. When we were returning from that mission we flew in two pairs, and I saw that the other pair was taking a different course or route, so I decided to show them the right course. I approached them twice and wagged my wings—we had no air-to-air radio contact—and then I returned back on course, but they wouldn't follow me. After the second attempt to get them to turn to the right heading, we left them and returned to base. Later we learned that one of them made a belly landing, and the other flipped over while landing. The com-

Pilot Klavdiya Pankratova in a Yak-9 fighter, 586th regiment

mander of our regiment reprimanded me for not bringing the other two aircraft back with us. I asked him, "How could I have done that, could I have tied them with a rope to my aircraft and returned them here?"

We were normally sent in pairs on a reconnaissance flight, but for some reason that I did not understand, I was always sent alone—alone without a prayer. One day I was given the mission to reconnoiter the area near Kursk, and I flew there and met another of our fighters, a man who was also without a wingman. He turned to me and said, "Brother, let's fly together." I growled out something indecipherable to him on the radio, being afraid to be recognized as a woman, accepting his offer. So we flew in a pair and fought as a pair, and I protected him in an attack on a Messerschmitt. When the fight was over, I decided to break away and finish the reconnaissance work assigned to me. He never knew I was a woman; we never saw each other's face.

In the four years of the war I was a night fighter, and I knew that in order to survive there should be no one on my tail, no fascist aircraft there. I always looked back, first over one shoulder and then the other, constantly watching behind my plane. When the war was over and I was walking down the street, I couldn't move without fear of someone behind me, a danger, a fear I carried with me from the war.

I had a very unpleasant experience with the commander of the regiment. I never tried to teach morals to anyone, but I was two or three years older than our commander, and I sometimes taught the girls how to do this and that, and he didn't like it. In the air I was constantly sent alone, not in a pair, and I always returned. The male commander didn't like my skillfulness; he didn't like me. And in 1947 he crossed my name off the list of those in our regiment who were to be awarded the Order of the Great Patriotic War, first grade, for deeds at the front. And he assigned me to night fighters where you flew alone always, never in a pair. Later on I was given another order, the Order of the Great Patriotic War, second grade, but I never saw the first grade.

It was impossible to locate the enemy aircraft at night to shoot them down, except when they were caught in a searchlight. Our fighters replaced one another; one took off and the other landed, and they alternated all night long. One night I was loitering in the area over Kiev, and I was caught by the searchlights. The German aircraft began shooting at me, and my plane was trembling but no shell penetrated it. I was swinging it back and forth like a leaf falling to escape the lights and the firing.

I flew 168 combat missions. I shot down a German fascist aircraft, a Ju-88. I also flew the P-39 Airacobra and the English Spitfire. I was the only Soviet woman pilot who did that. It all happened because at the end of the war, I married a fighter pilot and was transferred to his regiment, where all of the fighter aircraft were American and English; I married into the regiment. My husband and I flew in that regiment together for a year. I have a strong belief that it doesn't matter whether it is a woman or a man at the controls; a woman can be a military pilot, she can fulfill combat missions if a misfortune like war falls upon the heads of the people of a country.

And then it came to who should retire. It was not the men, of course; I was made to retire, and I didn't want to. Later I wanted to go into civil aviation, but they hated fighter pilots; they didn't take me. So I had to quit flying.

Senior Sergeant Zinaida Butkaryova-Yermolayeva, parachute packer

I was born in a village, and my parents were peasants. In 1931 my relatives who lived in Moscow decided to take me to live with them. It was the time of collectivization in the Russian countryside, known for its peasant riots and massive annihilation of farmers resisting this hated policy. It was dangerous to live in a Russian village at that time. So I came to Moscow and lived for some time with my relatives there, and then I went to the textile factory. I was under seventeen at that time; I worked there for five years. There was a campaign in the country to work as much as you could, to achieve outstanding results in labor, and I was one of those who joined this movement. The factory was a weaving mill, and I was a weaver.

I was fond of sports, and when the war started I was young and single, and I usually took the night shift at the factory. I lived in a dormitory, and I saw a note pinned on my bed that said, Zinaida, you should come to the drafting office. I was sent to the office of the Central Committee, and they told me to come back the next day to be sent to the front. I said I had to work in my factory. I was told I should quit the factory and be there the next day. We were all in a patriotic mood at this time, and I said I would go to the front with pleasure.

On September 11, 1941, we came to the Airforce Academy here in Moscow where the women gathered. They gave us military uniforms and high boots, and during the night we went to bomb shelters because the Germans were bombing Moscow. We met there with Marina Raskova, and then we were sent to Engels to the flying school. We all studied everything about the aircraft, and at the end of six months we were assigned a specialty.

I was appointed parachute packer, and I was very disappointed because I wanted to work on the aircraft. My commander was a major of the parachute section, and he tried to calm me, but I started crying. We had a field tent with a long table of fifty square meters where I could pack the parachutes. The rule was that before the packers started their work, they must first make some jumps. Of course there was no great desire to jump, but we considered it a duty. So I put on this parachute, and I had another parachute, a reserve one; I got into the cockpit, and we climbed to 900 meters.

The pilot told me to get ready. There is a cord from the pilot to the parachute so if you are not balanced enough, or freeze up and don't pull the ring yourself, it will open. I asked permission to get out of the cockpit and to stand on the wing. I climbed out on the wing, the pilot decreased the speed of the plane, I held onto the cockpit with my left hand, got ready, and asked the pilot which leg I should jump from. He told me either. I took the ring in my hand, and the pilot said jump, so I jumped and pulled the ring, but it was too difficult to pull. Then I took both hands and pulled it again, and then came the shock of the parachute opening. I felt something sliding off my leg; it was one high boot and then my sock, and I landed with one boot and one bare foot. Then everyone started laughing! I made three jumps in all.

When one of our aircraft was shot down and the pilot jumped with the parachute I had packed, I felt proud because it was also the result of my job that the pilot got down safely. For my good work I was given a medal. Every day I checked the parachutes that were in the cockpits. The minimum altitude for jumping was about two hundred to three hundred meters; otherwise, the pilot would hit the ground before the parachute completely opened.

I was at the airdrome whenever the planes were flying, and at times the Germans bombed our field. All of the airdrome personnel lived in dugouts underground and slept on bunks. In the winter it was so cold when you awakened in the morning that sometimes your hair was frozen to the wood of the beds; but you could hardly call them beds, because they were some thin logs with mattresses on them. We wore men's uniforms, trousers, and underwear. Our ration was a soldier's, and the pilots had their own rations.

Once at Voronezh city, where the military situation was very grave and the Germans were massively advancing, the logistics battalion couldn't bring us our rations for three days. We had no other food; we lived on herring, so we survived. When we were stationed near the villages we would exchange tobacco, cigarettes, bread, and sugar for milk, sour cream, eggs, and butter and sometimes meat. We seldom had meat, only cooked soup bones.

When we moved to another airdrome, a cargo aircraft with mechanics, ammunition, and some instruments was first to go, and sometimes our pilots took the mechanic into the cockpit of the fighter aircraft. There was some space inside the fuselage, and the mechanics flew with the pilots in that manner. It was forbidden, of course, but the front is the front. I had duty also at the command post of the regiment and in the officers' mess. I enjoyed that duty because I was close to the food. But we adjusted ourselves to the wartime food and seldom felt hungry.

The mechanics and the sergeants had a salary of seventy rubles a month, very good money at that time, and parachute packers and mechanics of armament and avionics got less. To bathe, we were carried in trucks to a nearby town bathhouse once every two or even three weeks; it depended on the situation. There were some marriages registered at the front. The regimental commander usually gave permission, and then the documents were sent to the division commander at the front. They approved of the marriages, but there were no proper conditions, no place to live together. If the wife was pregnant she was sent from the regiment to the rear to give birth and was gone about three or four months.

I married my husband at the end of the war; most of us married after the war was over.

Lieutenant Raisa Surnachevskaya,
senior pilot

I was born in Moscow on August 8, 1922. I entered a technical school when I was about fifteen and very romantic. Across the street was a glider school. I saw boys and girls entering there every day, and I was carried away by the idea. The next year I was admitted, and I studied there simultaneously with the technical school and finished both. I was seventeen. I had to choose then between work or aviation; I chose aviation and became a flight instructor.

When the war broke out I was brought with other girls in a truck to a stadium, where Raskova was founding the regiment. I was appointed to the 586th Fighter Regiment. We went through training at Engels and then to the front in the Yak-1. Our combat began in 1942 at the town of Voronezh. One of our pilots shot down a German bomber while we were still studying for combat!

At the front we flew in pairs, and Tamara Pamyatnykh and I flew together. Our mission was air defense, and we were sent up when there were German aircraft in our area. On one particular mission we were told that there were two German planes in our area moving in the direction of a Soviet railroad station that we were to defend. When we climbed up we could see that there weren't two bombers, there were two large groups of enemy bombers! We placed ourselves above them with the sun behind us as we approached the formations.

At first we thought they must be birds, there were so many of them. Then we realized they were German dive bombers, they were approaching the railroad station, and the station was full of trains. We wagged our wings to indicate to each other that we were ready to attack. Our first targets were the lead aircraft. On this attack we each shot down a German bomber, and then we quickly made another pass, and again each of us shot down another. My plane was not damaged by their gunfire but Tamara's plane was, and I was filled with despair when I saw her plane dropping away, spinning and on fire. I realized that I would have to continue the attack alone, and I continued making passes at the bombers, shooting, and setting sev-

Raisa Surnachevskaya, 586th regiment

eral more of them on fire, but I didn't shoot them down. Our task was not to shoot the enemy down so much as to prevent them from reaching their target; in this instance, the railroad station.

Then there was a jolt. My aircraft was hit, there was steam and smoke in the cockpit, and the oil temperature rose to the red line, but still I could handle the plane—it was controllable—and I chose a field to make an emergency landing. But first I also made sure that I was over our territory and not behind the German lines. I landed on a hill, with my landing gear up; it was a belly landing to try to prevent my plane from turning over. In the valley below there was a village, so I tried to land so as to not further damage the aircraft or the people in the village. I wanted to transmit over my radio that I was making a forced landing, but I couldn't transmit.

When the plane stopped I got out of the cockpit and took my parachute out, and I was thinking all the time about Tamara, because I saw her plane go down, and I thought she might have been killed. Then the civilians from the village and collective farm came toward my plane armed with sticks and spades and rushed to the aircraft, because they thought it might be a German plane. When they saw a girl, they stood still, fascinated! The chief of the collective farm came up to me and asked for documents. That area and farm had recently been occupied by the Germans, and they were very afraid. I said to the man, "First you show me your documents and then I will!"

I left my aircraft there and told the villagers that it would be taken away by the mechanics. When they came for my aircraft, they counted forty-three bullet holes in it. Afterward it was completely repaired, and I flew all my missions in that particular aircraft.

When I left my plane after I was shot down, I walked to the telegraph station to notify my regiment that I had been shot down and was returning to Voronezh. I was thinking about Tamara, and I asked the staff there if I could call my regiment to find out if she was safe. They said that already another young girl with a parachute had been there to notify Voronezh that she was safe. And then I saw her and she was safe!

Later, in another battle, I shot down another German plane. It was a reconnaissance aircraft, and I was flying with the commander of the regiment, and we shot the German plane down.

Senior Sergeant Galina Drobovich,
regimental mechanic of the aircraft

I was born in the town of Smolensk in 1921, and my mother and grandmother raised me, because my father started another family. He was a Russian intelligence officer. When I was three years old we moved to Moscow. I completed nine grades of a secondary school and then worked in an aviation plant, but I had never been in an airplane. I worked as a controller in the instrument laboratory of the plant.

I went in for mountain climbing, and I was among the mountain climbers who were to conquer the peaks of the Caucasus Mountains. When the war actually started I was climbing the highest peak, Elbrus. We got back to Moscow with great difficulty, because trucks, carts, and trains all were crowded with people being evacuated or trying to return home. Part of the time we traveled on the roofs of the train because the cars were overflowing. When at last we arrived in Moscow we went immediately to the Military Commissariat to enlist in the army. There were huge crowds of people trying to enlist. They wouldn't enlist me because I was a woman.

I attended courses to train medical personnel and continued working in the plant. Then the Germans started bombing Moscow, and there were many wounded civilians. We picked them up and took them to hospitals. Then I worked in a military hospital taking care of the wounded brought from the front. My working day at the aviation plant was twelve hours, and I worked in the military hospital at night. We had very little sleep.

I heard about Marina Raskova forming the women's air regiments, and I went to Komsomol headquarters and asked to be taken in to this regiment. Before I went to be interviewed by Raskova, I put on my Alpinist boots and overalls. When Raskova saw me, she smiled and asked me what I would like to do at the front. I told her I wanted to be a machine gunner. She then appointed me as a mechanic of the aircraft. I think she took me right away because I wore the badge of First Grade Alpinist on my overalls.

I trained in Engels, and then I was assigned to work with the Yak fighter plane in the 586th Fighter Regiment. I remember when the Yaks were first brought to Engels, because up until then we had only worked with models in the classroom, and it was altogether another thing to work outside when the wind was blowing and the temperature was forty below zero. When we touched the metal of the engine our skin would stick to it, and some of it came off on the metal. Our cheeks and foreheads were frozen too. On returning to the barracks our hands would be a deep blue color.

At the front, when our crews were flying combat missions near our airdrome, we mechanics could recognize the sound of our guns and machine guns as a mother can tell the voice of her child. If the sound stopped, we felt we had failed our pilots because we hadn't properly prepared the aircraft for the mission, and thus our pilots could become an open target for the enemy. We worried until our planes returned.

After the war I worked at the Kurtchatov Nuclear Research Institute. Then I married and had two children, and I still work as the assistant telephone station master in the Olympic Games Center in Moscow.

Captain Klavdiya Terekhova-Kasatkina,
secretary of the party organization of the regiment

My duty was to bring up the young girls to be real soldiers, real military people. My parents were peasants who moved from their village to Moscow to earn some money, and here I was born. I graduated from a technical school, and after that I entered the Moscow Textile College. I was a very brave girl: I jumped with a parachute, rode horses, drove a car, I could do everything!

When I was finishing the third course at the college, the Great Patriotic War broke out. I went to my father and said, "There are three of us in our family, and at least one member of the family must go to the front and defend our motherland. I can do a lot of things—I will join the army and fight the hated enemy."

On the second day of the war I went to the Central Body of the Komsomol League in Moscow and was enrolled among its staff, and my department received a lot of letters from female pilots asking to be permitted to go to the front. There were so many letters that Marina Raskova, who later on founded the regiments, calculated that the number was equal to that required to form three regiments. This was the start of the female regiments. I too submitted an application asking to be admitted to such a regiment. And when the regiments were formed, I was appointed the secretary of the party organization of the 586th Fighter Regiment with the rank of senior lieutenant, designated by three small stars on the ribbons. By the end of the war I was a captain, designated by four small stars.

When the girls came to join the army they all looked like girls, with long, curly hair and high heels. The first thing to do was make them look all alike, like soldiers, with hair cut short, military boots, and pants. It was really very difficult to make the girls part with their hair and feminine things and put them into men's military clothing.

In the army air force it was obligatory for the girls to jump with a parachute, especially the pilots. The commander of our regiment didn't make a single jump because she was deadly afraid of it. They even threatened that she would be relieved of command, but she still said, "No, I'm afraid to do that!" The commander of our squadron, Tamara Pamyatnykh, didn't make a single jump either. In 1943, near Voronezh, she and her wingman intercepted German bombers, and in that fight Pamyatnykh's plane was hit and she had to jump!

About the uniforms: we were not allowed to do anything about those too large boots. Once in the morning, when we were in training, we all lined up, and Raskova faced us and gave the command: to the right. One of the girls turned to the right, but her boots remained in the same place, and she swerved and the boots didn't move. Raskova was a very strict woman, and she was young, just twenty-seven; she could have reprimanded her, but she didn't— she burst out laughing. Soon after that one girl was to show that she could pack her parachute rapidly and then jump. When she was jumping one boot fell off, then the other, then the leg wrappings that replaced socks, and only then did she come to the ground— barefoot! Then we were allowed to resew the boots. We have a saying in Russia: if there hadn't been an unhappy incident there never would be a happy one!

Valentina Lisitsina, 586th regiment

When the girls were ordered to cut their hair very short, only one girl, Lilya Litvyak, refused to do it. I came to report to Raskova and said, "Comrade Major, your order has been carried out; everyone has had their hair cut but Lilya," and Raskova replied, "My order has not been fulfilled." I came to Lilya with tears in my eyes and asked her to please to do it, and at last she agreed.

When we were at the front, one of the regimental duties was to protect the aircraft of important people. Zoya Pozhidayeva was assigned along with five other female pilots and six male pilots from another regiment to guard the plane of a government official. When the aircraft landed and the guard planes took off to fly back to their respective airfields, Zoya decided to trick one of the male pilots and flew around his plane several times. He cursed her with very bad names. When our planes landed and our commander asked if the flight had been successful, Zoya said, "Yes, but we should never fly with the men again because they cursed and called me bad names." Our commander called the commander of the male regiment and told him that our girls refused to fly with them anymore because of their bad behavior. The male commander lined up the whole crew and said, "How could you do that? How dare you do that? There were girls in those planes, and you have to behave yourselves!" And the pilot who had done the cursing said, "Oh my God, I didn't know they were

girls! I would have never opened my mouth and uttered such words!"
He decided to apologize and got into his plane and flew to our regiment. He apologized to Zoya for what he had done, and they became
friends and corresponded throughout the war, and when it ended
they were married.

Besides my work, I was responsible for some amateur concerts, and
also our regimental newspaper that we wrote ourselves—not printed—
written by hand. The duty of a political activist was not only to speak
in the meetings and to do reports describing the political and military
situation but mostly to have very close contact with all the girls and
talk with them individually. When a girl was assigned a mission to
fly but had to wait for some time in the cockpit before the mission, I
would come up to her and talk about politics. The girls used to say,
"Well I'm sorry, but go to hell with your politics, let's discuss love
affairs!" They were patriots and would gladly talk politics, but they
would say that it might be their last flight and they might not return,
and they didn't want to talk politics, they wanted to review their
emotions. There was a pressure that filled their bodies, and those
personal talks helped me get to know them better.

I knew everything about the family affairs of almost every girl,
their love affairs, everything. Not like a mother, but still I was very
close to them; they were frank. Moreover, such intimate talks eased
pressure in their hearts. Before the flight they were fearless, but after
they returned from a mission they felt a nervous strain and emotional
outburst.

One day the two girls who flew a mission in which they engaged
forty-three bombers returned and were having a rest under the wings
of their planes. I asked them if they experienced great fear while
fulfilling their missions, and they said, "Yes, very much," and their
legs were trembling still. One of them, Raisa, said that she was so
frightened and overstrained that she would never fly again. Well, after
she calmed down and pulled herself together, she went on performing
her missions—it was an immediate reaction.

It was especially hard mentally and emotionally to come through
the experience of losing our friends. It was a great strain, and it took
strength for me to somehow raise their spirits. In our regiment twelve
girls perished. When the brilliant commander of one of our squadrons
returned from a mission and suddenly crashed before our eyes and
died, we wanted to find her body, her remains, and we didn't find
anything at all. There was no special ceremony when someone perished. There was a coffin, and we stood beside it and said something

Leaving headquarters (a dugout) for a mission in 1942, 586th regiment

about the dead person and cried, and then buried them right there in the fields.

Our first losses were at our training site at Engels. We lost two crews, two pilots in each aircraft. It was a shock for us and a misery, and we sobbed beside their coffins, and Raskova turned to all of us and said, "My darlings, my girls, squeeze your heart, stop crying, you shouldn't be sobbing, because in the future you have to face so many of them that you will ruin yourselves completely." And since that time we have suffered great losses and overcome the gravest experiences, and we were, and we remain, the closest of friends. We swore that after the war ended, each year we would have our reunion. And we do.

Senior Sergeant Inna Pasportnikova,
mechanic

There is a monument to Lilya Litvyak, and each star on it is for a German aircraft she shot down. When they erected the monument to Lilya, they left a blank space on the stone so that one day "Hero of the Soviet Union" could be added. They searched for her plane and body for fifteen years. Only in May, 1990, was she awarded the Gold Star.

Lilya Litvak, 586th Fighter Regiment

Lilya had crash-landed in a field and died there, and persons unknown buried her under the wing of the plane. Later people came and disassembled the aircraft, and no one knew Lilya was buried there. I was her mechanic when she joined the male regiment at Stalingrad but not before, in the female regiment. She flew the Yak fighter during the war. When the war broke out, she was a flight instructor.

Engels, on the Volga River, was our training base. We went to Engels in October, 1941, and were given our winter uniforms in November. Once, when we were all standing in formation, Lilya was told to step forward. She was in winter uniform, and she had cut the tops off of her high fur boots and made a fur collar for her winter flying suit. Marina Raskova, our commander, asked when she had done this, and Lilya replied, "During the night." Lilya wanted to have this fashion. Raskova said that during the next night she shouldn't sleep but must take the fur collar off and put it back on the boots. She was arrested and put in an isolation room, and all night she was changing it back. This was the first time she was noticed by the other women. She was a very small person. It was strange: the war was going on, and this blonde, this girl, was thinking about her collar. I wondered, What kind of a pilot will she make when she doesn't think of more important things than the collar and how she looks! After this I started to watch her, and she was one of the best pilots; she flew her program perfectly. I never thought the time would come when I would be her mechanic.

Our regiment, the 586th Fighter Regiment (Air Defense), was the first to be formed from the training regiment with about twenty pilots. In the beginning there were only two squadrons, and the regiment's first assignment was to protect Saratov city on the Volga River. The most important thing there was the bridge across the river—the only bridge in that area. The first woman pilot to shoot down a German aircraft in that vicinity was Valeriya Khomyakova, who was later killed in a dogfight.

In September, 1942, some of our pilots, including Lilya, were sent to different male regiments protecting Stalingrad during that terrible battle, and I was sent there also, to be Lilya's mechanic. Lilya bleached her hair white, and she would send me to the hospital to get hydrogen peroxide liquid to do it. She took pieces of parachute, sewed them together, painted it different colors, and wrapped it around her neck.

Lilya was very fond of flowers, and whenever she saw them she picked them. She would arrive at the airfield early in the morning in the summer, pick a bucket of flowers, and spread them on the wings of her plane. She especially loved roses. In the winter she wrote to her mother in Moscow asking for a picture with roses. Her mother couldn't find a picture, so she asked me to write to my mother, who sent a postcard with roses, but the roses were yellow and Lilya liked red. She put the picture of roses on the left side of the instrument panel and flew with it. She was pretty and thin and looked like the actress Serova, who was quite famous. Lilya was born in 1921, and at that time she was twenty years old and I was twenty-one.

The day Lilya didn't come back from a mission—when she perished—I was not there at the airdrome. I had been sent to take the entrance examinations for the Airforce Academy, so that day, unfortunately, I wasn't there. I was the only woman who entered the academy and there were no barracks for women, so I had to come back to my regiment. When I arrived I was told Lilya had not returned yesterday. I served on her crew for about eight months.

It was very difficult to work as a mechanic—that is a man's job. The airdrome was often bombed by the Germans, and there was some artillery shelling, but I wasn't afraid for my life. I was just waiting for Lilya to come back; I was impatient for her to return from her flight. The aircraft flew about five flights a day when the weather was good, starting at sunrise. The pilots stayed in a village nearby, and we mechanics slept at the airdrome near the aircraft in open trenches. When it became cold in the winter, we took the engine cover and put it over ourselves, and in the morning we would wake up with ice on our hair and faces.

My hands are scarred and misshapen because of the kerosene we used. Many parts of the engine were very hard to get to, and it was impossible to wear our gloves when we worked. When it was very cold I would touch the engine, and my fingers stuck to it, and it pulled the skin off. The brakes worked by air pressure, and the compressor air container weighed sixty kilograms. In the summer I could roll it, but in the winter I had to carry it. I would put it on my shoulder and carry it from one plane to another, because the engines started with pressurized air.

Sometimes men flew the same aircraft as Lilya, for there was a shortage of planes. Lilya was very small and short, and each time the men flew it I had to fix the pedals, then fix them again when Lilya flew, and it took time. My friends used to say, "You are always with your legs up," because I had to go head first into the cockpit to change the rudder pedals; I had to dive into the cockpit.

Lilya was wounded twice before she perished. She was first wounded in her leg, and even after this she kept on fighting. She managed to land the aircraft, but she couldn't taxi or get out of the cockpit because of her wound. The second time she was wounded she belly-landed on German territory, and she could see them running toward her but she escaped them. It happened that if you were shot down and landed, one of your aircraft would land next to you if they saw it. At that time another Soviet fighter pilot landed and picked up Lilya, and she escaped. There were two different airdromes in our area, and when the pilot flew back with Lilya, he landed on the other airfield so nobody knew who he was; she never found out.

Lilya shot down twelve enemy planes by herself, including a balloon; she shared three others. The balloon was a threat to that whole area of the front, and it was protected by many anti-aircraft guns and had a German officer observing from it. Many Soviet airmen tried to shoot it down but turned back, because there was a wall of fire from the guns. Lilya volunteered to shoot it down. She was just out of the hospital from her wounds, promising the doctors she would go visit her mother and recover, but she spent only one day, then returned to her regiment. She went to the regimental commander and said, "Let me shoot down the balloon." He said she could not, for she was still ill and had no right to fly. She told him that if he did not let her do it she would do it without his permission, and he told her in that case she should tell him how she was going to do it.

She took off and flew—not straight to the front line, but parallel to it, to the area where there were no German troops or artillery. She crossed the front line and flew to the rear, choosing the time of day when she could approach the balloon from the direction of the sun. Nobody expected her to appear from that side; she fired, and it caught fire and went down. This was in the spring of 1942. She was a senior lieutenant. Lilya's real name was Lydiya. Her mother called her Lilya, and Lilya herself liked to be called that name because in Russian *lilya* means lily-flower.

When Lilya approached the airdrome after a victory, it was impossible to watch her; she would fly at a very low altitude and start doing acrobatics over the field. Her regimental commander would say, "I will destroy her for what she is doing, I will teach her a lesson!" After she landed and taxied to her position she would ask me, "Did our father shout at me?" And he did shout at her, and then he admired what she had done. She flew over the field so low the covers of the aircraft would flap and fly around, she created such a wind! When she was shot down the first time, she received a new Yak-1 aircraft. Men pilots tried to stop her from flying because they wanted to save her, but it was impossible. She was a flight commander; there were three aircraft in a flight.

Earlier Lilya flew as wingman with the squadron commander, Alexei Salomatin. They loved each other, and he taught her about combat. One day Lilya was sitting in the cockpit in readiness two—readiness one is on the runway. Lilya and I were talking, with me sitting on the wing of the plane while she was waiting for her turn to take off, and at this time the squadron commander and a new, young pilot were up flying. Alexei was training him, doing aerobatics with engines roaring, and then one of the aircraft started coming down with a roar, crashed, and exploded. Everyone thought it was the new pilot, but no, it was the squadron commander, it was Alexei. Something happened to his plane, and he didn't have time to bail out. We buried him, and after this happened Lilya didn't want to stay on the ground, she only wanted to fly and fight, and she flew combat desperately. This happened in May, 1943, and Lilya perished on August 1.

She was returning from a mission of escorting the Il-2 aircraft, sometimes called the flying tank, and from somewhere behind the clouds, two German aircraft appeared. Lilya and her wingman, who were flying along the edge of the bomber squadron, were attacked, and she was shot down. She tried to escape by diving into the clouds, and at this point another Soviet pilot, Ivan Borisenko, saw this scene and tried to find her after she dove. He looked everywhere but couldn't find her. He never saw an aircraft explode or a pilot jump with a parachute. She never returned from that mission.

In reality she managed to belly-land the aircraft near a village. She was buried under the wing of the plane. We don't know who buried

Left to right: Valentina Guozdikova, Klavdiya Pankratova,
Lilya Litvyak, 586th regiment

her, the fascists or the Soviet soldiers who liberated the village the
next day. And we also don't know whether she was mortally wounded
in the crash or killed by the Germans on the spot.

In August, 1943, the commander of her regiment wrote all the
documents to posthumously award her the title of Hero of the Soviet
Union. But because there was no evidence of her death, no trace of her
or the aircraft, this procedure was stopped, and the rumor was that
she might have become a prisoner of the Germans. There were many
rumors of various sightings of her as a prisoner in camps and speculation about what happened to her, but until this year (1990), there was
no evidence. I personally searched for her plane for three years with
my husband and grandchildren, using a metal detector. We found
thirty aircraft but not hers.

Lilya's father was killed in 1937 during the repressions, and Lilya
was very afraid to die somewhere unknown. It was her feeling, and
she was very afraid of it. Lilya's brother had to change his name to his
mother's name. He said his father was tortured and killed in 1937, and
he changed his name to save his own life. I don't blame him; nobody
would blame him who lived in that time. He said his father was killed

in a concentration camp; his sister, no one knows where; and there were rumors about her going over to the Germans. It was very hard times for him. Lilya's mother decided to treat me as Lilya's sister. She never knew about the happy ending of this story.

A few years ago, two boys were playing in a field in Belorussia and saw a snake that went into a hole. They decided to widen the hole to take the snake away, and they found a body—her body. So they dug it out and invited the commission, the specialists, to inspect the remains. This commission wrote a paper that said it was the body of a woman pilot, very small; and they found hair, her flying suit, and a gold tooth. Then the commission reburied her in a village nearby. People had been searching for her body for fifteen years. In May, 1990, President Gorbachev signed the decree that made Lilya Litvyak posthumously a Hero of the Soviet Union. Now I have a right to die. I swore that I would find Lilya before I died and that has happened, so now I can die.

NOTE: Lilya Litvyak's brother, with great pride, showed me her Gold Star of Hero of the Soviet Union medal and the citation signed by Mikhail Gorbachev.

Senior Sergeant Valentina Kislitsa,
mechanic of the aircraft

My parents were teachers in a small village settlement where I was born in 1922. It was in the region of Stavropol in the Caucasus, the same region where Gorbachev was born. My father was killed in 1922 in the Civil War. In 1938 I finished secondary school and came to Moscow, where I enrolled in the Moscow Aviation University. I was a third-year student when the Great Patriotic War began. It was summertime and I was supposed to go home to spend my holiday, but because of the war I stayed in Moscow to work in a plant as a controller. My university was evacuated to an Asian republic. So at that time I decided to volunteer for the army and was accepted into Raskova's regiments. After training I was assigned to the 586th Fighter Regiment, and we went to the front. I stayed with the regiment until the end of the war.

After the war I returned to the university, and upon graduation I worked for the Central Aerohydrodynamic Research Institute. This institute resembles NASA in its research. I am not retired; I still work as an engineer economist. I have been working at this institute for forty-two years.

Lieutenant Valentina Volkova-Tikhonova, pilot

Valentina Volkova-Tikhonova,
586th regiment

Before the war, I was a pilot instructor in the glider school. I had a great amount of flying hours. When the war broke out, I taught the young men to fly the U-2. I was twenty-three when I started flying. When I went into the women's regiment in 1942, I was twenty-seven. We flew the Yak-1, and we guarded certain important places on the ground. When we moved forward into Voronezh, the remains of the Germans and Soviets killed in the fighting had not yet been removed, and when snow and ice started melting and the river began moving, the river was red with blood.

We landed in an area formerly occupied by the Germans, and the town was completely destroyed. Apart from the wreckage we could see gallows everywhere, used by the Germans to hang their own people. The airfield was mined, and they couldn't find the mines because they were a special kind, so only the runway was clear. There were a lot of aircraft in the air, and one of my girlfriends who was a pilot stood on the side of the runway and shot a rocket into the air to identify the airfield for our pilots. A rocket malfunctioned and fell into the grass at the side of the runway and started burning the dry grass. My friend threw a blanket on it to put out the fire and started jumping on it to smother the flames, and she jumped onto a mine. She was thrown into the air, and I was thrown aside by the explosive force. She was taken to the hospital, and none of us could tell whether she was alive or dead—she was alive. Gunpowder got under her skin, and the doctors could do nothing about that. Her face remained dark with powder burns for the rest of her life.

When I was young during the war, I was convinced it was a job for a woman to fly combat. In those times our only thought was to defend the motherland, to save the country. I didn't think of it as emotional and physical pressure. I had become a pilot before the war, and it was only natural for me to become a military pilot. Now I realize that the stress was very great and that it is not a female job. The task was even more aggravating because when you are the sole person in the plane, you have to be extremely alert and aware; you are the gunner, navigator, and pilot all in one person.

We constantly had two aircraft on alert. As soon as the enemy was spotted, we took off to attack. Our planes flew at 600 kilometers per hour, our altitude was as high as 10 kilometers (33,000 ft.), and we flew with oxygen. Our job was to keep the enemy from getting to their target.

I was considered to be a second-generation military pilot. I joined the regiment in 1942. I flew in the daytime, and some of my friends were night fighters. The night flights were the most dangerous. The night fighter pilots said goodbye before they left and kissed each other at dawn when they returned. We waited for them to return, and when they all came back we were happy.

I had 518 hours of combat flying during the war.

Sergeant Nina Shebalina,
mechanic to the commander of the regiment

First I was a mechanic of the regiment, and then I was the mechanic to the commander of the regiment. I was surprised when it happened; I was proud and at the same time a little afraid. It was a very important and responsible position. When the war started I was a third-year student at the Moscow Aviation Institute preparing to acquire the profession of designing aircraft. Like all girls at that time I was a patriot, and I tried to volunteer. I wrote a special letter asking that I be allowed to go to the front, and at last I was allowed to join the regiment that Raskova founded. My knowledge then was completely theoretical—I was a student.

At first I was mechanic to Raisa Belyayeva, the commander of a squadron, and she was killed. She was returning from a combat mission, and suddenly I saw her aircraft dive into the ground. We never knew what happened to her or why this happened. She was in communication with the field and the other aircraft in her squadron, and abruptly the communication stopped, and the plane just dove into the ground. We think she was overstrained or fainted. No bullet had hit her. It was a terrible shock to me. When she perished I had already been reassigned to the aircraft of the regimental commander, even though I was fearful of having such a responsibility on my shoulders. I remained in this assignment for the remainder of the war.

I was never arrested while I was in the army—it wasn't common. I remember two or three times girls were arrested, but it was because they violated some established rules or discipline, and you know that the army is the army, and discipline is the first and foremost thing. Probably they were most often arrested because they ran away to a dance when they were supposed to guard the planes. Some were very strong-headed, and they didn't want to obey orders.

The living conditions were really very difficult for us. The pilots were provided with very primitive quarters, but we lived in trenches that we dug on the airfield at the tails of our planes. These trenches were covered only with canvas, so we lived underground. First of all, there was no place to live; and second, there was no time to sleep. In daytime the pilots flew combat missions, and in the nighttime we had to repair the aircraft. We worked at night with a cover over the engine and used torches for light. In some areas we lived in destroyed houses or in barracks if they were available.

The first shock of being at the front came at Stalingrad. We arrived by fighter-bomber, and when our aircraft landed and we emerged from the plane, the artillery shelling began; we were caught in the shelling. I was a young girl and I was frightened. The regiment had not been informed of our arrival, and they didn't come to meet us. When the girls began jumping from the fighter-bomber and the men in the regiment saw us being shelled, they ran to us and pushed us into their trenches, covering us with their bodies. Thus we lay still all together until the shelling ceased. None of our flying personnel perished in the bombings and strafing during this period, but I did see one girl from the logistics battalion, who had served us our dinner, killed carrying a tray with dishes.

During the four months that I was a mechanic for the aircraft I lost two male pilots. At that time there was a great shortage of planes, and the planes we did have had to alternate between pilots. So when a woman pilot would return from a combat mission, a male pilot would take the aircraft on another mission, and the aircraft were flown nearly all the time. We had to examine the aircraft after every mission and to fuel it if it had sustained no damage.

In the 586th there was one squadron of male pilots and two of women with ten planes and pilots in each. During the war we lost ten women pilots. Both the commander and chief navigator of our regiment were men.

After the war I went back to my undergraduate work and graduated as an aeronautical engineer five years after the war ended. It took so long because I had two brothers who became invalids from the war, my father was an invalid of war, and my mother was very old, so I had to go home to the Ukraine to help the family. I worked at the Research Institute of Radio Electronics as an engineer. The war added much to my courage and much to my character, and later on, when I received my diploma for a master's degree, it was very different from the mechanics work I had done in the war.

During the war my attitude toward my aircraft was really like it was a living creature, like a baby. I cared for it every day and night, and I had to go through lots of tears when I lost my plane. I saw it off and said goodbye to it when they went on a combat mission, and then I was impatiently awaiting their return. If it didn't come back it was a misery, a misfortune. When I received a new plane, it took some patience and time for me to accustom myself to it. We all knew our own aircraft: you didn't have to see it, you just heard it and you knew. In between flights, when we were waiting for our planes to return, we had a little time to sit on the grass to talk and laugh.

Sometimes we had a day off, and we gathered in the barracks or wherever, combed our hair, and trimmed ourselves. We wanted to make ourselves look pretty and attractive and womanlike, in spite of the uniform clothing. Our regiment was a female regiment, but there were a lot of male pilots and mechanics, and we wanted to make an impression. Lots of us fell in love, and after the war we married, having been through the war together. Yes, we had time to fall in love—life is life!

Once before a combat mission my aircraft got out of order. I had to fix it quickly, but it was a complicated task, and I couldn't finish it in the short time before the mission. Two male and two female mechanics helped me—that was the way we were—we all helped each other.

The regiment consisted of very intelligent girls, graduates of universities and institutes. We even had a poet. She studied at Moscow University in the philology department, and she composed verses and we recited them; moreover, we sang those verses using the melodies of well-known songs. We danced a lot, made fun, teased each other, and laughed.

All of us at the front were obsessed by the idea that our land must be liberated.

Senior Lieutenant Galina Burdina,
pilot, commander of the formation

I was born into a very large and poor family. We had to exist without a father, and I had never dreamed of becoming a pilot. At the age of fourteen I had to work as a laborer, and simultaneously I was attending secondary school in the evening part time. When I was seventeen I was admitted to glider school. Then I was sent to continue my studies at the civil aviation pilot school in Ulyanovsk. I graduated and was sent back to Sverdlovsk to work as a pilot instructor. In September, 1941, our school was turned into a military pilot school; I trained military pilots there.

When war broke out, all the girls volunteered into the army and wanted to help the country. At that time we were flying the Ut-2, a sport aircraft. It was a transitional plane between a training and a military aircraft. It had a covered cockpit—a canopy. Later we three girls who were instructors received orders to be in Moscow within twenty-four hours, and when we arrived we were told that we were to be admitted to the women's regiment. When we arrived at Engels, the training base for the regiment, Marina Raskova looked at us and said that we three were going to be fighter pilots!

At the front, Tamara Pamyatnykh and I first flew as a pair in the Yak fighters. While I was in Tamara's squadron I was trained to fly at night. Then I became a night fighter. Our main task was to fly over the major industrial areas of the cities located close to the front line and safeguard important positions. We also escorted our dive bombers over the front line and guarded transports carrying important persons.

We were stationed in the Ukraine, and on April 5, 1943, which is in the middle of spring, it began snowing. It is a rarity for that time of year, and all the airfields were shut down and incapable of receiving any aircraft. It snowed very heavily during the night again, and the snowstorm blew huge drifts. That night we were to fly combat missions. In spite of the fact that the runways had been cleared, heaps of snow were here and there. We were lined up and told the flight could be very risky, and were there any volunteers? Tamara and I were the first to volunteer, to risk it in any weather. It kept on snowing heavily, and we wondered how we would take off. It would be very difficult. Then we received a radio signal that the enemy was approaching; a large group of German bombers was flying in the direction of the railroad. We didn't believe we would be given permission to fly, for that flight might very well be our last in those conditions. But then a

Left to right: Galina Burdina, unidentified, and Alexandra Makunina, 586th regiment

rocket was shot into the air signaling me to take off. It was snowing, and the white reflected light and that helped.

I was ordered to fly to the area of the railroad where the German planes were approaching. When I saw the German planes I ascended a bit, to be higher than the enemy. I heard on the radio that Tamara was also ordered to take off to help with the mission. When Tamara joined me, we saw a large number of German bombers dropping flares by parachute to light the area they were to bomb. They thought that with the bad weather there would be no Soviet fighters in the air. We were the only two that made it. We were above the bombers, and we could see that there was a great black mass of them, and I dove into the mass and fired all my weapons. Then we both turned and made another run through them, and then again, so that the Germans would think there were many of us. The bombers began dropping their bombs a distance from the railway; they didn't reach their target and turned back.

When the bombers turned back we too were ordered back. Then we were told that it would be impossible for us to make a safe landing, and we were ordered to jump from our planes. I just couldn't jump; I loved my aircraft and I begged them to think of some other way. I couldn't give up my aircraft. Beneath us was an airfield of a male bomber regiment. They didn't want us to die, and their commander had an idea. He had his men gather all the flares from their planes, and they shot them into the air a few at a time and lit the runway for me to make a landing. I made a safe landing, but because of the heavy snow the aircraft nosed down into the snow but wasn't damaged.

I was very anxious about Tamara and calculated that her plane was running out of fuel. Moreover, I lost radio contact with her. Tamara knew that it was impossible to make a safe landing at our own airfield, and she had decided to change her course to Kiev. She told me later that she had flown to Kiev, but she couldn't land there either because of the heavy snow. She turned back and decided to jump by parachute over her own regimental airfield. Then she saw the flares being shot into the air, and she too made a safe landing. The very moment she landed the engine quit; she was completely out of fuel.

Another time Tamara and I were to carry a very urgent message to the Stalingrad front. We landed at a male fighter airdrome, and a fighter pilot met us and questioned us, asking who we were and where we had flown from, and we told him we were from the female fighter regiment. He didn't believe such young girls could be fighter pilots. Then he accompanied us to headquarters, and we delivered the message. We were told not to take off because by then it was nighttime; moreover, in the air over the Stalingrad front there were heavy battles every day. The Germans were constantly loitering over the airfield, and every time an aircraft took off, they tried to shoot it down. The commander told us to wait until early morning and take off with the male fighter regiment stationed there, so they could protect us.

But the next morning we overslept. When we came to the airdrome they had already taken off. The commander ordered us to wait until the next formation went out on a mission. We decided we didn't need protection and made up our minds to fly alone. We got into our aircraft and told the commander we only wanted to warm up our engines. We took off, and the weather was cloudy. We could see the German aircraft behind us, but they didn't like to fly in cloudy weather, so we dove in and out of the clouds and made it back to our airdrome safely.

In the Kiev region the Germans were retreating. Large groups of German troops and armament were encircled by the Soviet troops, and the Germans tried to break out. I flew my plane along with the commander of our regiment to loiter over the area. We were assigned the mission of shooting down the aircraft sent in by the Germans to fly out their high-ranking officers from the encirclement. We shot down two Messerschmitts and a cargo aircraft.

It was in the territory of Romania, where the Romanian troops had already gone over to our side, that I met a Romanian pilot. Our regiment was stationed on the same airfield as a Romanian regiment. One of their pilots came up to me and told me that he knew me. He said he had seen me in the battle over Kiev. In that battle I had been covering my commander, and all my attention had been concentrated on that duty. This pilot had flown quite close to me in that battle, and when he recognized that I was a woman, he decided not to fire at me, not to shoot me down. So he gave me back my life.

I participated in many combat missions, and the one time that my plane was shot down, I made a belly landing. I was wounded in my head, face, and mouth. Part of my lower lip was torn, and it was hanging down. I was never shot down or wounded again. All in all I shot down four enemy aircraft.

After the war I returned to a pilot school and taught flying to cadets, and then I flew for fifteen years in civil aviation for Aeroflot.

Sergeant Irina Lunyova-Favorskaya,
mechanic of armament

When we meet every five years in October, we tell each other time after time that the reason we never tire of each other over all these years is because we all came together at the same time and volunteered to join the regiment. I was a student in the Institute of Geology in Moscow, a second-year student. I was born in 1921, and in 1940 I finished secondary school, then entered the institute. I wanted to join the army to help the country beat the fascist Germans, to liberate the motherland. My comrades in arms, I discovered, all joined for the same reason.

When we heard it was Raskova that was forming regiments, and she was so attractive, so intelligent, we all wanted to serve under her very much. It happened that on October 10 all of us had submitted our papers to the Central Committee asking to be allowed to go to the front. On the sixteenth the Hitlerite fascists were located only twenty-four kilometers from Moscow. I am a native Muscovite as were my parents and grandparents. All were born here, and it is the loveliest and dearest place in the world, and I didn't want it to be captured by the Germans—it was an emotion of my heart!

The war broke out on June 22, and on July 3 many of the students from my institute along with other colleges and universities were called to the front line to dig the trenches around Moscow, not far from the town of Smolensk. Two units had been formed at the geology institute to dig the trenches. One unit consisted of the first- and second-year students, and I was a part of that unit.

When we were called we were asked to take meals for three days. Concerning clothes and other things, we were not warned about anything, so we were in our summer dresses—light summer dresses. It was a very hot summer, and all we had with us was the clothes we had on. We were loaded into trucks and driven on the Minsk highway to near Smolensk, where we dug antitank trenches. It was a really hard job for us girls because our hands were not used to this work, and after the first day of digging, our hands turned to a mass of skin and blood. We covered them with bandages, and it took much time for them to recover. We couldn't hear the guns at all. The soldiers helped us by exploding the soil with gunpowder to make it easier to dig. Sometimes it was very useless. At one place we had been digging for three days, and on the third day a commander came to us and said, "Girls, you have to go because the enemy is advancing, and we have to retreat." So we put the spades on our shoulders and walked back to a new location and dug there. When we moved from one place to another, it was almost always at night. We were working along the forest, and at that time the German aircraft would fly over and begin dropping bombs on Moscow. When they flew raids over our city we couldn't fall asleep for two or three hours. We became very tired, and we would cry when we heard the sound of the engines overhead.

In order not to fall asleep while we were working, the girls would ask me to sing out loud. I had a beautiful voice when I was young. I was singing and crying at the same time; we were so tired. I started singing what the girls called concerts when we were marching; then I drifted to romantic songs, then folk songs to keep our spirits up, to help them keep walking, walking—not to fall asleep. Later on I began to sing to myself. Finally, when everybody was exhausted at night and I couldn't sing anymore and they couldn't walk anymore, we all fell into the dust. Because the village roads are not paved, they are dusty; we fell into this dust and went to sleep.

As I said, when we went to the front to dig we were told to take food for three days and nothing extra, so we went in our dresses. The summer was extremely hot, and it was impossible to dig trenches in those clothes. We spared our dresses because we were haunted with the fear that one day we would finish and return to Moscow and what would we wear! So in the daytime when we dug trenches we took off our dresses and dug in our underwear. The native population, the village population in our country, is very superstitious, old-fashioned, and traditional. When they saw us almost naked they said, "It is crazy people, how they appear in the daytime before all the men and women in their underwear!"

At that time, when our dresses became so very shabby, the Central Committee of the Komsomol remembered about us, and they sent Alexandra Makunina to the front line with clothes for all of the girls, and that is when I met Alexandra for the first time. Since that time we have been friends, and it turned out that we were later assigned to the same air regiment.

We were out there digging for more than a month. The choice of food was very primitive. They brought loaves of bread, sugar, and some grains from the military in Smolensk, and we had to cook it ourselves after digging all day. In the morning before we went to dig we had white bread, a cube of sugar, and water for breakfast; sometimes boiling hot water, but without tea.

When we had done our job there we asked the commander of the nearest regiment if we could stay, but in vain. When we returned to Moscow we again tried to volunteer for the army, but we were refused. Always we were sent to local committees. But suddenly I read in the Komsomol newspaper that the army might take us, and so we went to be interviewed. They talked with us before determining where we would go and inquired if we were afraid of fighting—to go to the front. No one got frightened at that time; we were young and brave. Later I heard about Raskova founding three regiments and that I was going to be in one of them.

At Engels, where we trained, I was assigned to armaments. In the winter of 1941, the cold was the most severe of the whole war. The temperature dropped to thirty-five degrees below zero centigrade; it was unbearable. We had to fix instruments on the aircraft with our bare hands, our skin stuck to the metal, and our hands bled. I wrote to my mother saying that it was unbearable to work with bare hands, and she sent a parcel to the front with a pair of pink silk ladies' gloves! I wore them, and all the girls laughed and made fun of me.

When I started as a mechanic of armament it was hard for me. There was supposed to be a technician assigned also, but there was none, so I performed all the work myself. The Yak fighters were new and intricate, and our education was limited. In March, 1942, the regimental commander brought in a male technician who was to help with our armament duties.

Later on, this man became the chief armament mechanic of the squadron. He assigned some work to me, and I didn't succeed in performing it successfully. I told him that I performed it as best I could, but he reprimanded me for that. Being not very reserved I blurted out some not very good words, and he heard them. His order, and his punishment, was to transfer me from mechanic of armament to motorist. That job was as an assistant to a mechanic of an aircraft. I washed the plane and did all the minor work. I was very cross and angry with this man, but I revenged myself on him; later on he became my husband!

In 1944 we were married, and last year he passed away. We not only fought at the front together; we also made merry, we fell in love, and he courted me for two years. I constantly refused to marry him. I told him, "The idea for my joining the army was to fight for our liberty, to serve, not to marry you!" Later on, I accepted. We have three children; we were married forty-five years. We have grandchildren and even one great-grandchild. My oldest daughter was born in 1945—victory year. I always say that my daughter was born together with the victory.

When we were stationed on the Volga River, again we experienced shortages of everything: food, bread, soap; we suffered great hardships. We had to patrol the airdrome, we had to work in the open air, and the conditions were difficult. My husband, Fyodor, had courted me for two years, and there was a rule that we must submit papers to the commander of the regiment asking for permission to marry. My husband submitted the papers, and the commander responded as follows: "I permit Senior Lieutenant Fyodor Favorskaya to marry Sergeant Irina Lunyova." But there was not a single mention of my acceptance to marry him! At that point I felt hurt. It is also customary to register a couple's marriage in a special establishment called the Palace of Matrimonial Procedures. There are two palaces in Moscow, and one branch of each in all Moscow districts. There at the front there was no palace, no establishment, no branch. There was nowhere to register our marriage. My husband was in a hurry to register because I was not an obedient girl; I was strong-willed and could decline his proposal, and God knows what could come into my mind. Moreover, he was seven years older than me, and in the regiment he was called Uncle Fedya because all the staff of the regiment were very young. My girlfriends tried to persuade me not to marry him—they said he was too old.

My younger son, having lived with his wife for five years, decided to get a divorce, and he did. He explained to me that they quarreled a lot, and they didn't want to be married any longer. I asked my son, "Do you think that we have lived for forty-five years together and never quarreled?" We did, and at one point my husband came to me and said, "Irina, I want to tell you we haven't quarreled for a long time," and I said, "Yes, I have noticed it." He asked, "Why?" and then answered for himself, "Because why should we quarrel when we know that in a few moments we'll have to reconcile!" If he hadn't been a really kind and wise man, always helpful to me with the children and household duties, I would never have given birth to our three children.

When I retired I joined the War Veterans Council here in Moscow, and I was responsible for the work in the Propaganda Committee, which gave many lectures at schools and institutes.

About our regiment: we haven't only cherished all these relationships for so many years, we have doubled them! When we don't see each other for a long time, we feel we lack these attachments, we lack these feelings, we miss each other greatly.

Junior Lieutenant Tamara Voronova,
pilot

I was born in the Volga region in 1922 in the town of Yaroslavl. When I was in the last grade of high school I learned to fly, and then I became a flight instructor. I graduated three groups of pilots, and then the war started. I flew my aircraft to a combat military regiment—it was a male fighter regiment—and I retrained to fly the Ut-4 aircraft. When a plane needed to be repaired, I was assigned to work in the regiment as a dispatcher.

The division commander came to my regiment, and when I told him I was very eager to fly, he transferred me to the liaison unit. I flew in that section one year and was given the rank of junior lieutenant. I carried messages from one unit to another. The commander of my regiment wanted me to retrain to fly the Yak-3 fighter, and I flew the Yak-3 as the only woman pilot in that regiment.

Later I flew the Yak-7 aircraft, and about that time I was transferred to the 586th Fighter Regiment. I arrived at the regiment in June, 1944, not long before the end of the war. I stayed with the 586th until the end of the war, when I was among a group of pilots ferrying aircraft to Vienna, Austria, and from there to Ploesti, Romania.

When I came to the female regiment I had a short training course with the commander of the squadron, and then I was assigned as a combat pilot. I was put on patrol over the Danube River. When I wasn't flying, I was in the cockpit in a state of alert called readiness one, waiting to intercept enemy aircraft when the remainder of our regiment was away on a mission. By the time I joined the regiment the Germans were retreating, and we seldom had encounters with enemy planes—we controlled the skies.

When the war ended, it came so suddenly that even though we expected it, it was a shock. We cheered and cried and shot our pistols off in the air. Our regiment met the victory in Hungary, not far from Budapest. The civilian population there was very friendly to us; we felt no hostility at all. I was discharged from the army in November, 1945.

After the war I returned to my native town, married an Il-2 pilot, and had four daughters. They all graduated from universities. Now I have four grandchildren.

Senior Sergeant Marina Muzhikova,
mechanic of the aircraft

I was born in 1923 in the Urals. When I voluntarily joined the regiment I was a second-year student at the Moscow Aviation Technical University. I served in the 586th Fighter Regiment from the first day of its formation until our release in 1945.

After the war, I returned to Moscow and entered a university to study law. Before the war, I was studying to be an aircraft designer. I changed my mind drastically after the war—only a woman who possesses the mind of a designer should connect her life with aviation. Being a mechanic of the aircraft was very difficult, both mentally and physically. It is not a woman's job. All our work at the front was hard labor.

I really wanted to study languages at the Linguistic University, but unfortunately they didn't provide hostels for the students and the university did, so my choice was influenced by that. I have been a lawyer now for thirty-six years and have never regretted my decision. It is my dedication. For the last eighteen years I have been a state arbiter in the Supreme Court of Arbitration. But I couldn't escape aviation—I have been considering cases connected with aviation all these years.

Lieutenant Yelena Karakorskaya,
deputy engineer of the squadron in special aircraft equipment

I was born in July, 1917. I was the sixteenth child in the family. My father was a Cossack peasant of pure Russian stock from the area of the Don River. Some of my brothers and sisters and I moved to the town of Novocherkask. I moved there to get an education. One of my sisters, who was nineteen years older than me, was married, and she and her husband adopted me because my parents by that time were very old. My stepfather was the commander of the North Caucasian Military District in Aviation. One of my brothers was a pilot in the Civil War and perished at the front.

In 1935 I entered a pilot training school in the navigation department; then that department was closed. At that point I could enter any aviation institute, and I did apply to enter, but my stepfather was repressed by Stalin, and I was not accepted. I stayed on at the school and entered their instrument department. In 1939 I became an engineer in aviation instruments. I was sent to the Finnish front and worked there as a technician in aircraft instruments during that war. The instruments were very primitive, and my work was manual labor under difficult conditions, because it was very cold there.

After the Finnish War I was transferred to the Moscow Central Aviation Detachment, where we worked on the Li-2 version of the American Douglas transport aircraft and other planes. This was on the eve of the Great Patriotic War. I already had the rank of a junior lieutenant, but I did all the work myself, checking the instruments after flights and repairing them.

When the war started, Marina Raskova selected me for her regiment. I became the engineer, and I supervised a group of five women who were specialists in instruments.

In September, 1942, I lost my close girlfriend, a pilot in our regiment, whom I had known for many years before the war. She took off on a mission and was climbing up to join the other aircraft when something happened to her plane, and it fell and crashed onto our airdrome. It was a great shock and loss for me.

When our regiment was stationed in Voronezh, a famous Russian pilot, A. I. Pokryshkin, three times a Hero of the Soviet Union, landed at our regimental airdrome. The Germans were afraid of him, and they even recognized his voice in the air. Our commander was away, and the deputy commander of our regiment, who was a former Tsarist officer, came to me and ordered our group (of engineers) to refuel Pokryshkin's aircraft. I replied that the manual forbade the engineers from fueling the aircraft; it was the duty of the mechanics. He grabbed me by my collar, and I pulled away; his hand slipped down onto my breast, and I slapped him on his face instinctively. He pulled out his pistol and wanted to shoot me, but the girls hung on his arm and prevented it. He then ordered me to be imprisoned for ten days, even though the officers' manual forbid the imprisonment of officers in the guardhouse.

The guardhouse of our regiment was situated in the basement of a house, and I was ordered to whitewash the walls. Every day he came there and checked my work. The basement had no electricity, and I had to whitewash the walls with the aid of a torch. There were lots of rats in the cellar, and I was without light. Only when I was working on the walls did I have light. I was afraid that one night a rat might bite me. I had to sleep in my uniform, and I wore my gloves, a cap on my head, and a scarf around my face to keep from being bitten.

While I was imprisoned I was the last to be fed in the mess, and the people on duty there sympathized with me and gave me extra food. I was always guarded, even when I went to the bathroom.

When the commander returned from his trip to Moscow, I called to him. He came to the cellar, saw the conditions, immediately released me, and gave me a day off to recover. The deputy commander was cruel to everyone, and for that he was discharged from the regiment.

Senior Sergeant Kareliya Zarinya,
mechanic of the aircraft

I was born in Saratov in 1919. My father was an economist. After finishing secondary school, I entered an automobile engineering university. Before the war I had attended a parachute school and made three jumps. When the war broke out, I voluntarily joined the 586th Fighter Regiment as a reinforcement. Until the end of the war I served in that regiment.

I was discharged from the army in August, 1945. I returned to my civilian profession and graduated from the university as an engineer. I am still working in Riga, Latvia. I come to Moscow to attend our regimental reunion.

NOTE: This interview was cut short because she had to catch a train back to Latvia.

Lieutenant Zoya Pozhidayeva,
senior pilot

I lived and worked in Moscow after I graduated from a trade school. In the evenings I attended a glider school. Then I was sent to pilot school to become a pilot instructor. When I graduated, I returned to Moscow to instruct. We flew both the Po-2 and the U-2 aircraft.

When the war broke out, we all went to the military commissariat and asked to be taken into the army. I was then twenty-two. I applied to the Komsomol Central Committee and the Communist Party Central Committee in Moscow, to no avail. I wrote to Marina Raskova, who received millions of letters from young girls all wishing to join the army and go to the front. She had received so many letters that she went to the government with a proposal to form a female air regiment. But so many girls had applied that it was decided to form three separate female regiments.

When our regiment, the 586th Fighter Regiment, was stationed near Saratov in September, 1942, I knew the grief of the first loss. My friend Olga Golisheva and I were to protect a railway and bridge. We fulfilled our mission and were returning home when we were assigned a training flight over our airdrome. I don't know what happened to her plane, but it nosed down into a dive and crashed. She might have been diving and couldn't pull it out of the dive. She didn't respond when I cried out to her over the radio, "Jump!" She never got out; she perished right in front of my eyes. I felt so terrible—it was not only my first loss but the first loss of the regiment.

I mainly escorted important people to the front, but I never knew who they were. They usually were flying to the Stalingrad front. Six of us were ordered to escort a high-ranking military officer from the Stalingrad front to the town of Kujbishev. We missed him because the weather conditions were very misty with poor visibility. When we were landing, the commander of our squadron, Yevgenia Prokhorova, crashed because we got into a dense fog and couldn't tell the earth from the sky. We were held at that airdrome for a long time while they investigated the cause of the crash, and it was at that time we also learned about Raskova's death.

In 1943 our regiment was transferred to Voronezh, and there I flew with two different wingmen. On one mission I took off with my wingman at 5 A.M., on an alert signal, to an altitude of 8,000 meters where we intercepted a German reconnaissance aircraft, a U-88. I transmitted that we had in sight an enemy aircraft and were approaching it. The German made a left turn and made it easy for us to attack. To escape, he made a deep dive and we followed, but the speed of our aircraft was so high it was impossible to attack. Very close to the ground, he pulled out of the dive and I followed, but I lost sight of my wingman, thinking she must have run out of fuel. I went on attacking him, and I could see the white trail of steam coming from his aircraft. But he crossed into German-held territory, and I ran out of fuel over the neutral ground between the Soviet and German lines and had to make an emergency landing.

All in all, I flew 237 combat missions. My husband was also a fighter pilot, and after the war I applied to the commander of the air army to be transferred to his regiment. I flew together with my husband until 1946, when I had a child. My husband was forming a fighter division in the Urals area, and we lived there until 1985, when I buried him. He flew the American Airacobra during the war and was a Hero of the Soviet Union.

I returned to Moscow to my daughter, and now I raise her two children.

Sergeant Zoya Malkova,
mechanic of the aircraft

We lived in a small textile city near Moscow where I graduated from a secondary school, and then, in 1937, my parents moved to Moscow and I entered the Moscow Aviation Institute. That was in 1939, so I finished a two-year course and wanted to be an engineer. It was a very prestigious institute. When the war broke out, all the young people were so very, very patriotic, and we visited military offices asking them to take us and send us to the front. That September, when I came back to the institute, my friends from the Young Communist League Committee told me to please be in a hurry and go to the Central Committee. That was in October, and I saw a long line of young people standing in line to join the army. I joined the army and I was nineteen.

At that time we looked at Raskova as a rather old woman, but we were very young then. She was an outstanding woman in our country; she was a military officer and navigator. Stalin's son, Vasily, was a pilot, and Stalin's favorite military field was aviation. That's why before the war, aviation was held in such high prestige, and that's why he liked three women fliers, Grizodubova, Osipenko, and Raskova. He liked and admired them greatly. He had made them Heroes of the Soviet Union even before the war. When Raskova wrote a letter to Stalin asking him to authorize a women's detachment and permit her to organize such a unit, he granted her request.

At that time and now, my position is that war is not for women; women shouldn't participate. In a way it's against their nature, because women's first purpose is to preserve peace and not to permit conflicts. Now, looking back from 1990, I think that at that time we didn't need this women's detachment, because 1941 was an awful time for the Soviet army and people. The fascist army was eighteen kilometers from Moscow, and even men pilots wasted their time because there were not enough aircraft for all of them. To some extent it was a kind of propagandist action, but still and all we were mostly happy that we joined the army.

We were elitist because students from aviation and pedagogical institutions and universities joined the army, and that is why the atmosphere in our detachments was intellectually high. We had serious discussions, we took a record player with us and listened to classical music, and then we swore not to be in love with anybody until the end of the war. We thought that our main task was to fight and not to have dates.

In 1943 there was a kind of breakthrough in the war at Kursk. At last our people realized and could see the victory, and that's why we permitted ourselves to be loved! Our detachment often had the same airfield as the men. We had dates and were in love with the boys. But I want to tell you that I speak rather often before young people, and I tell them that only during the war did I feel an atmosphere of man's nobility, a readiness to help. After the war, I never felt that in men's attitudes toward myself or the ladies.

I was a mechanic, and my duty was to prepare the planes for flying. There was severe frost at Stalingrad, our fingers stuck to the metal, and we had to carry very heavy things such as oxygen containers. At the same time this life gave me a lot. From my point of view, all the people should have some hard life to stimulate their energy, to open their abilities, and simply to bring them up adequately. I think that owing to my war experience I am strong, and I learned how to reach a goal and not to postpone or retreat but to be persistent, to be strong-headed. War gave me wide experience; my wartime service taught me how to live in a collective body, to communicate with other people, to subordinate my wishes, and to coordinate with the needs of other people.

After the war I was fed up with aviation, and I decided to choose the most humane profession—teaching. I graduated from a teachers' training institute and worked as a teacher for ten years in secondary schools. Then I defended my dissertation, took the doctor's degree, and finally moved up to the position of director of the Institute of Theory and History of Education. And really I am happy.

It was a noble war for our people; it was a great patriotic, enthusiastic feeling for all young people. For example, my younger brother was seventeen years old, and he added one year to his age to be accepted into the army. He was only at the front one year when he was killed near Kiev. His friend wrote to me how he had been killed, and I went there because it was twenty kilometers from where our regiment was stationed. I rushed there and opened his grave, and with their help I put him into a coffin, and then we reburied him. I could never do that now, when I'm sixty-eight years old, but then I was so young and brave, and he was so young, eighteen years old, and he had never even kissed a girl. Eighteen, and he was a commander of some detachment. We lost so many, and the best people, the best men. Some specialists think that we spoiled our genetic fund because we lost the best. The first to fight and the first to be killed.

The last of my war experience is that I have more than one hundred sisters. We regularly meet twice a year in front of the Bolshoi Theater on the second of May and the eighth of November. Outsiders look, and they can't understand old ladies that sing and make noise. Of course this war was a just war, and that is why we are proud of our participation.

Five
Women Fliers
in Male Regiments

Introduction

Women not only flew in the three regiments organized by Marina Raskova but in other diverse units of the Red Air Force. Anna Timofeyeva-Yegorova, deputy commander of the 805th Ground Attack Regiment, was the only woman pilot in that organization. She flew the powerful Illyushin Sturmovik.

Anna Popova flew with the 10th Guard Air Transport Division as a flight radio operator on an Li-2 twin-engine transport aircraft.

Pilot Olga Lisikova, also in the Transport Division, later flew in the Intelligence Directorate of the General Staff in C-47, lend-lease, American transport aircraft.

A number of other women who were later transferred to one of the women's regiments began the war in male units. Marina Raskova attempted to gather all the women serving in the air force into her regiments but was not entirely successful.

Senior Lieutenant Anna Timofeyeva-Yegorova,
pilot, deputy commander and navigator of the regiment
Hero of the Soviet Union
805th Ground Attack Regiment

When the war ended I returned to college for a master's degree in history and, later, another master of technical science degree at an aviation technical college. My husband was a pilot and our division commander during the war. He died ten years ago. I have two sons, and one of them is an air force pilot. I never sleep when I know he is flying.

I was born in 1918 in the town of Torzhok, between Moscow and Leningrad. When my father died, my brother brought me here to Moscow where he was working. I finished secondary school in Moscow, entered a trade school to become a locksmith, and then worked on the metro construction. In those days either you quit the Komsomol or you went to work building the metro. The metro was considered to be the most gorgeous and fabulous creation of the century, and all the young Komsomol members were expected to work on it.

While I was working, I also managed to complete some courses called *Rubfuk*, or workers' faculty, a four-year course. I also attended a glider school. When I finished that program I was transferred to the powered-aircraft pilot school in Kherson, where I trained to became a flight instructor, and then I taught cadets to fly. When the war broke out in 1941 I volunteered to go to the front.

It was September, 1941, the month of my first combat mission. I began flying the Po-2 aircraft with a male air regiment, making reconnaissance flights in the daytime. It was very dangerous to fly the Po-2 in daylight, because it was a slow, defenseless aircraft made of fabric, which made it very vulnerable to enemy fire. The German fighters often shot it down. My only armament was a pistol. The Germans were given the highest order for shooting down and capturing Russian pilots if they remained alive.

In the spring of 1942 my plane was set on fire by the Germans, and I managed to land the burning aircraft. We were given no parachutes at all. When I landed I jumped out of the cockpit and ran for the woods, luckily in Soviet territory. While I was running the German fighters were firing at me from the air. I fell down several times and again ran. There was a cornfield, and the stalks were still there from the previous year. When I fell, I dug my head into the heap of corn and lay there while they fired at me. The plane burned completely.

I was on a mission to bring a secret, urgent message to the staff of our Air Army. I had it with me and knew I had to somehow deliver that message, so I started out on foot and ran. Our troops were retreating, and the Germans were rapidly advancing. Here and there I could see fascist tanks and infantry from a distance. Then I was picked up by our troops and made my way toward headquarters. It was difficult with all the troops and traffic on the road, so I combined walking and riding. I had burns on my hands and feet, especially on the knees, because I was dressed in a skirt and had suffered the burns before I could land. Finally I delivered the message to headquarters, and they bandaged my burns there and sent me back to my squadron by truck.

I served in a squadron with staff headquarters on the southern front. The dream of all the pilots in my squadron was to fly combat and not to carry messages. We all wanted to fight back. Finally I was

Anna Timofeyeva-Yegorova,
805th Ground Attack Regiment

allowed to join a male regiment where I could be trained as a combat pilot. Later, I heard that Raskova wanted me to join her regiment. She sent six messages requesting that I join, but the staff did not even let me know about it. Only after the war did I find out.

When I first started flying the Illyushin Sturmovik Il-2 aircraft, it had one cockpit only. Because we were shot down very regularly, they added the second cockpit in the fuselage with a gunner facing to the rear armed with a large-caliber machine gun. We usually flew at an altitude of about eight hundred meters to drop bombs and at a lower altitude of about four hundred meters for attacking and strafing. Every pilot wanted to fly the Il-2, because it was a heavy plane carrying 600 kilos of bombs and two machine guns and rockets. It was used as a close ground support aircraft at the front lines against tanks, airdromes, railways, ships—everything.

I had a very strange reaction when I was flying over the target: my lips would bleed. They were very dry and would bleed, but not from biting them. In the summer of 1943, a third of the flying personnel in the regiment were killed over the Black Sea. Over the sea we flew very low, and even though the aircraft was well protected we suffered heavy losses. During the war my heart sank when I was flying combat missions over the sea; even now I am afraid of the sea. My regiment was stationed on the coast, the coast of the Sea of Azov, and these awful, frightful storms would develop over the sea.

The so-called Blue Line was a fortified area made by the Germans, and it had been impossible to break through it. So they decided that we should make a smoke screen to cover our troops while they moved forward to penetrate these defenses. Before this operation, the commander of our regiment lined us up and said that he needed nineteen volunteers. Everyone volunteered. He selected commanders and deputy commanders of the squadrons, and he called my name. This mission was by order of the commander of the front.

In the morning before the mission we lined up and handed in all our documents to the staff. The planes were disarmed, and balloons filled with gas were affixed instead. We were not to deviate from our course, not to take any evasive action, and fly one after another. We flew down the Blue Line, a distance of eleven kilometers. I was told to count three seconds and then release the gas. We were fired on constantly; the front line was completely on fire. I wanted to look behind to see what was happening but I couldn't, for I would then perhaps have deviated from the course.

When we had fulfilled our mission and were returning to base, our commander radioed that, thanks to God, we all were here and were returning to the airdrome. Meanwhile, anyone who had damage to their aircraft should land first. It was transmitted to us that all the pilots who had completed the mission successfully had already been awarded the Order of Red Banner. When we landed, got out of our cockpits, and lined up, the commander of the army awarded us the decoration right there.

Once, in the Taman region, I was to make a reconnaissance flight. Our attack planes were usually protected by the fighter aircraft. The fighters were stationed closer to the front line, and as I flew past the airdrome I saw the two fighters that were to protect my plane taking off. I transmitted to them that I was going to reconnoiter the ground and photograph it and to please protect me. After my transmission I heard, "Why are you speaking in such a tiny voice?" and "You are called a fighter? You're not a fighter!" and several bad expressions after that. I realized they didn't know I was a woman.

The flight was very successful; I managed to photograph the front line even though they made some holes in the plane. I visually reconnoitered the landscape; then I turned back with the two fighters still protecting me. I reported from the air to my airdrome, and the fighter pilots could hear the conversation. After I had reported, the person on the ground said, "Thank you, Anechka," and only then did they realize I was a woman. They began circling around and wagging their wings at me. We arrived over their airfield, and I told them, "Thank you, brothers; land, please." They did not land at their airdrome but escorted me to my field, wagged their wings again, and flew away. When I landed and came into the headquarters, they were all laughing and smiling at me, saying, "See, Lieutenant Yegorova has found bridegrooms!" When at last we liberated the Taman Peninsula in 1943, our regiment was transferred to the First Belorussian Front.

It all happened on August 20, 1944, Aviation Day. The commander promised to throw a party after we returned from our combat mission (this was in Poland). By that time I was already the regimental navigator. Our troops had crossed the Vistula River; the Germans wanted to eliminate this bridgehead, and they had sent in reinforcements of tanks, artillery, and guns. Our mission was to stop this force. Half the attack planes were led by the commander of the regiment, a force of fifteen aircraft, and the other half were led by me, as deputy commander. The first group took off, and after an interval of ten minutes my group followed. Ten fighters protected our fifteen planes. We proceeded to the area of the bridgehead. When I was making my first pass, the antiaircraft guns started firing at my plane and hit it. The pilots in my group saw that my plane was hit and that I did not have complete control. They asked and even begged me on the radio to turn back, but I didn't listen to reason. Now, so many years have passed and I still don't know why I didn't listen to them, but I went on and made the second pass over the target.

It was very difficult to be the leader of a male squadron. They trust you—not because you are a woman, but because you are a skillful and trained pilot. The Germans always fired at the lead plane, because if the leader could be shot down, the formation would disperse and leave without a commander. My aircraft became more uncontrollable; it was continuously going nose up. They fired at my plane with great intensity, and my gunner—a woman—was killed. I saw the glass dividing the two cockpits covered with her blood. The instrument panel was smashed, and the engine was burning. The radio was damaged, and I had no communication. By then I had no vision of the ground or the planes. I tried to open the canopy but it wouldn't open. I became choked with the smoke and fire. The plane exploded; I was blown out of the cockpit and lost consciousness.

When I opened my eyes, I was free of the aircraft and falling through the air. I pulled the ring and the parachute opened, but not completely. When I hit the ground I was falling very fast. I don't know if I lost consciousness, but when I opened my eyes there was a fascist standing over me with his boot on my chest. I was seriously injured: I had a broken spine, head injuries, broken arms, and a broken leg. I was burned on my knees, legs, and feet, and the skin was torn on my neck. I remember the face of the fascist; I was very afraid that I would be tortured or raped.

I remember very little of how I was carried to the fascist barracks, but I was very much afraid of the Germans and the atrocities they could inflict on me. My only wish was that I be shot, and the sooner the better. I was brought initially to a fascist camp in Poland. I lay motionless, and I was given water through a straw by the prisoners. The Germans tore off the ribbons from my uniform. I heard Polish speech but very little else. I recall that two Germans dressed in rubber aprons came up to me in the barracks, and they poured some powder over my burns. I shouted and cried and screamed so loud that the Polish imprisoned there thought I was being tortured. But it was my injuries that made me cry out. I couldn't breathe because all my ribs were broken.

I was never treated medically by the Germans. Soon I was loaded onto a cargo train, and in five days, under a guard of four soldiers, we were taken to a prisoner-of-war camp on Polish territory. In the same carriage was a nurse who was standing next to me all the time, crying. The German guards dragged her away and beat her, but all the same she crawled back to me and never left me alone. She cried and begged me not to die.

The camp was international, and there were prisoners who were doctors. A Russian, Dr. Sinyakov, treated me. Sinyakov went to the Gestapo headquarters of that camp and asked, in the name of all the prisoners of the camp, that permission be given to treat the Russian pilot. All of the prisoners, except the Russians, received a parcel with food and medication from the Red Cross Society. Stalin had said during the war, "We do not have prisoners of war, only traitors"; and he forbade all help.

On January 31, 1945, Soviet troops liberated the camp. I, being a woman, was suspected of being a collaborator. When Russian prisoners were released from the German prisons, they were immediately imprisoned in the Soviet Union. They were deprived of their rank and all their medals and were forced to stay in work camps for long periods. While I was in the German camp, the Russian doctor who treated me kept safe the documents of my two orders and my party membership card. When the Soviet troops were advancing and approaching the camp, the Germans transferred westward to another camp the Soviet prisoners who were able to be moved. Those of us who couldn't be moved stayed in the camp. The Germans started shooting those of us that remained, but the Soviet tanks rushed into the area before they could finish and liberated the camp.

Russian prisoners were sent to Lansberg to be tested. But I was considered to be a special kind of a traitor, the worst sort, and as such I was sent to a Soviet organization called SMERCH, which meant "death to the fascists." I was to be tested there, where the fascists were tested. It was operated by the NKVD (the secret police). There were many fascists in the basement where we were confined. They all lay on the lower bunks; I lay on the upper bunk. Above that cellar was a room where NKVD officers questioned me. Through a small hole in the ceiling I could see an NKVD officer examining my orders and medals through a lens.

I was questioned every night for ten days. They wanted to know how I had gotten to that camp: if I had really been a traitor, I would have come to the camp voluntarily and offered myself into German hands. They examined my orders and papers each night. But the doctors who treated me in the camp, who described in detail my condition when I was brought to the camp, told how they had taken care of me and how I had been imprisoned. They asked that I be released and sent to the camp at Lansberg to be tested with the other Soviet prisoners. The officers would not do that; they questioned me every night—ten of them. The soldiers on guard duty there called me bad names: German bitch, fascist bitch, swine. I was constantly guarded by soldiers, and a gun was directed into my back when I was going to the bathroom.

On the eleventh night of the eleventh day, I pulled myself together. I felt some strength inside my body, and I ran up to the second floor. I had wanted to speak to the colonel every night, but they wouldn't let me. While I was running upstairs a soldier behind me was shouting, "Stop, or I will shoot you," but I rushed on into his quarters, a well-furnished room with a rug. The NKVD officers lived quite well in the rear, even during the war. I cried out, "Shoot me, but I will not let you torture me."

I don't know what happened then because I fell unconscious. When I regained consciousness, lying on the floor, I saw a glass of water standing on the table. I was in the colonel's room, but it was empty. I got up from the floor, sat on the sofa, and pulled myself together, and in a moment the colonel came in and asked if I had calmed myself. I said yes. He looked at me and said, "You are released." I asked him then to give me a certificate that said I was released and that I had been tested, and he said that he would not do that. I asked him if a woman had really given birth to him—I doubted that he could ever have had a mother if he tortured everyone like me, who came from the concentration camp wounded and burned, with all the bones in my body broken and having undergone in the camp what I had to endure.

He didn't speak right away, and then he said that he would give me the certificate. The officer then gave me a horse and cart with a soldier as a guide who brought me to a control line. There I told an officer that I was from the 16th Air Army and wanted to return to my unit. They sympathized with me, put me on one of the trucks, and sent me back to the army.

When I returned to the regiment everyone was so happy to see me and to know I hadn't been killed in the crash. The regimental commander gave me an apartment to myself. They all brought me small presents, like sweets. Captain Tsikhonja came to me with dresses—long dresses—and said that he was going to give these to his wife, but the moment he heard I was still alive he decided to present the dresses to me. Then he burst out crying.

I stayed in the army until the end of the war, but I did not fly. The doctors have never let me fly since that time. They said I was an invalid.

I found out that the commander of our regiment was also shot down but managed to land the plane in Soviet territory. They all saw my plane crash and were sure that I had perished. They never saw my parachute. At that time the commander of the regiment sent an application to the Supreme Council of the Soviet Union to award me the Gold Star of Hero of the Soviet Union posthumously. They sent my mother a *pokhoronka*, a document saying her daughter had been killed.

My mother suffered greatly; she became sick after that news and stayed motionless in bed for some time. She sent my sister to a nearby village to a fortune-teller, because she had a feeling that I was still alive. The fortune-teller said it was the truth that Anna was no longer alive. My mother began going to the church to have the priest sing an orthodox song for the dead.

The moment the camp was liberated, I wrote a letter to my mother and passed it to the tankers, who sent it to her. When she received the letter, she thought she had gone mad and that it was all a dream; she thought it was a vision. Then she went to the neighbors and asked a young boy there to read the letter. He read it word for word, and then she did believe it was true. She went home and put on her best clothes and went to the army staff that was headquartered near the village. When she had been informed that I was killed, she began receiving a small pension. So at the local army headquarters she told them to please not send her that damned pension any more!

NOTE: Anna Timofeyeva-Yegorova was the only woman pilot in her regiment. She was granted the Hero of the Soviet Union medal only in 1965. The award had initially been granted posthumously in 1944, then withheld when it was discovered she had not perished but had become a prisoner of war.

Senior Sergeant Anna Popova,
flight radio operator 10th Guard Air Transport Division

I finished the war in the rank of senior sergeant. I began flying in the so-called Group of Special Role formed in Moscow, and by the end of the war it grew into the 10th Guard Air Transport Division, which consisted of three regiments. This division used pilots from civil aviation. I started flying on Li-2 aircraft, then on C-47s. These were twin-engine American transport planes, ferried from Alaska to our country in the Second World War. But I came to the air forces as a ground radio operator and went to the front trained as a flight radio operator.

Before the war I attended courses in Morse code. I cannot say I was willing to become a ground radio operator in my youth, but in the 1920s and 1930s it was more or less obligatory for a Komsomol member to actively participate in the sociopolitical life of the country. So each young person of my age was supposed to join a club, an after-school activity course or movement, to manifest loyalty to the political system as well as readiness to defend the regime when needed. An adult's extracurricular activity was normally recorded in her graduation grade list and was very significant when applying to any educational establishment or for a job. Many young girls went to glider school for reasons far loftier than demonstrating their loyalty to the system—they dreamed of flying. But I didn't join any glider school, because I was fully engaged in Morse code training.

In order to accomplish what I've done in my life I had to break stone walls and apply unfeminine energy and effort to each step, but I have always been inspired by the real feelings of my heart. When the war was declared, a great number of young people went to the front voluntarily. I applied to the Military Commissariat several times and each time was rejected. Here is my story.

I was born on December 31, 1923, in the town of Vitebsk in Belorussia. When at school, like every Soviet youngster, I actively participated in the socioeconomic life of the country. But in 1939 the NKVD (secret police) arrested a group of schoolchildren in our town, all of them age fifteen—I among them. There were two girls and seven boys in that group. The people who arrested us were vigilant hawks of the Stalin regime who spared nobody to curry favor with their governors. They totally ignored child psychology and completely lacked an understanding of a child's fantasy. They were uneducated and ignorant, ready to find anyone guilty of never-committed crimes; perhaps even newborn babies who appeared to cry non-Stalinist tears! They converted the whole great country into a big concentration camp of life-term inmates. They would turn people into programmed robots stuffed with slogans and cheers for the great Stalin.

My story, or rather the story of my group, is only one tiny, modest example of how this evil machine operated. The boys who fell under suspicion and were jailed were just like boys all over the world who like to read lots of science fiction, adventure stories, thrillers, and travel novels. Under the spell of world-famous literary characters, three of them decided to run away from their homes and rode to Odessa on their bicycles. Of course they were found and brought back to their parents. After that they wanted to intrigue the girls and seem mysterious, and they began signing any messages or notes to their friends as 3+X. Several years passed. This childish game was forgotten, and no one even thought of it again.

On the eve of May 1 (May Day), celebrated in our country as the Day of International Solidarity of Workers of the World, I was summoned to the secretary of the Regional Komsomol Committee to report on the May Day preparations at my school. When I left that committee one of the members asked me to accompany him to meet his friend, who had allegedly returned from the Far East. I consented; we climbed the stairs, the door opened, and ahead of me lay an NKVD office. I still remember the man who played that evil trick on me and so dramatically affected my life. His name is Vasilij Korsakov. He asked me to repeat the information I had just told the committee about the May Day festivities at school, about my schoolmates and their grades, and about our after-school activities, when out of nowhere came a question about the 3+X group.

I explained to him the meaning of 3+X and the origin of this boyish game. Then I was allowed to leave, but several months later, all of us were arrested. We were accused of founding an anti-Soviet, subversive, underground youth organization in the territory of Belorussia. I was included in the group because we were close friends, and we spent our free time together. We were all sent to the central prison in Minsk, capital of Belorussia, where I was held for six months in solitary confinement.

By the time we were brought to trial a new secretary of the Regional Komsomol Committee, Ponomarenko, was appointed. He easily understood that we were innocent and did what he could to soften our sentences. We were tried by the regional court behind closed doors. We were sentenced, according to Article 58, for counterrevolutionary activity and anti-Soviet propaganda. At the trial it became obvious to everybody, including the jury, that the accusations had been fabricated. That nightmare affected me and changed my future dramatically. Mariya Veitzer, the other girl, and I were released, and I returned to my native town, but the boys were not released. I was expelled from the Komsomol, and I was looked upon as a spy and an enemy. If anyone had sympathized with me they would have had to conceal it so as not to fall themselves under suspicion of the NKVD.

I returned to school and completed ninth grade; then I moved to live with my aunt in Smolensk, where I didn't have to hide from people. But in December, 1938, my parents called me and said that the group had again been arrested and put into prison, because the verdict hadn't satisfied the NKVD. In my youth I had a strong belief that the state as governed by Stalin had nothing in common with the evil people who performed such injustices on innocent citizens. I thought Stalin was being deliberately deluded by enemies who paralyzed the whole country with a spy network. Stalin himself, I believed, was not involved in it and did not know about the Soviet concentration-camp system. We believed that if only Stalin could learn of the crimes of the spy machine, he would punish them severely. Ours was a boundless faith and an unbreakable love of Stalin—our God, as we symbolized him. Even after being imprisoned I only desired to prove that I was a genuine Soviet girl, honest and loyal; a real patriot who loved her motherland dearly and was ready to give her life for it and for Stalin. My faith was boundless. Now that we all know the real truth about what happened during those times—the system that caused it, the horrors and crimes committed during Stalin's reign, the millions of people victimized and murdered—I cannot perceive how shortsighted we were, how Stalin managed to charm and hypnotize the whole country. It's beyond my understanding.

To continue my story, I was restless staying with my aunt and couldn't stand the idea of just waiting to be arrested again by the NKVD. The trial was in Minsk, and I went there with the idea of surrendering myself, but my uncle wouldn't allow it. He believed that I must go to Moscow to prove to the Central Party and the Komsomol that I was innocent and had committed no crime. On the night train I shivered with fear that at any moment the NKVD would board the train and arrest me. In Moscow I hurried to Pravda, the Communist newspaper, to tell my story, to plead my case, and to beg for their intercession. They listened, then called the Central Komsomol Committee in pretense of helping me. In truth, they were closely connected to the NKVD and were busy fabricating big lies for the party. Never thinking of the consequence, I even left my aunt's address with them.

I returned to Smolensk to continue with my studies. Two months later NKVD agents intruded into my aunt's apartment while I was at school, searched it inside out, grabbed some family photographs, and left me an order to be in their office that day. Again I was to be arraigned with the group before the Supreme Court of Belorussia, also behind the closed doors. I asked the Central Komsomol Committee to send a representative to the trial, which they did. But it was a sham; they only pretended to help my case. In the end, all but one of us were released. One boy was sentenced to five years of imprisonment for anti-Soviet propaganda. This was because once, at school, he said that collective farms in this country, in the period of agricultural reconstruction of the 1920s and 1930s, had been conducted against Lenin's general plan of agricultural rejuvenation.

Later I moved to Moscow and attended courses in Morse code. I tried to be readmitted into the Komsomol. I wrote many appeals and knocked on many doors, but in vain. The war started, and I attended a special class to prepare to be flown behind enemy lines and work with the partisans. Upon completion I filled out a questionnaire; one of the questions asked if I were a member of the Komsomol, and if not, what was the reason. For the whole period of Soviet rule it was obligatory for all young people from the ages of fourteen to twenty-eight to be Komsomol members. I answered that I had been expelled. We had been informed by the selections board that if we were accepted as volunteers, the risk of being killed was ninety-nine percent—one percent would survive. I did not hesitate a second in my determination to go to the front. When I was summoned before the board for the final determination, I was rejected. The reason was my expulsion.

My parents had left our native land of Belorussia and walked to somewhere in the Volga River region as the Germans advanced into our country. I decided to try to find them, and luckily I did. But my grandparents were killed by the fascists in their village during the first days of German occupation, for they shot all the Jews on the spot, irrespective of their age. They were old and sick and could not think of abandoning their home to walk long kilometers to somewhere else—they preferred death.

I returned to Moscow and renewed my efforts to be reinstated into the Komsomol and thus be eligible to volunteer for the front. The Komsomol then summoned me and told me my appeal would be granted if I went on a special mission behind the enemy lines. Those terms sounded as though I had committed a crime and were expiating my guilt, so I couldn't accept them. In despair I wrote to Lavrentij Beriya, chief of the NKVD. By a miracle my letter was read by a general, a very honest man, who believed my story. He placed me before him and interviewed me. He told me that I should never ever mention that I had once been expelled from the Komsomol. He then supported me, and I was able to join the Komsomol. After that I became a ground radio operator stationed at one of the Moscow airdromes.

But I had a burning desire to be a flight radio operator and requested a transfer. Soon I was sent to take a brief training course, and in 1942 I was assigned to the 10th Guard Air Transport Division as a flight radio operator. Our division was stationed at Vnukovo airdrome near Moscow. We flew behind the front line to the enemy's rear, dropping medicine, food supplies, ammunition, and weapons to the partisans who conducted subversive activities on enemy-held territory. Sometimes we dropped paratroopers deep into the rear. At the front we dropped oil barrels for our tanks and trucks, and on other missions we landed at the front to carry the badly wounded to the rear so they might survive. Occasionally we were attacked by fascist fighters. When we flew to the besieged city of Stalingrad to drop supplies and bring out the wounded, we were escorted by fighters even though our Lisunov Li-2 aircraft was equipped with machine-gun turrets.

In Belorussia, in 1943, the partisans were waging the so-called Rail War. They blew up the tracks so the German cargo trains could not deliver supplies to their troops. We delivered supplies to these partisans hiding in the dense Belorussian woods. We dropped the cargo at night. They would signal us from the ground with identification fires, and the code changed each night. One night it might be fires laid in a triangle, another night a cross or rectangle. We talked with the land forces through radio. It often happened that German intelligence intercepted the partisan code and laid out fires of similar shapes to trap the Soviet transport aircraft. But we outwitted the

Germans; we had auxiliary codes in addition to the fires. The partisans would shoot up a signal flare of a certain color, and the aircraft would respond with a prearranged answering signal color—only then did we drop the cargo.

I had many experiences in the war that made my heart sink. But one is especially unforgettable. On one mission, when we were about to drop supplies to the partisans, we were very unexpectedly attacked by a German fighter. The aircraft commander asked me to check why the tail gunner was silent. I rushed to the tail compartment and saw that the turret and machine guns had been hit and were unusable. The right fuel tank was leaking and flaming. The fighter made another pass on the right and attacked the pilot's cabin. The commander could hear the bullets bouncing off the armor plate in back of him where my station was located and thought I had been killed. But I was still in the rear of the plane. I ran to the commander to report that we were on fire. We were flying at only 200 meters, and he started to climb so we could bail out of the aircraft. But our parachutes were all piled into the tail of the plane, and it was on fire. Our only chance to survive was to land the plane in the area of the partisan fires beneath us. While the pilot struggled to control the aircraft, we were throwing weapons, ammunition fuses, and detonator cargo out of the plane so it wouldn't explode when we landed. The pilot, our commander, called to me to help him hold the aircraft, and I saw that he was wounded in his chest and right arm. Our copilot became so frightened he left the cabin and cowered near the back of the plane. I couldn't help hold the control stick—it was beyond my physical capacity—so I dashed to the flight engineer for help, but he was on the floor, bleeding from six bullet wounds. Our commander was barely conscious but still managed to control the aircraft as we bellylanded. My life flashed before my eyes in an instant. My last wish was that everyone who had made me unjustly suffer in my youth for crimes never committed would learn now that I was dying for my fair motherland.

We touched the ground—we were safe! When we belly-landed I opened the hatch and pulled the flight engineer out of the cabin. The navigator and tail gunner had already jumped out and helped me lower the engineer to the ground. Now I can hardly give an account of how I energized myself to drag our commander through the hatch, but I did. I was the last to quit the plane. When I felt myself firmly on the ground I heard the commander's order to crawl away from the plane. We might be on enemy-held territory, for we hadn't had time to signal the partisans on the ground. The fuel tanks blew up, and the whole plane was burning. Then the men who were not wounded went into the forest to reconnoiter. Our commander wanted us to leave him because he was so badly wounded, and he had his pistol ready to shoot himself if the fascists came. I didn't obey him and stayed with the wounded. I was in despair, for I didn't know how to stem the bleeding of the chest wound. I remembered that I always had many handkerchiefs in my greatcoat, because in the daytime when we were not flying I passed the time embroidering them. I used them now for bandages, pressing them against the chest wound. The flight engineer was also bleeding. I tore his high boot with a knife and bandaged the wounds with his foot wrapping.

In about an hour the crew returned with a partisan, a horse, and a cart. We loaded the wounded onto the cart and made our way to a village controlled by the partisans. The wounded were carried into a hut, and the surgeon extracted splinters and bullets from their bodies. There was no anesthesia, so he used pieces of ice to freeze the area. The partisans radioed to the their headquarters in Moscow that we had crashed, and two weeks later, two small aircraft were sent to ferry us out. Before we left we were visited by the secretary of the underground Komsomol. Our commander praised my courage and self-control, and the secretary turned to see me. His dismay and astonishment showed on his face when he recognized me as the girl whom he had arrested and expelled from the Komsomol!

While awaiting the rescue aircraft, the navigator and I returned to our burned aircraft to search for the Order of the Red Star, the award our pilot commander had been wearing when we were forced to land. He valued it highly and mourned its loss. It was nowhere to be found at the aircraft site, but we did find, to our horror, that we were in the middle of a mine field! Later, when in a Moscow military hospital, surgery was performed on our commander, and when they entered the wound, they extracted the medal from his chest! It had deflected the bullet from his heart and saved his life.

Our flights to the landing strips behind the lines in the Crimea were very risky. The partisans built short strips in the mountains where they were hiding, and fog and overcast made it difficult to locate these rocky fields. They could not light fires at night because they were visible everywhere, and in the daytime German fighters loitered over them. On one such mission we searched five days to locate the small landing strip. When we finally landed to take out the severely wounded, we packed the aircraft to capacity, for the men would die there if we could not fly them out. On each trip we would carry thirty-five or forty people, our maximum load. We had no nurses on board, and we attended them ourselves as best we could. It was impossible to take a breath in the passenger compartment, for the bodies were decaying and stinking. On one mission one of our engines quit over the Black Sea, and we were forced to turn to an auxiliary field. It took forty minutes to get to that field, and all the way there we realized we could crash any minute—it seemed like an eternity.

Many of our missions lasted for two or three days. My crew always granted me the best conveniences, while they nested in worse. Moreover, they cared not only about my comfort but also about my long braid I couldn't bear to cut. Each time we were stationed near a small rivulet, pond, or lake, my crew would bring me several buckets of clear water to wash and rinse my thick, long hair. I gave them my ration of vodka and cigarettes, and they gave me their chocolate. They never dirty-mouthed in my presence; they treated me in a most gracious manner. And in their presence I never gave way to emotions, no matter how grave the situation. Every day we saw such grief, death, and destruction that my thoughts merged into one desire—to liberate my motherland from the fascist barbarians. On board the aircraft I felt sheltered and protected. My plane was my home; I stood on the flooring of the plane as if on the land.

In 1944 the war was moving toward its end. We were flying to the Belorussian front, where the Germans were vehemently resisting, for they were losing superiority on all fronts. They threw the main German air forces to that front. On those missions we were attacked again and again, and on each flight we returned with bullet holes in the fuselage. I feared each flight. But when my commander transferred me to Kiev to another crew I sobbed for several days. Not only was I losing my crew but I would never cross the front again, because I was being assigned to domestic duty behind the front. No longer was I defeating the enemy; I was assigned to fly with the Ukrainian government within Soviet-held territory. My commander made this decision to transfer me because he felt that he bore responsibility for my life. Once I had saved him when I pulled him out of a burning aircraft, and now he was saving me from a wild bullet. My younger brother lost his life at age eighteen, in 1944, and now my commander was forcibly preventing me from losing mine. Soon I quit flying completely. I entered the Military Academy of Foreign Interpreters but was soon transferred to a civilian college, the Linguistic University, for I was expecting a child.

I majored in Italian and Spanish, then completed postgraduate courses and defended my dissertation. For ten years I taught Italian at the University of Foreign Economic Relations. Later I translated feature films for Mosfilm. Then I moved into film production, where I am now managing producer for joint Russian-Italian films.

Lieutenant Olga Lisikova,
pilot, commander of the aircraft
Intelligence Directorate of the General Staff of the Red Army

Olga Lisikova, transport pilot

I completed flying school in 1937 and was assigned to Aeroflot, operating on the Leningrad-Moscow line. Our aircraft was the P-5, difficult to fly, especially for a newly trained pilot. It could only carry 500 kg, and the flight lasted three to four hours. We flew at low elevation so there was often turbulence, and we had few instruments in the cabin.

One day my commander told me I was to make a solo flight to Moscow, and I knew that only very skillful pilots flew on that air route. It was a miraculous dream come true: I had become a professional pilot! So I flew the P-5 and then the PR-5—it had the shape of a cigar and carried four passengers. Later I became the copilot on the K-5 aircraft, and the commander of the plane, Vasilij Lisikov, became my husband.

For the rest of my life I will remember the years 1939–40 because of the senseless and brutal war with Finland. I had to participate in that war. I flew the Red Cross aircraft carrying severely wounded soldiers and officers and many who hadn't been wounded at all; they had frozen in the bitter northern frost. The temperatures were sometimes forty to forty-one degrees below zero centigrade. The soldiers were poorly equipped for such weather, so they lost their extremities—it was terrible. I made many flights in that war. I myself was wrapped in warm clothing so that I was unrecognizable, with a helmet, a mask for my face, fur high boots, gloves, and fur overalls. I flew an open-cockpit plane—open to the wind—and in spite of the armistice concluded on March 13, we went on flying out the wounded. My life was complicated by the fact that I was carrying a child.

At the front we landed on a lake covered with a thick layer of snow, because the aircraft was provided with skis. We would taxi to the bank of the lake, where we loaded the wounded and flew them to the hospital in Leningrad. When in June I announced to the commander of the detachment that I was expecting a baby, he was astonished. He had never even noticed that I was pregnant. He asked me how I managed to fly and carry on missions. I told him that being the only female pilot in the detachment was both an advantage and a disadvantage at the same time! It had never occurred to him that there should be a gynecologist on the medical test board.

The Great Patriotic War began when my child was only ten months old. In spite of that, I was drafted to the front in the first days of the war. I flew the medical plane, an SP-2, and on one of the missions I loaded two badly wounded soldiers to carry them to the hospital. About seventy kilometers from the front line, I saw a fascist Messerschmitt Me-109 circling around to my tail. What could I do—how could I protect my small, defenseless biplane with wounded aboard? He could easily see the large red cross on my plane. But nothing seemed to stop the beast; he was rapidly approaching my aircraft. Now he would fire at me with his machine guns. There in the rear of my plane lay the two wounded men; they didn't even sense the danger. And I was perfectly sure that our last minutes were ticking away. I had always wondered, in such a situation, how fast your life flashed in front of your eyes. At that point, I visualized all of my life, and now I will tell you.

I was born in 1917 in the Far East. My school was on the bank of a small bay near the village of Americanka, and my father was a schoolteacher—he brought us up. When I was four years old I could swim very well; I climbed trees like a monkey. At eight, my father instructed me to bring my brother home from a village 50 kilometers away. I made my way alone through the *taiga* and brought him home—100 kilometers in all. I heard all of the *taiga's* mysterious noises but strangely had no fear. Now we were living in Leningrad and I was in secondary school, physically more mature than my classmates and good in school. They tried many tricks to humble me. Once they bet that I would never sit the whole night through in the cemetery. That night I went to the oldest cemetery in the city and sat the whole night in the lap of a monument erected to Tchaikovsky. I also dove into water from a tower ten meters high and sat the night in a basement full of rats! I won the right to lead.

Sixteen of us girls went to flying school, where we were issued flying uniforms. I put mine on, and it was terrible—I looked like a monster! It was so awfully oversized that I couldn't move in it. I cut it drastically, as well as the high boots. Out of the remainder of the overcoat, I stitched a beret. In my new uniform I appeared in the formation, and I was given ten days in the guardhouse for destroying state property! The other girls decided to support me and express their solidarity, and the next day they all appeared for roll call in their altered uniforms. The commander of the battalion could do nothing but release me from the guardhouse. And that is what flashed before my eyes in that second while the enemy fighter approached. I didn't want to die. A painful feeling seized my heart: a mixture of grief, misfortune, and anger for my own helplessness.

Now my brain worked clearly; not far ahead I saw a precipice and the thin thread of a rivulet—a tiny hope for survival. I dove at the moment the fascist fighter pulled the trigger, and then he flew past me. I saw explosions in the air, but I was not hit. I dropped between the river-banks, very low, close to the water. Now the thought of death didn't seem so bitter—it was mixed with triumph. I knew he had lost me, and he would need to gain altitude to look for me. He would be furious— the fighter plane not being able to cope with a small flying bug. The river narrowed; the banks closed in on the plane. My hands numbed, so hard did I grip the control stick. I didn't have the nerve to look back, but intuition told me he was somewhere very close. Suddenly the river abruptly turned to the right. I made a sharp turn, and at that instant the aircraft shook very hard; the enemy machine gun had hit my tail. Fortunately the control cables weren't damaged. But I saw that I couldn't fly farther up the canyon, or I would crash into the narrowing banks. I climbed up, and five minutes later I landed at my airdrome, the 14th Air Force Army. The commander and other pilots watched the Messerschmitt firing at something, but they did not see my aircraft. When I landed they understood what had happened. My plane was shot through in many places, but none of us was hurt. They told me what had happened to the enemy fighter: when he dove on my tail that last time, he came too low to the ground and crashed into the riverbank. The pilots congratulated me for my victory over the fascist fighter, and the commander of the 14th awarded me the Order of the Red Banner.

After that episode, I was sent to the flying center to be retrained to fly the Li-2 aircraft, a version of the American Douglas C-47 built under license in the Soviet Union. I had my doubts about it because the Group of Special Role consisted of male personnel, and the crew I was assigned to comprised six men. I wondered how the male pilots would accept me. Also, my experience up to now had been in simple aircraft of the Po-2 type. The Lisunov Li-2 aircraft was equipped with two engines of 1,000 horsepower each, to give it a load of 2.5 metric tons of cargo or thirty paratroopers with equipment. It also had a gun turret on the fuselage with a machine gun. It was a very sophisticated aircraft with many instruments: some for blind flying, an automatic pilot, de-icers, and much more. And I had to master all that knowledge in a short time. At that time I had 1,600 flying hours.

I was hospitably accepted at the center, and I finished the course with distinction. I was transferred to the Flying Division of Special Role, which was assigned to the State Committee of Soviet Defense. This organization completed missions on all fronts, from the Black Sea to the Barents Sea. The main base was at the Vnukovo airdrome, not far from Moscow. When we were fulfilling our combat missions, we flew out of auxiliary airfields closer to the front lines or to the location of our mission. The pilots were experienced airline pilots with many hours. Our missions were to bail out paratroopers, drop supplies for encircled troops, transport fuel and spare parts to advancing troops, fly to the partisans in the rear, drop intelligence officers to the enemy rear, and bring supplies to besieged Leningrad.

I was assigned to the 1st Regiment. The regiment was commanded by Colonel K. Bukharov, although among ourselves we called him Uncle Kostya. He was fifteen or twenty years older than us and had graduated from flying school in 1925; he was deeply respected. He came from a noble Russian family. After the great October Revolution he had concealed his origin. He had deep roots of genetic nobility in him and preserved them, undestroyed by the regime. After hard, devastating flights deep into the enemy rear, the commander, having taken off his flying jacket, sat at the piano and played the Moonlight Sonata by Beethoven.

Our deputy commander, Captain A. Kalina, was full of energy and was gifted with a good sense of humor and a sophisticated mind. He decided to take me as his copilot on a difficult night mission to the enemy rear, to drop two intelligence officers by parachute. He was astonished that I didn't feel fear. All my actions were thoroughly calculated; I was confident. On that flight there was no time for fear.

We flew over the front line at a very high altitude; there was enemy antiaircraft fire, but we were not hit. Then we were attacked by fascist night fighters, and I could see the missiles exploding in the air. The commander ordered me to maneuver in a sideslip and then to dive down to the earth and hedgehop over the ground. It took me several minutes to accustom myself to the darkness, and then I began discerning rivers, highways, and forests. We changed course constantly: flying on one heading for ten minutes, changing to another course until I could see a lake, then changing again. It was a confusion—I didn't know where I was! Several seconds before we reached the target, he took the controls, climbed to 300 meters, and gave an order to the intelligence officers to bail out. The whole crew knew their jobs perfectly and worked in silence. On the way back he placed me in the pilot's seat and entrusted me with the aircraft.

The next day I was assigned to the crew of Captain Ivanov as copilot. Our mission: to fly cargo to the besieged city of Leningrad. My heart beat to the sound of my fair city—Leningrad, Leningrad. Our aircraft was filled with cargo for the people exhausted and devastated by the war: the bombings, the famine and cold. I knew we were bringing help to my friends and family.

In a month I was appointed commander of the aircraft. But a few days later I was ordered to fly to Siberia to be assigned as a copilot ferrying aircraft from America. It turned out that the commander of my division learned that I, a woman, was flying in his division, and he was determined to get rid of me. But then he was ordered to another command, and my chief rescinded the order.

One day I was assigned to carry cargo and two passengers, the directors of a plant situated on the Volga River. We took off in the morning with clear skies, but the weather soon began to change for the worse. On the approach to the airfield the fog had completely covered the city, and I was not allowed to land. I wasn't worried about that, because we had enough fuel on board to land at another field until the fog lifted at our destination. The mechanic, a crew member, came to me and told me we had only a twenty-minute fuel supply. He had fueled the aircraft the night before, and someone had poured off fuel from the tanks. He had not checked the tanks before takeoff.

I had to save the plane and the passengers! I flew to another town, where I could see the chimneys and smoke appearing from the fog. I entered the overcast on a heading toward the lowland along the river. The copilot was very fearful and was of no help to me. I chose a field and decided to land with the gear down. We touched the ground, and I braked abruptly because the field was small. Only because we had a heavy load of cargo did the aircraft not nose up. When we came to a stop, I leaned over the control wheel and nearly fainted. I knew I was alive only by the shivering in my knees. I had used all my willpower, skill, and energy to save the plane, and now I was speechless! The directors of the factory were angry that we had to make an emergency landing, but the crew said they should thank me for saving their lives. I never told about the lack of fuel, the real reason for the forced landing. I don't know why I did not report what had happened—possibly for fear of being prosecuted, or because of the awe of my crew, who were overwhelmed with my flying skills and praised me to everyone.

I actively took part in all the combat missions my division carried out. The new commander of the division summoned me and told me that I, being the only female pilot in the division, had a great responsibility, because all eyes were on me. Each flight, every landing was closely watched by the staff. And where the failure of a male pilot could pass unnoticed, mine would be always under surveillance. Any blunder, or worse—an accident—would not serve me well. He cautioned me to be demanding of myself. After that talk I changed drastically; I didn't look or act like myself. Everything congested inside; I became very strict with myself and my subordinates. Before, I would go to rest and relax after a mission; now, I went to the navigators' room and scrupulously studied the route of the next mission. When the crew went to see a movie, I went to the meteorological station and studied the weather reports. I would do everything better than the men.

I was totally trusting of my crew with the exception of the mechanic; he had failed me once by not checking the fuel tanks, and another time he didn't warm up the engines in the winter. Besides, he was so dirty-mouthed I couldn't stand it. I was brought up with real Russian intelligentsia who survived the socialist revolution in Leningrad. My family lived in a roomy house, with six families and eleven children in one apartment. Our parents treated us carefully. In our big flat lived a novelist who read us poems and stories, and we children sat near the fire and absorbed all those wonderful pieces of literature. Her elder daughter played the piano and sang for us. All the tenants of our flat added much to our upbringing. We never heard rude words, shouts, or swearing. So back to the crew: no matter how much the mechanic pleaded to be left in the crew, I replaced him. The crew comprised a pilot, copilot, tail gunner, navigator, mechanic, and radio operator.

We were transferred to a division of the long-distance flights, closer to the front. After this redeployment, the commanding staff of the division invited me to a division dinner with their major-general at the head of table. As the dinner came to an end, I noticed that the general's staff were quietly sneaking out of the room. I tried to follow their example, but I was stopped by the commander of the division. I understood that the general wanted to bed me down. Yes, I was only a lieutenant, but apart from that I was Olga Lisikova, and it was impossible to bed me down. His pressure was persistent. I had to think very fast, because he was in all respects stronger than me, and I knew well that nobody would dare to come to my rescue. In desperation I said, "I fly with my husband in my crew!" and he was taken aback. He didn't expect to hear that. He released me; I immediately rushed out and found the radio operator and mechanic of my crew. I didn't make explanations. I, as commander of the crew, ordered that one of them was to be my fictitious husband and gave them my word of honor that nobody would ever learn the truth! Then I released them.

I couldn't sleep all night; I couldn't believe any commander would behave like that. I thought, Were generals allowed to do anything that came to mind? I couldn't justify his behavior. The only explanation that seemed appropriate was that I was really very attractive in my youth. Thank God we flew away early the next morning.

I already had 120 combat missions when our division began receiving the C-47 aircraft. It was a most sophisticated plane, beyond any expectations. We pilots didn't even have to master it—it was perfect and flew itself! Before I was assigned a mission in it, I made one check flight. My next flight was a combat mission, to drop paratroopers to liberate Kiev. Later, when Kiev had been liberated, I flew there again. There were few planes on the landing strip, and in the distance I saw an aircraft of unusual shape, like a cigar. I realized at once that it was an American B-29. I taxied and parked next to it. My radio operator, tail-gunner, and I were invited aboard by the American crew. We spoke different languages, but my mechanic knew German and an American spoke it also; thus, the communication took place. The outside of the aircraft was no surprise, but when you got into it, touched it, and saw the most sophisticated equipment, you realized that it was the most perfect aircraft design. The Americans received us very warmly. The news that we flew the American C-47 made them respect us more. The most astonishing news for them was that I, a woman, was commander of the plane. They couldn't believe it. It was an instant reaction—I suggested that I would fly them in my plane to prove it! I put the crew in the navigator compartment and placed the copilot in the right seat beside me. The flight was short, six or seven minutes, but it was hilarious. After that I was strictly reprimanded by my commander.

By the time I had made 200 combat missions, I was entrusted at last to fly in the Intelligence Directorate of the General Staff of the Red Army. I will tell you about one of those flights. I was assigned a mission to drop six paratroopers into the deep rear of the enemy. When we ascended to the altitude of 3,000 meters the tail-gunner reported a Focke Wulf 190 on our tail, but not attacking. I couldn't understand why; then decided that it was a reconnaissance aircraft, and the pilot was interested in what cargo we carried. I knew if I changed course or dove, he would start firing. I climbed up a little and hid the aircraft in the clouds. The fascist instantly began attacking us but made another mistake by firing while he was facing the moon, which blinded him. There were bullets bouncing against the fuselage but so far no serious damage. He attacked once more but with no success, because we were by then deep in the clouds.

We had changed course, so now we corrected it and crossed the front line. In the enemy rear we usually flew at a very low altitude, because the Germans had detectors sensitive to flights above 300 meters. Our path to the enemy rear was a crooked route, because we avoided flying over towns and other places where we might be detected. It happened that we flew directly over an enemy airfield—bombers were circling around it. I knew that these fields were surrounded by antiaircraft guns and sound detectors that could easily tell we were Russian. More experienced pilots had told me to quickly change the engine sound if this happened to me, so I ordered the mechanic to change the synchronization of the engines so we might sound like a German Junkers aircraft. It worked; we flew through the area without an attack.

At last we arrived at the appointed spot, and my passengers bailed out. We held to that course so the Germans couldn't identify the place where the men jumped; then we took a course back to our base. After about forty minutes at low altitude, the mechanic inquired if I had touched the fuel-tank switch. I was angry, because in my crew we had a strict rule: never interfere with other crew members' work. But then he showed me the fuel-tank switch circling of its own accord. I understood what had happened: the German fighter had shot the fuel lines, and now we had fuel only in one tank, only enough for one and one-half hours. The other fuel tanks had been cut off.

We chose the shortest route to the front line, but when the red light began signaling that we were running out of fuel, goosebumps ran back and forth over my body. I even felt dizzy at the very thought that in a few moments we would crash. I continued flying in a desperate hope to cross back over the front line—and we did! At night the terrain is clearly perceivable, and I decided to land the plane. At any moment the engines could quit. I ordered the crew to go back to the tail of the aircraft, but nobody moved. I throttled back and began gliding down. I did not lower the landing gear, having decided to belly-land. But at this moment, the lights of a landing strip lit up. The mechanic managed to lower the gear, and we touched down. It turned out to be a front-line airdrome for small planes. When the aircraft stopped and we were to deplane, we saw that we were surrounded by military carrying guns. I ordered the mechanic to open the door and say a few phrases in both German and Russian. Then the misunderstanding was cleared up. The day before, a German bomber had landed at that airdrome, and when he found that he had landed on Russian territory, he very quickly took off again.

In another episode I was assigned a mission to fly to the enemy rear and drop supplies to the partisans. I crossed the front line at 4,000 meters, and at the appointed place began a dive. The altimeter showed me to be lower and lower, but I could see nothing through the clouds. Finally the altitude read zero and then less than that. Judging by the meter I was to be deep in the soil, but still I held the dive. I couldn't return to base without completing my mission: I didn't want to be reproached after the flight that I hadn't fulfilled the risky mission only because I was a coward, because I was a woman. Then I glimpsed the ground, and below me was the target where we were to drop the cargo. The area was covered with dense, patchy fog. We dropped the supplies to the partisans and returned to base.

When we arrived we learned that all the crews had turned back, not having managed to fulfill the mission. Everyone was astonished. How could I, a woman, do what other male pilots hadn't managed to accomplish? The division commander said he would promote me to be awarded the Gold Star of Hero of the Soviet Union, but I never received that award, because my crew consisted of males. If the crew had been female, it would have been awarded.

I flew with that division almost the whole war and completed 280 combat missions, but I was never awarded a single order. Although I was promoted for awards, it was always denied. The deputy commander of the division staff told me that it was totally his fault and responsibility that I had never been given an order. He had decided that I might get a swelled head in the purely male division if I had been given a high award. Instead, he thought it quite healthy for stories about me to be published in the press. Twenty years later, when I met him at the reunion of our division, I saw that his breast was pinned with high awards. I told him that during the whole war I had made more than 280 combat flights as commander of the aircraft, while he had all the traces of distinction on his body although he hadn't made a single combat flight.

I had a funny episode in 1945 when Kiev was liberated. I was assigned to pick up football players from Kiev and bring them to Moscow. I was sitting in the cockpit watching them approach the aircraft, swaying and hardly moving their feet. No doubt they were drunk. Their looks made me laugh until I heard dirty words—it enraged me. They didn't know that the commander of the crew was a woman. I decided to teach them a lesson. I climbed to 4,000 meters and totally disconnected the passenger compartment from the heating system. Some time later their coach entered the cockpit. I demanded an apology for their swearing; otherwise, I would freeze them to death. All together they cried out, "Olga, forgive us." When we landed and I passed by them, they stood with their heads bowed. I smiled, and thus our friendship started.

Later, in 1945, I flew the same team to play a match with another football team. In the airport where we landed they asked me to be their guest and gave me a seat at the commentator's booth. I was hurrying to my seat when I met a friend, a press correspondent, who introduced me to a young man, Volf Plaksin by name. It was my fate; I have lived in love with my second husband for forty-five happiest years. Then, two years ago, he died.

NOTE: Olga Lisikova, who lives in St. Petersburg, was not available for an interview, and her reminiscences were obtained by correspondence. There is no present-day photograph of her.

Nina Raspopova

Irina Rakobolskaya

Mariya Smirnova

Polina Gelman

Serafima Amosova-Taranenko

Klavdiya Ilushina

Yevgeniya Zhigulenko

Olga Yerokhina-Averjanova

Mariya Tepikina-Popova

Nina Yegorova-Arefjeva

Larisa Litvinova-Rozanova

Zoya Parfyonova

Irina Sebrova

Matryona Yurodjeva-Samsonova

Nadezhda Popova

Nina Karasyova-Buzina

Raisa Zhitova-Yushina

Alexandra Akimova

Mariya Akilina

Valentina Savitskaya-Kravchenko

Valentin Markov

Antonina Bondareva-Spitsina

Yevgeniya Gurulyeva-Smirnova

Yevgeniya Zapolnova-Ageyeva

Antonina Dubkova

Mariya Dolina

Anna Kirilina

Antonina Pugachova-Makarova

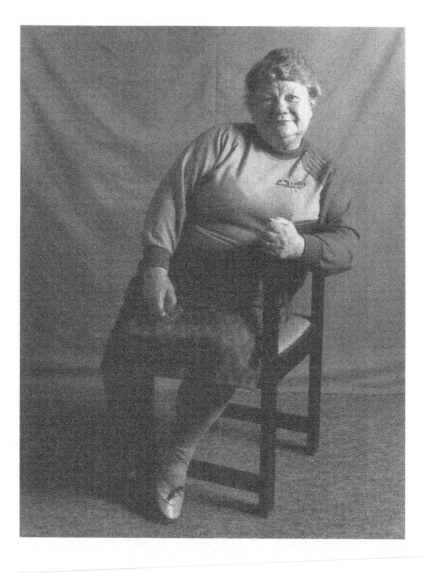

Antonina Lepilina

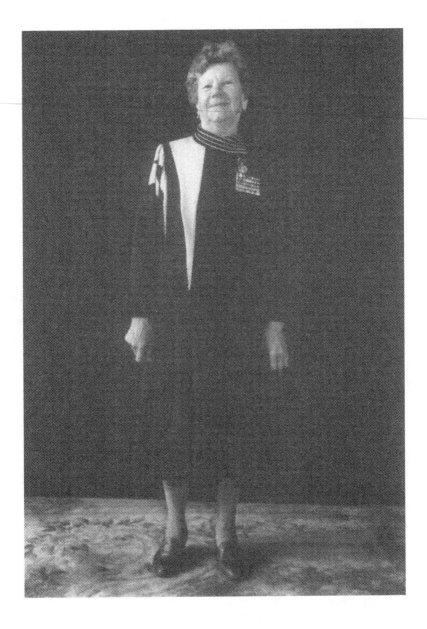

Yelena Kulkova-Malutina

Nataliya Alfyorova

Galina Brok-Beltsova

Marta Meriuts

Galina Chapligina-Nikitina

Yekaterina Chujkova

Ludmila Popova

Yekaterina Musatova-Fedotova

Mariya Kaloshina

Galina Tenuyeva-Lomanova

Nataliya Smirnova

Tamara Pamyatnykh

Yekaterina Polunina

Alexandra Makunina

Mariya Kuznetsova

Nina Yermakova

Valentina Kovalyova-Sergeicheva

Valentina Petrochenkova-Neminushaya

Nina Slovokhotova

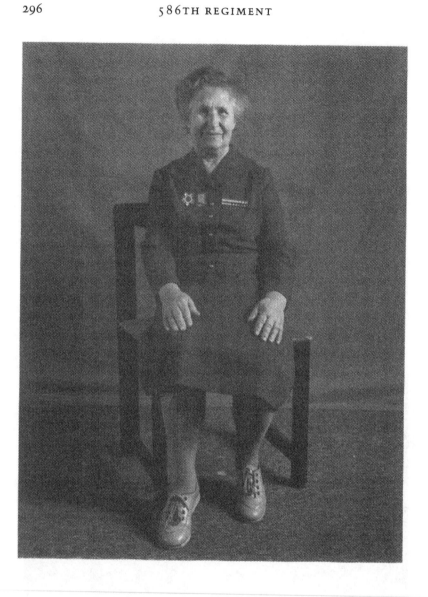

Anna Shibayeva

Klavdiya Pankratova

Zinaida Butkaryova-Yermolayeva

Raisa Surnachevskaya

Galina Drobovich

Klavdiya Terekhova-Kasatkina

Inna Pasportnikova

Valentina Kislitsa

Valentina Volkova-Tikhonova

Nina Shebalina

Galina Burdina

Irina Lunyova-Favorskaya

Tamara Voronova

Marina Muzhikova

Yelena Karakorskaya

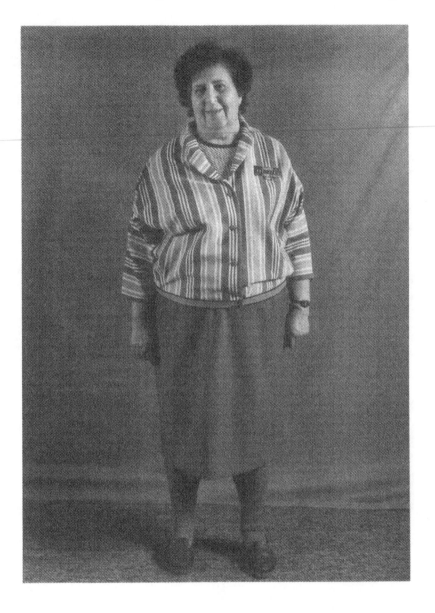

Kareliya Zarinya

Zoya Pozhidayeva

Zoya Malkova

Anna Timofeyeva-Yegorova

Anna Popova

Each year since the end of World War II, the three women's airforce regiments meet in a small park in front of the Bolshoi Theater in Moscow on May 2. In 1990 I was invited to be the guest of the 125th Guards Bomber Regiment at their luncheon after the annual meeting.

The 46th Guards Bomber Regiment proceeded to the steps of the Bolshoi for their group picture. They then read aloud letters from fellow members unable to attend, while graciously accepting flowers, interviews, and attention from admirers old and young. They were very much the center of attention.

The 586th Fighter Regiment formed a tight group farther into the park and began serenading me, singing wonderful minor-key war and love songs and rousing melodies of their aircraft and victory.

The 125th regiment had gathered on the far side of the park and were quieter, holding flowers, smiling, and embracing one another. My friend Margarita Ponomaryova was with me. We had worked together in harmony for so long that conversation flowed easily as she murmured to me and spoke my thoughts to them. At that point we began walking out of the park toward the Moskva Hotel, where the regiment had reservations for our luncheon. When we arrived at the hotel our banquet table was not ready. The regiment waited in a reception area, where they spontaneously began to sing their songs from the war.

They had gathered as a remembrance, a celebration. They are sisters, they will tell you—closer to one another than to their own relatives. Ultimately their *memento mori* is one of survival, haunted by the ghosts of those not so fortunate. As they perished, so came others to fill the vacancies, and so the regiments endured. So if you are they, you sing and you remember, and the memories that lie beneath the surface most of the time are living, throbbing realities this day.

We are seated at the banquet table, and the festivities begin. One of the ladies rises from her chair, lifts her glass, and proposes a toast. We all rise, and our glasses touch with a musical note. A husband, who had also been a pilot, marvels at their absolute mastery of the bomber aircraft, so heavy and unforgiving. The political commissar speaks at length about the deeds of the regiment. A pilot toasts the skill and dedication of the mechanics—they are comrades. Later we stand for a moment's silence honoring those who are gone.

Then their attention is turned toward me, the American, who represents the Women Airforce Service Pilots, who also flew during the war. The focus is on me, who represents America in World War II—America, with whom we all desire peace forevermore. I, too, am fervent. I respond with affection and admiration; I toast them. I am presented with a regimental postwar medal worn by all the members of the 125th regiment, and I am made an honorary member of the regiment.

Everyone talks and eats, and there are more toasts. Yevgeniya Gurulyeva-Smirnova stands and sings a haunting melody in a clear, melodious voice, then seats herself. Everyone sings together. I hum along, feeling this nostalgia, feeling the vodka; and all around me, their past that I never knew but nevertheless am touched by. I propose another toast, with greetings from the Women Airforce Service Pilots in America. I am filled with the dignity of the occasion, with the mantle bestowed on me to represent my country. My small glass is filled to overflowing. We all drink the toasts in a gulp. It is the way it is done. Later, we file out of the dining room. Aleksandr Panchenko, our other translator, loses his way, and we are diverted through the hotel kitchen.

I am on the street in Red Square. I breathe deeply. My next remembered breath is late at night, and I am in my hotel room, on my bed, with the medal still pinned to my chest, the lost hours never recalled, I am assured by my friend Jim that I conducted myself properly, rode the metro, went to my room, and disappeared for the night. My dear, dear country, I did not disgrace you after all!

CPSIA information can be obtained
at www.ICGtesting.com
Printed in the USA
BVHW072322020320
573891BV00001B/10